Motor Learning in Practice

Motor Learning in Practice explores the fundamental processes of motor learning and skill acquisition in sport, and explains how a constraints-led approach can be used to design more effective learning environments for sports practice and performance. Drawing on ecological psychology, the book examines the interaction of personal, environmental and task-specific constraints in the development of motor skills, and then demonstrates how an understanding of those constraints can be applied in a wide range of specific sports and physical activities.

The first part of the book contains three chapters that offer an overview of the key theoretical concepts that underpin the constraints-led approach. These chapters also examine the development of fundamental movement skills in children, and survey the most important instructional strategies that can be used to develop motor skills in sport. The second part of the book contains 17 chapters that apply these principles to specific sports, including basketball, soccer, boxing, athletics field events and swimming.

This is the first book to apply the theory of a constraints-led approach to training and learning techniques in sport. Including contributions from many of the world's leading scholars in the field of motor learning and development, this book is essential reading for any advanced student, researcher or teacher with an interest in motor skills, sport psychology, sport pedagogy, coaching or physical education.

Ian Renshaw is Senior Lecturer in the School of Human Movement Studies at Queensland University of Technology, Australia.

Keith Davids is Professor of Motor Control and Head of the School of Human Movement Studies at Queensland University of Technology, Australia.

Geert J. P. Savelsbergh is Professor in the Faculty of Human Movement Sciences at VU University Amsterdam, the Netherlands, and Visiting Professor at Manchester Metropolitan University, UK.

Motor Learning in Practice
A constraints-led approach

Edited by Ian Renshaw, Keith Davids and
Geert J. P. Savelsbergh

Routledge
Taylor & Francis Group

LONDON AND NEW YORK

First edition published 2010
by Routledge
2 Park Square, Milton Park, Abingdon, Oxon, OX14 4RN

Simultaneously published in the USA and Canada
by Routledge
270 Madison Avenue, New York, NY 10016

Routledge is an imprint of the Taylor & Francis Group, an informa business

© 2010 selection and editorial material, Ian Renshaw, Keith Davids and
Geert J.P. Savelsbergh; individual chapters, the contributors.

Typeset in Goudy by Pindar NZ, Auckland, New Zealand
Printed and bound in Great Britain by CPI Antony Rowe, Chippenham,
Wiltshire.

British Library Cataloguing in Publication Data
A catalogue record for this book is available from the British Library.

Library of Congress Cataloging-in-Publication Data
Motor learning in practice : a constraints-led approach / edited by Ian
Renshaw, Keith Davids and Geert J.P. Savelsbergh. — 1st ed.
       p. cm.
    Includes bibliographical references and index.
    1. Motor learning. 2. Physical education and training. I. Renshaw, Ian. II.
Davids, K. (Keith), 1953- III. Savelsbergh, Geert J. P.
    BF295.M68 2010
    612.8'11—dc22   2009040593

ISBN10: 0–415–47863–4 (hbk)
ISBN10: 0–203–88810–3 (ebk)

ISBN13: 978–0-415–47863–2 (hbk)
ISBN13: 978–0–203–88810–0 (ebk)

Ian Renshaw: This book is dedicated to my parents Ernie and Margaret Renshaw, my wife Alison, and children Hannah and Matthew.

Keith Davids: I dedicate this book to the continuing love and support of my mother Pearl Janette Davids.

Geert J. P. Savelsbergh: To all the kids that love sport, especially to my daughter Rocio Maria and son Cristian David Savelsbergh.

Contents

List of contributors   x
Preface   xiii

PART I   1

1 The constraints-based approach to motor learning: implications
  for a non-linear pedagogy in sport and physical education   3
  KEITH DAVIDS

2 Instructions as constraints in motor skill acquisition   17
  KARL M. NEWELL AND RAJIV RANGANATHAN

3 Building the foundations: skill acquisition in children   33
  IAN RENSHAW

PART II   45

4 Perceptual training for basketball shooting   47
  RAÔUL R. D. OUDEJANS AND JOHAN M. KOEDIJKER

5 Saving penalties, scoring penalties   57
  GEERT J. P. SAVELSBERGH, OLAV VERSLOOT, RICH MASTERS AND
  JOHN VAN DER KAMP

6 Stochastic perturbations in athletics field events enhance skill
  acquisition   69
  WOLFGANG I. SCHÖLLHORN, HENDRIK BECKMANN, DANIEL
  JANSSEN AND JÜRGEN DREPPER

7 Interacting constraints and inter-limb co-ordination in swimming   83
   LUDOVIC SEIFERT, CHRIS BUTTON AND TIM BRAZIER

8 The changing face of practice for developing perception: action
   skill in cricket   99
   ROSS PINDER

9 The "nurdle to leg" and other ways of winning cricket matches   109
   IAN RENSHAW AND DARREN HOLDER

10 Manipulating tasks constraints to improve tactical knowledge and
   collective decision-making in rugby union   120
   PEDRO PASSOS, DUARTE ARAÚJO, KEITH DAVIDS AND RICK
   SHUTTLEWORTH

11 The ecological dynamics of decision-making in sailing   131
   DUARTE ARAÚJO, LUÍS ROCHA AND KEITH DAVIDS

12 Using constraints to enhance decision-making in team sports   144
   ADAM D. GORMAN

13 Skill development in canoeing and kayaking: an individualised
   approach   152
   ERIC BRYMER

14 A constraints-led approach to coaching association football: the
   role of perceptual information and the acquisition of co-ordination   161
   MATT DICKS AND JIA YI CHOW

15 Identifying constraints on children with movement difficulties:
   implications for pedagogues and clinicians   173
   KEITH DAVIDS, GEERT J. P. SAVELSBERGH AND MOTOHIDE
   MIYAHARA

16 Augmenting golf practice through the manipulation of physical
   and informational constraints   187
   PAUL S. GLAZIER

17 Skill acquisition in dynamic ball sports: monitoring and
   controlling action-effects   199
   NICOLA J. HODGES AND PAUL R. FORD

18 A constraints-based training intervention in boxing   211
   ROBERT HRISTOVSKI

19 Researching co-ordination skill   221
   DANA MASLOVAT, NICOLA J. HODGES, ROMEO CHUA AND
   IAN M. FRANKS

20 Skill acquisition in tennis: equipping learners for success   231
   DAMIAN FARROW AND MACHAR REID

   Index   241

Contributors

Ian Renshaw is Senior Lecturer in the School of Human Movement Studies at Queensland University of Technology, Australia.

Keith Davids is Professor of Motor Control and Head of the School of Human Movement Studies, at Queensland University of Technology, Australia.

Geert J. P. Savelsbergh is Professor in the Faculty of the Human Movement Sciences, at VU University Amsterdam, the Netherlands, and Visiting Proffessor at Manchester Metropolitan University, UK.

Duarte Araújo is Assistant Professor of Sport Psychology in the Faculty of Human Kinetics at the Technical University of Lisbon, Portugal.

Hendrik Beckmann is a PhD student in Training and Movement Science at the University of Mainz, Germany.

Tim Brazier is Lecturer at Otago Institute of Sport and Adventure at Otago Polytechnic and High Perfomance Coach and Swimming Specialist for Triathlon NZ, New Zealand.

Eric Brymer is Lecturer in the School of Human Movement Studies at Queensland University of Technology, Australia.

Chris Button is Associate Professor in the School of Physical Education at the University of Otago, New Zealand.

Jia Yi Chow is Assistant Professor of Physical Education and Sports Science at the National Institute of Education at Nanyang Technological University, Singapore.

Romeo Chua is Professor of Motor Control in the School of Human Kinetics at the University of British Columbia, Canada.

Matt Dicks is Lecturer at the Institute of Cognitive and Team/Racket Sport Research at the German Sport University, Germany.

Jürgen Drepper is a teacher of physical education and biology in a secondary school in Bocholt, Germany.

Damian Farrow is Senior Skill Acquisition Specialist at the Australian Institute of Sport, Australia.

Paul R. Ford is Post Doctoral Research Fellow in Sport and Exercise Sciences at Liverpool John Moores University, UK.

Ian M. Franks is Professor of Motor Learning and Control in the School of Human Kinetics at the University of British Columbia, Canada.

Paul S. Glazier is Post-Graduate Researcher at the Centre for Sport and Exercise Science at Sheffield Hallam University, UK.

Adam D. Gorman is Skill Acquisition Specialist at the Australian Institute of Sport, Australia.

Nicola J. Hodges is Associate Professor in the School of Human Kinetics at the University of British Columbia, Canada.

Darren Holder is Director of Cricket at Brisbane Grammar School and is a sessional staff member in the School of Human Movement Studies at Queensland University of Technology, Australia.

Robert Hristovski is Professor of Theory and Practice of Sport Training in the Faculty of Physical Culture at the University of Ss. Cyril and Methodius, Macedonia.

Daniel Janssen is a PhD student in Training and Movement Science at the University of Mainz, Germany.

Johan M. Koedijker is Postdoctoral Fellow at the Institute of Sport Sciences at the University of Berne, Switzerland.

Dana Maslovat is Lecturer of Human Kinetics at Langara College, Canada.

Rich Masters is Assistant Director (Research) at the Institute of Human Performance at the University of Hong Kong, China.

Motohide Miyahara is Senior Lecturer in the School of Physical Education at the University of Otago, New Zealand.

Karl M. Newell is Professor and Head of the Department of Kinesiology at the Pennsylvania State University, USA.

Raôul R. D. Oudejans is Senior Lecturer in the Faculty of Human Movement Sciences and Research Institute MOVE at VU University Amsterdam, the Netherlands.

Pedro Passos is Assistant Professor of Motor Control in the Faculty of Human Kinetics at the Technical University of Lisbon, Portugal.

Ross Pinder is Post-Graduate Researcher in the School of Human Movement Studies at Queensland University of Technology, Australia.

Rajiv Ranganathan is Postdoctoral Fellow at the Rehabilitation Institute of Chicago at Northwestern University, USA.

Machar Reid is Sports Science Manager of Tennis Australia.

Luís Rocha is Technical Director of the Portuguese Sailing Federation, Portugal.

Wolfgang I. Schöllhorn is Professor in Training and Movement Science and Head of the Department of Sport Science at the University of Mainz, Germany.

Ludovic Seifert is Associate Professor and Coordinator of the International Relationships in the Faculty of Sports Sciences at the University of Rouen, France.

Rick Shuttleworth is Skill Acquisition Specialist at the Australian Institute of Sport, Australia.

John van der Kamp is Assistant Professor in the Faculty of Human Movement Sciences at VU University Amsterdam, the Netherlands. He is also Visiting Assistant Professor at the Institute of Human Performance at the University of Hong Kong, China.

Olav Versloot is Exercise Physiologist at Ajax Amsterdam Football Club, the Netherlands.

Preface

The purpose of this book is to demonstrate how the constraints-based approach can be used, in a non-linear pedagogy, to shape practice in different perform-ance contexts. This book builds on an existing book, published in 2008, by Keith Davids, Chris Button and Simon Bennett entitled *The Dynamics of Skill Acquisition: A Constraints-Led Approach*. That book provided a comprehensive theoretical overview of processes of motor learning from a constraints-led per-spective. It was the first text to outline a conceptual model of co-ordination and control with a multidisciplinary framework, capturing the different interlocking scales of analysis (e.g. neural, behavioural, psychological) and the many different subsystems (e.g. perceptual and movement) involved in producing skilled behav-iour. The book showed that a conceptual model of co-ordination and control, and their acquisition, is important for designing learning environments, and for ensuring that learners gain positive experiences when acquiring motor skills. The current book seeks to build on that scientific application by enlisting contributions from a number of authors across the world who are actively engaged in applying the conceptual model of constraints in learning environments in different sports.

The task for the chapter authors in this book was to describe and illustrate how key concepts and ideas from the constraints-based framework can be used to design learning tasks in sport. Specifically, contributors were asked to examine principles of learning programme design in their specialist area by answering the following questions: What are the implications of your research for practitioners in sport? How can/have these ideas been incorporated into training and practice programmes in your area of expertise?

Structure and organization

The book is organized into two parts. Part I consists of three chapters. In Chapter 1, Keith Davids starts off by providing a brief overview of key theoretical concepts in the constraints-based approach and in particular examines the implications for a non-linear pedagogy in sport and physical education. Key ideas in dynamical sys-tems theory and ecological psychology have been developed into a constraints-led approach to motor learning. This particular pedagogical approach is predicated on the notion of a learner as a non-linear dynamical system. These insights have been applied in a non-linear pedagogy for sport and physical education. The principles of non-linear pedagogy are based on the key characteristics of non-linear dynamical systems in nature, including self-organization under constraints, emergence and co-adaptation in metastable regions. The basis of non-linear pedagogy advises how practitioners might help each individual performer search for functional information movement couplings to satisfy unique constraints impinging on him/her during learning. Implications for learning design are illustrated with reference to research examining task organization, interpersonal interactions in team games, and feedback processes during motor learning.

Chapter 2, by Newell and Ranganathan, covers the instructional strategies in motor skill learning from a constraints perspective. The focus of this chapter is on *one* aspect of instructional strategies: the strategic role of instructions in learning and performing motor skills. They make the point that information from instructions is a forward-looking category of task-relevant information for the learner (i.e. directed at future performance) compared to the well-studied category of information feedback, which by definition provides information about some aspect of past movement and behaviour. Newell and Ranganathan emphasize the role of instructions as constraints in channeling the search for task-relevant solutions in motor learning.

In Chapter 3, Ian Renshaw discusses the importance of this model for teachers and coaches who wish to adopt the ideas of non-linear pedagogy in teaching children. Examples are provided that identify individual constraints in children and the unique challenges facing coaches when these individual constraints are changing due to growth and development. The second part of Chapter 3 aims to develop an understanding of how cultural and environmental constraints impact on children's sport. This is an area that has received very little attention but plays a very important part in the long-term development of sporting expertise. Finally, Renshaw looks at how coaches can manipulate task constraints to create effective learning environments for young children.

In the second part of the book, 17 chapters have been written to target the application of a constraints-based approach to learning environments in a variety of sports and physical activities. Each chapter focuses on a particular sport or physical activity, as an exemplar, and aims to provide insights and ideas on how the main theoretical tenets of the constraints-based approach can be applied by practitioners to design learning environments in a variety of specific sports and physical activities. Contributing authors were invited to exemplify how key theoretical ideas may be applied in specific learning and practice environments, emphasising how they may shape the design of practice tasks and interactions with athletes. Key practical issues discussed included: practice structure, organization and design of task constraints; instructional constraints, including coaching methods; types of KR (knowledge of results) provided exposure to discovery learning; use of video, simulations and models for practice; adaptations to specific rules, boundaries, surfaces, media, and equipment used in task performance; specific activities undertaken during practice time; and design and scaling of practice equipment and practice areas.

The chapter by Oudejans and Koedijker (Chapter 4) investigates perceptual training for basketball shooting. It attempts to answer important questions such as: How do expert shooters succeed? When and for how long should a player look at the rim of the basketball ring for an optimal shot? How can this be trained?

In the chapter by Savelsbergh, Versloot, Masters and van der Kamp (Chapter 5) the topic is saving and scoring penalties in association football. For goalkeepers, the authors explain the role of visual perception and discuss recent evidence that shows perceptual training can improve anticipation of penalty kick direction. They also highlight evidence that goalkeepers can present barely perceptible information cues to penalty kickers, which influences kicking behaviour. The chapter concludes with some rule of thumb suggestions for both penalty takers and goalkeepers.

In a chapter examining learning design in athletic events, Schöllhorn, Beckmann, Janssen and Drepper (Chapter 6) explain and examine the role of differential learning in sport. They review research showing its efficacy and examine how it envisages the role of variability in practice compared to traditional theories such as schema theory and contextual interference. They draw attention to the counter-intuitive manner in which random variability might lead to instabilities in learning environments and eventual stabilization of successful movement solutions adapted for achieving successful task outcomes in athletic events. They refer to a case study in the following part to highlight their theoretical arguments.

In the chapter by Seifert, Button and Brazier (Chapter 7) a review is presented of recent findings on inter-limb co-ordination in swimming. The implications of this data for designing training and learning programmes in swimming are highlighted. They lead readers through a detailed analysis of how task and personal constraints can shape the acquisition of co-ordination in the front crawl and breaststroke, referring to two case studies (see Case Study, p. 94).

In the first of two chapters devoted to learning and practice in cricket (Chapter 8), Ross Pinder analyses evidence on the role of ball projection machines in practice, an ubiquitous part of training for many ball games. He highlights data showing how movement patterns differ when batters face a real bowler compared to a projection machine. He argues that an important problem with learning design involving ball projection machines is that it unintentionally eradicates key sources of perceptual information used by batters to regulate their actions. However, there is no doubt that ball projection machines can provide learners with flexibility to practice on their own and also helps avoid bowling over-use injuries in teammates asked to help in batting practice. Pinder highlights the integration of video-based imagery and ball projection technology as a potential solution to ensure that task constraints of batting include information for action.

In a second cricket-oriented chapter (Chapter 9), Renshaw and Holder demonstrate how the ideas of non-linear pedagogy can be used by cricket coaches to help players to overcome movement system rate limiters in the skill of running singles. They identify technical, perceptual and mental rate limiters on batting performance and refer to a case study to show how cricket coaches can use variability in practice learning design in order to enhance adaptability in developing players.

There are also three chapters devoted to the training of decision-making in team sports. This is explored in the context of rugby union in Chapter 10 by Passos, Araújo, Davids and Shuttleworth; sailing in Chapter 11 by Araújo, Rocha and Davids; and AFL in Chapter 12 by Gorman. In each chapter an ecological dynamics perspective is presented and each of the chapters demonstrates how decision-making emerges from the interaction of multiple constraints in both environments (e.g. cognitions, performer morphology, specific opponents, space constraints, natural characteristics such as field dimensions and wind direction). Each chapter shows how decision-making can be developed through active exploration of situational constraints. It is argued that generally performers at different skill levels can achieve their task goals (i.e. they do not act "irrationally"), through acting on reliable information. Rather than solely using a knowledge base stored in memory, decision-making seems to be predicated on exploratory activities in the performance context. The acquisition of expert decision-making entails a transition from using non-specifying information to a greater attunement to relevant informational variables. Furthermore, decision-making in sport is based on a symmetry-breaking process, e.g. changes in wind-line angle selection in sailing and alterations in relative velocity and distance between an attacker and defender in team games. For the coach, different expertise levels entail different information-action couplings, where different processes should predominantly occur (education of intention, attunement, calibration). The transition between different levels of decision-making performance may be achieved with the manipulation of performer, environment and task constraints in a representative task or practice context. Gorman considers these issues with specific examples from Australian Rules football (AFL). He argues that designing representative training tasks is paramount for scientists supporting skill acquisition in sport. He exemplifies his argument in the sport of AFL by showing how making training tasks more open and dynamic is essential to challenge performers during practice. In this approach the coach acts as a facilitator for the development of decision-making performance, more than a prescriptor of the best decisions. All three chapters refer to excellent training examples in the case studies section.

In his chapter on skill development in canoeing and kayaking (Chapter 13), Eric Brymer advocates an individualized approach and focuses on the nature of the introductory session for complete beginners. He argues that the quality of the learner's experiences in this session can decide whether or not he/she will continue with paddlesports. He compares a traditional approach to the introductory session with a constraints-led approach suggesting that a key strength of the latter is the adoption of an individualized approach in learning design, along with a commitment to avoid task decomposition in practice and to ensure that learners are given opportunities to pick up affordances for action.

In their chapter (Chapter 14) Dicks and Chow review the perceptual anticipatory literature in football before providing evidence that demonstrates that changes in ecological task constraints (i.e. information display and response requirements) can directly influence the visual anticipatory behaviour of goalkeepers. They also examine research on co-ordination of a football kicking action. They highlight how task constraints provided in the learning environment help to shape the emergence of different yet equally successful movement solutions among novice learners. In the case study section there is an example of how practitioners can exploit understanding of empirical evidence on task constraint manipulation and movement co-ordination for the design of coaching activities.

The chapter by Davids, Savelsbergh and Miyahara (Chapter 15) discusses how individuals with movement difficulties produce actions that satisfy constraints on them, highlighting implications for a non-linear pedagogy. Data from selected studies of constraints on functional locomotion and reaching behaviours of individuals with cerebral palsy are discussed. The main implication for a non-linear pedagogy is that pedagogues should not adopt a "one-size-fits-all" approach in trying to ensure that all individuals, regardless of movement difficulties, adhere to hypothetical, idealized motor patterns. Rather, inter- and intra-individual movement variability can be viewed as adaptive functional behaviours that emerge when individuals with movement difficulties attempt to satisfy the unique interacting constraints impinging on them.

Paul Glazier (Chapter 16) looks at the burgeoning industry in augmenting golf practice through the manipulation of physical and informational constraints. Every year it seems that golfers are exposed to a variety of gadgets, such as training and feedback systems, that often come with nothing more than overly inflated claims of a drastically improved game. He points out that rarely are these devices subjected to scientific analysis. In his chapter, he reviews the limited number of scientific investigations that have been published in the literature on coaching and practice tools and critically analyses their effectiveness from a constraints-led theoretical perspective. He concludes that some training and feedback systems might be useful in inducing performance increments if they are used sparingly and in the correct manner.

Nicola Hodges and Paul Ford (Chapter 17) review a number of studies where they and others have examined how external action-effect information (e.g. ball trajectory) and external action-percept information (e.g. visual monitoring of other players) constrain action. Although the majority of this research has been conducted in relatively controlled, laboratory-based tasks, in order to allow isolation of critical performance features, Hodges and Ford attempt to contextualize the findings of this research for sport. They finish by discussing the implications of this research for coaches and practitioners, particularly those involved in invasion, net, target and field sports.

Robert Hristovski's chapter (Chapter 18) illustrates how a constraints-based training intervention in boxing can be undertaken, showing that one of the key 'control' parameters (i.e. constraints) in attacking and defending behaviour in boxing is not physical distance, but scaled distance to a target. Scaled distance is the ratio of the physical distance and the arm length of the attacker, to a target/opponent. Hence, Hristovski concludes that boxers use an intrinsic, body-scaled metric of distance, rather than an objective physical distance in punching a target. Moreover, it has been shown that what boxers perceive for guiding their behaviour are the affordances (i.e. perceived opportunities for specific punching actions). Punching actions have been defined as angles (directions) of impact of an attacker's fist with the target and were considered as 'order' parameters, (i.e. variables that contain the collective information of the organization of the upper limbs of the attacker with respect to a target). In other words, the direction of fist-target impact is most probably a variable that organizes the trajectory formation of different punches.

Maslovat, Hodges, Chua, and Franks (Chapter 19) look at the learning of new limb co-ordination patterns and skills. Topics include the effectiveness of various practice conditions including instructions, demonstrations, feedback, order of skill presentation and amount of practice. Other areas of discussion include how timing constraints can be manipulated to assist learning and how various task constraints affect the assessment of individual abilities and the acquisition of new co-ordination skills. Although the research will primarily focus on laboratory-based tasks, applications to new movement patterns such as dance routines, music and juggling will be discussed.

Damian Farrow and Machar Reid (Chapter 20) discuss trends in international tennis to reduce the amount of time spent teaching specific movement techniques to learners in favour of spending more time playing games. This game-based approach, named 'Play and Stay', is predicated on the manipulation of important task constraints such as key racquet dimensions, ball characteristics and practice court sizes. They discuss the way that such an arbitrary approach may benefit from the provision of a sound theoretical rationale in the form of a constraints-led perspective.

Embedded within a number of the applied chapters of the book are exemplar case studies which are included with the aim of demonstrating to practitioners how the range of key ideas incorporated in non-linear pedagogy can be incorporated into the design of practice programmes in sport and physical activity. Our aim is that as a result of reading the practical chapters and exemplar case studies, readers will be stimulated and challenged to apply the key model ideas to their own practice. The book is intended to engage reflective practitioners working at a variety of different skill levels. The theoretical chapters are intended to act as a platform through which readers may be stimulated to interpret the exemplar practical applications and decision-making of the contributing authors in different performance and learning environments.

Target audience

The book provides a novel contribution to the literature on sport pedagogy and practice. It is aimed at undergraduate students training to enter pedagogical and applied professions who will be charged with the task of creating practice and training environments in a range of different sports and physical activities. Degree programmes that these students would typically be taking include Sport Science, Coaching Science, Coaching Studies, Sport Studies, Physical Education, Sport Psychology and Kinesiology. Additional target groups include advanced researchers working in coaching education, motor learning, sport pedagogy and sport psychology programmes as well as coaches, teachers and sport scientists who support their work. In order to ensure a sound basis for practical applications, contributing authors were selected because of their applied research in motor learning from a constraints-led perspective and/or because they work as skill acquisition specialists and consultants for sport performance organizations including professional sports clubs and national institutes of sport in different countries across the world. In this respect, the authors provide a global perspective for the targeted readership.

Part I

1 The constraints-based approach to motor learning

Implications for a non-linear pedagogy in sport and physical education

Keith Davids

Introduction

Recently, a constraints-led approach has been promoted as a framework for understanding how children and adults acquire movement skills for sport and exercise (see Davids *et al.*, 2008; Araújo *et al.*, 2004). The aim of a constraints-led approach is to identify the nature of interacting constraints that influence skill acquisition in learners. In this chapter the main theoretical ideas behind a constraints-led approach are outlined to assist practical applications by sports practitioners and physical educators in a non-linear pedagogy (see Chow *et al.*, 2006, 2007). To achieve this goal, this chapter examines implications for some of the typical challenges facing sport pedagogists and physical educators in the design of learning programmes.

The theoretical basis of a constraints-led approach

A systems-oriented perspective, informed by ideas from dynamical systems theory, the complexity sciences and ecological psychology, conceptualizes humans as complex, neurobiological systems that exhibit several fundamental properties (Davids *et al.*, 2008). These include:

1   composition of many independent degrees of freedom and different interacting levels in the system (e.g. neural, hormonal, biomechanical, psychological levels);
2   inherent pattern-forming tendencies which can emerge as system components (e.g. muscles, joints, limb segments), and spontaneously co-adjust and co-adapt to each other;
3   openness to constraints (e.g. information that can regulate actions);
4   capacity of complex systems to exhibit tendencies towards stability and instability;
5   the potential for non-linearities in behaviours emerging from the system exemplified by small skips, jumps and regressions in motor learning.

Research has shown that neurobiological systems are able to exploit the constraints that surround them in order to allow functional patterns of behaviour to emerge in specific performance contexts. They tend to settle into stable patterns of organization (behaviours) because of intrinsic self-organization processes. A neurobiological system's "openness" to energy flows allows them to use that energy as informational constraints on their behaviour. These ideas show that the type of order that emerges in neurobiological systems is dependent on initial conditions (existing environmental conditions) and the range of constraints that shape their behaviour.

Constraints and movement co-ordination

The key idea of pattern formation under constraints in complex neurobiological systems is most useful for physical educators and sport pedagogists. Pattern forming dynamics emerge under interacting constraints in neurobiological systems by harnessing the body's mechanical degrees of freedom during learning. Bernstein (1967) argued that the acquisition of movement co-ordination was "the process of mastering redundant degrees of freedom" (p.127), or the conversion of the human movement apparatus to a more controllable, stable system.

The constraints-led approach views influential factors within the learning environment as constraints that guide the acquisition of movement co-ordination and control (Newell *et al.*, 2003). According to Newell (1986), constraints can be classified into three distinct categories to provide a coherent framework for understanding how co-ordination patterns emerge during goal-directed behaviour (see Figure 1.1).

1   *Organismic constraints* refer to characteristics of individual performers, such as genes, height, weight, muscle–fat ratios, and connective strength of synapses in the brain, cognitions, motivations and emotions. These unique characteristics represent resources that can be used to solve movement problems or limitations that can lead to individual-specific adaptations by a performer. Newell's (1985) model of motor learning captures how Bernstein's (1967) degrees of freedom problem can help elucidate the distinction between performers of different skill levels. Early in learning, novices at the "co-ordination" stage are challenged with harnessing available motor system degrees of freedom to complete a task. At this stage a functional co-ordination pattern is assembled to achieve the task to a basic level. However, if environmental conditions change, the basic pattern may need to be adapted. This is the next challenge for learners as they explore how to adapt an action to different performance conditions. Performers who can flexibly adapt a stable co-ordination pattern for use in changing performance environments are at the "control" stage of learning. Finally, expert performers reach the "skill" stage when they can vary the degrees of freedom used in a co-ordination pattern in an energy-efficient, creative manner to fit changing circumstances in dynamic environments (Newell, 1985; Davids *et al.*, 2008).

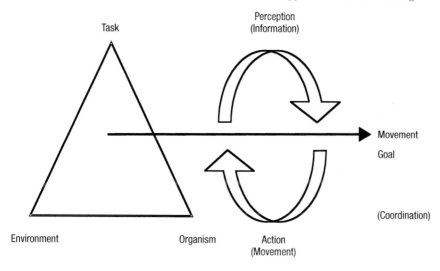

Figure 1.1 How co-ordination and control (in the form of functional information-movement couplings) emerges from the interaction of key constraints on the performer.

2 *Environmental constraints* can be physical in nature, such as ambient light or temperature. Gravity is a key environmental constraint on movement co-ordination in all tasks, as experienced by all athletes including skiers, divers, gymnasts and ice skaters. Some environmental constraints are social rather than physical. Spectators provide an influential environmental social constraint for learners and more experienced athletes during sport performance.
3 *Task constraints* are usually more specific to particular performance contexts than environmental constraints and include specific performance goals, rules of a specific sport, equipment and implements to use during a physical activity, performance surfaces and boundary markings. The functional movement patterns of an individual performer may vary, even within seemingly highly consistent activities such as a gymnastic vault, a long jump approach run or a golf swing, because the task constraints differ from performance to performance. A significant task constraint is the information available in specific performance contexts that athletes can use to regulate their actions.

Information constraints on action

James Gibson (1979) argued that neurobiological systems are surrounded by huge arrays of energy flows, which can act as information sources (e.g. optical, acoustic, proprioceptive) to support decision-making, planning and movement organization, during goal-directed activity. For example, informational constraints can be used to continuously guide actions as a player navigates through a defensive formation in a rugby union field. Gibson's ideas imply that pedagogists need to understand the *nature* of the information that regulates movement (i.e. "what" information). The structure of energy in the surrounding arrays carries information for a performer that is specific to certain contexts and that is available to be directly perceived. For example, light reaches the eyes of a netball player after having been reflected off surfaces (i.e. the ground and the goal posts) and moving objects (i.e. other players and the ball) in the busy, cluttered performance environment. Movements in the performance environment cause changes to energy flows that provide specific information on environmental properties that can be used by individuals as affordances for action (see Kugler & Turvey, 1987). Because flow patterns are specific to particular environmental properties, they can act as invariant information sources to be picked by individual performers to constrain their actions.

Gibson (1979) argued that movement generates information that, in turn, supports further movement, leading to a direct and cyclical relationship between perception and movement. This position was summarized by his statement that "We must perceive in order to move, but we must also move in order to perceive" (p. 223). According to ecological psychology, the use of information to support movement requires a law of control that continually relates the current state of the individual to the current state of the environment. That is, a law of control relates the kinetic property of a movement to the kinematic property of the perceptual flow (Warren, 1990).

The implication of these ideas is that, in sport, learners need to acquire specific information-movement couplings, which they can use to support their actions. They achieve this process by becoming *attuned* to relevant properties that produce unique patterns of information flows in specific environments (e.g. different sport contexts). Jacobs and Michaels (2002) argued that there are two processes involved when learners enhance their attunement to information for action. First, learners educate attention by becoming better at detecting the key information variables that specify movements from the myriad of variables that do not. During practice they narrow down the minimal information needed to regulate movement from the enormous amount available in the environment. Second, learners calibrate actions by tuning movement to a critical information source and, through practice, establish and sustain information-movement couplings to regulate behaviour.

From a constraints-led approach there are a number of principles that can guide the design of learning environments. These principles have been captured in a non-linear pedagogical framework (Chow *et al.*, 2006). In the remaining sections of this chapter, we will focus on how pedagogists might manipulate information to constrain the emergence of functional movement patterns in learners and how they might design learning environments so that decision-making behaviour can emerge from the constraints of practice. In this design approach the *interaction* of the main classes of constraints on learners during sport performance and physical activity results in the emergence of functional states of movement co-ordination.

Learning design and informational constraints on action: implications for a non-linear pedagogy

The mutual interdependence of perceptual and action systems suggests that these processes should not be separated in practice tasks by coaches and physical educators. The idea of designing learning environments that couple key sources of information together with specific movements has been supported in previous research on dynamic interceptive actions such as the table tennis forehand drive (Bootsma, 1989) and volleyball serving (Davids *et al.*, 2001). Research on volleyball serving showed that, for the visual flow information from the dropping ball to constrain the initiation of the striking movement, the task should not be decomposed during practice so that the ball toss is decoupled from the strike phase. The traditional pedagogical strategy of breaking up the serving action into the toss and hit components, for separate practice, may reduce attentional demands on the learner. However, it also decouples the ball placement phase from the ball contact phase of the action and disrupts the development of key information-coupling for performing such a self-paced extrinsic timing task. Practising both phases of the serve together without decoupling them permits the learner to explore an emerging relationship between informational and task constraints.

The principle of information-movement coupling proposes that learning design of interceptive actions should involve the process of *task simplification*, rather than traditional methods of *part-task decomposition* and *adaptive training* (Davids *et al.*, 2008). Task simplification refers to a process whereby scaled-down versions of tasks are created in practice and performed by learners to simplify the process of information pick-up and coupling to movement patterns. In these scaled-down tasks, important information-movement links are maintained in practice and are not disrupted in practice task design. For example, evidence shows that long-jumpers use information-movement couplings to regulate the stride pattern towards the take-off board during the run-up (e.g. Montagne *et al.*, 2000). The pedagogical implication of this finding is that the run-up and jump phases should not be practiced separately. Rather task simplification could involve novices starting a few strides from the board and learning to accurately place the take-off foot on the board, before gradually extending the run-up further back during practice. This type of task organization ensures that learners practice to run and jump together at all times and maintains information-movement couplings for the athlete (Davids *et al.*, 2001).

These ideas of information-movement coupling and task simplification have implications for learning in many ball games such as tennis, baseball, softball, hockey, and volleyball. An important issue that needs to be considered with respect to maintaining information-movement linkages is the use of artificial aids such as ball machines during batting, hitting and catching practice (see Figure 1.2). These machines are used in tennis, cricket, batting, hockey and other sports. For example, in cricket, batters need information to predict where the ball will pitch often under severe time constraints (some deliveries are bowled at around 140kph by fast bowlers). Cricket bowling machines are used in net practices with complete

Figure 1.2 Practice in hitting and batting tasks commonly involves practice against ball machines to ensure standardized ball feed.

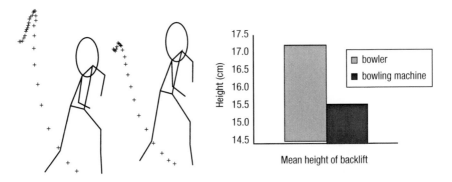

Figure 1.3 Kinematic data illustrating differences in peak height of back-lift of the bat from the ground against a bowler (left-hand figure) and bowling machine (right-hand figure).

beginners as well as international players. Since performers couple movements to the information present during practice, what exactly is the role of ball projection machines during learning?

To address this question Renshaw *et al.* (2007) investigated batting performance in cricket under two different but ubiquitous practice task constraints: against a bowler and a bowling machine. The forward defensive stroke is generally played to a straight ball on a "good length", the intention being to stop the bowler's delivery from hitting the batter's wicket.

They examined whether co-ordination of the forward defensive stroke differed under two different practice task constraints. Four skilled batsmen were filmed from a side-on position while batting on an indoor wicket against a skilled medium-pace bowler. Kinematics of body segments during the forward defensive stroke were compared when facing a bowler and bowling machine delivering balls at the same speed. Their data on the segment angle of the elbow showed a variation between the two task constraints. At the moment of ball release, the mean front elbow angle against the bowler was 101 degrees compared to 88 degrees for the bowling machine. At the peak height of back-lift the front elbow flexed to 116 degrees, a difference of 15 degrees, and against the bowling machine the elbow flexed to 124 degrees, a difference of 36 degrees. Significant differences were also observed between the back-lifts of the two strokes. When facing the bowler the mean bat height was raised to a point 172 cm vertically from the ground. However, when facing the bowling machine the mean peak height dropped to 156 cm from the ground (see Figure 1.3). This data suggests that batsmen can begin their shots prior to ball release, because their movements become tightly geared, with practice, to information from the bowler's delivery. However, when facing the bowling machine there is no information available from the bowler's run-up and delivery action and batsmen have to rely on ball flight information alone. These tasks differ considerably in the *nature* of the information present, which ecological psychology proposes as instrumental in forming specific information-movement couplings (Gibson, 1979).

Renshaw *et al.* (2007) also observed differences in movement timing when batting against a bowler and a bowling machine. They examined three phases during the forward defence, at front foot movement (FFM), downswing (DS) and front foot placement (FFP). When facing the bowler batsmen initiated their FFM 0.5 s (± 0.089) pre-impact compared to 0.41 s (± 0.059) against the bowling machine. Average downswing times began marginally earlier when facing the bowling machine (0.32 s ± 0.029 pre-impact) than when facing the bowler (0.3 s ± 0.031 pre-impact). Front foot placement against the bowler occurred 0.12 s (± 0.039)

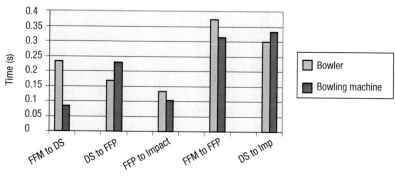

Figure 1.4 The duration (s) between key stages of the forward defence played under two different task constraints of practice.

pre-impact compared to 0.1 s(± 0.034) pre-impact against the bowling machine. Differences in duration of the front foot placement stride were greater against the bowler (0.375 s) than against the bowling machine (0.31 s). Stride length was greater against the bowler (0.8 m) than the bowling machine (0.72 m). The durations of different phases of the forward defence when facing bowler and bowling machine set to the same speed are summarized in Figure 1.4.

To summarize, the data showed clear differences in movement patterns between the two distinct practice task constraints. The significantly higher back-lift, earlier front foot movement, greater flexion at the front knee at lift off and greater stride length and duration, all signal great diversity of movements between the two task constraints of batting against a bowling machine and a real bowler. Although the patterns appear similar, these findings suggest that a different movement pattern is being practiced under the different task constraints.

Designing learning environments for emergent decision-making in practice

Modelled as dynamical systems, team sports display characteristics of complexity due to the potential for interactions that emerge between performers over time. For these reasons, the complexity sciences have been identified as a useful framework for studying decision-making and action in team games (Passos *et al.*, 2008). During a competitive game the decisions and actions of each player are constrained by multiple causes that produce multiple effects, such as game rules, environmental features including performance surface and weather, as well as significant others including teammates, opponents and spectators. From this view, attackers and defenders can be considered to form subsystems during performance, for example in a 1 v 1 dyad or a 2 v 3 sub-phase of a game (see Schmidt *et al.*, 1999; Guerin & Kunkle, 2004; McGarry & Franks, 2007; Passos *et al.*, 2006, 2008). The behaviour of a single player becomes dependent on what neighboring players (either teammates or opponents) are doing and on the immediate events prior to a sub-phase emerging. Players' decisions and actions suddenly become context-dependent and constrained by the interactions occurring in the complex system. This contextual dependence in behaviour signifies that player interactions are not deterministic (entirely predictable), nor completely random (entirely variable). These ideas suggest how the behaviour of interacting players can be interpreted as an emergent process resulting from the inter-individual spatio-temporal relations occurring during game situations. Team ball sports can be described as a series of sub-phases each constraining the co-ordination of different players to different extents (Schmidt *et al.*, 1999).

In order to understand the practical implications of these key concepts from the complexity sciences in team games, an example of emergent behaviour in rugby union during a ubiquitous 2 v 1 situation (i.e. two attackers against one defender) might be considered. For an attacker who carries the ball, the decision when and where to perform a pass is constrained by several factors, such as the position of teammates and nearest opponents, the approaching speed of adjacent opponents, the running line speed, the proximity of his/her nearest teammate, and key bound-ary markings such as the tryline and the sideline. The relative position of each player (i.e. teammate and opponent) is dependent on the ball carrier's behaviour and there is an interdependence of decisions and actions between those players.

Interdependence of the system makes it challenging to predict in advance the final outcomes of player interactions (i.e. tackle, pass, dribble, or try). This is because the characteristics of the interactions between neighboring components for each performance of the players in the 2 v 1 subsystem are unique. Although the players can display similar patterns of movement on different occasions, those movements are never repeated identically (e.g. the players' respective velocities and running lines are never the same; the players' relative positions differ; the locations on the field with respect to the tryline and sideline are never identical). Since the constraints imposed by neighboring components always exhibit differ-ent characteristics, it follows that each individual players' specific decisions and actions must satisfy those constraints. This type of rapid and refined behavioural adaptation is made possible by variability in movement behaviour by each player. The degrees of freedom of the movement system provides the players with the means to adjust their behaviour in order to maintain goal directed activity (i.e. adapt their running line to avoid an approaching defender or adjust the position of the ball in their hands to pass the ball to a teammate). A consistent outcome (move the ball towards the tryline) can be achieved or maintained by variability of actions of individual components (pass, dribble, kick). Players' variability leads to system unpredictability, which sustains the consistency of actions (attack or defend a tryline). Therefore, an implication for practice is that performers should not be encouraged to develop specific 'optimal movement patterns' as performance solutions. Instead, practice task constraints should aim to get players to search for a functional 'emergent' action, based on the current context. The use of practice drills to produce highly repeatable actions is unlikely to provide the adaptive behaviour needed to cope with dynamic performance environments.

Gibbs (2006) highlighted an important implication of these criticisms of traditional approaches to decision-making behaviour: "Perception cannot be understood without reference to action. People do not perceive the world statically, but by actively exploring the environment." (p. 49) In a team game, an attacker can create information by moving to perceive a defender's behaviour. In turn, the defender needs to act to perceive the attacker's behaviour. In team games like rugby union, such movements create information that is specific to the game environment that each player must learn to explore (become attuned to) through his/her actions.

Through using information to regulate action, information-movement cou-plings can be developed to adjust to environmental demands (i.e. an immediate opponent's actions) and support anticipation. However, anticipation is only pos-sible if the players are attuned to the most relevant sources of information needed to maintain their goal-directed behaviours. To be attuned to the most relevant perceptual variables in a performance context provides the basis of outstanding decision-making behaviour in team sports. Skilled performers are more sensitive to relevant sources of information to successfully perform a task than novices. In order to improve decision-making, training programmes should attune the interaction that a player has with the performance environment (i.e. by including relevant task constraints information from boundary markings, pitch surface, teammates, and opponents). To achieve this aim, the information available to be actively explored by players during practice must represent the same task and environmental constraints that exist during performance (e.g. speed of approach to an opponent; the space left available by defenders; the depth of the players in a defensive line; the body orientation of a defender). Otherwise, the information-movement couplings that emerge during practice will be attuned to perceptual variables *different* from those available during performance (as evidenced in the bowling machine and bowler example discussed earlier). The design of training programmes should be soundly based on the interactions that will occur in performance. Decision-making practices should be based on *performer-environment* interactions rather than a traditional *performer-* or *task-centred* approach. In the next sections of this chapter such ideas are exemplified by research on decision-making in rugby union.

Learning design for decision-making in rugby union

The aim of constraints manipulation by the practitioner is for the player to become better attuned to the relevant perceptual variables required to successfully perform a specific task. Manipulating constraints allows performers to search for alternative task solutions (improving their ability to cope with inherent performance variability) in dealing with unpredictability. But as Warren (2006) suggested, skilled action demonstrates two balancing features that need to be accounted for: stability and flexibility. He stated that: "These patterns are stable in the sense that the functional form of movement is consistent over time and resists perturbation and reproducible in that a similar pattern may recur on separate occasions. On the other hand, behaviour is not stereotyped and rigid but flexible and adaptive." (p. 359) Warren's (insights show that there is no single stable solution to a movement problem (no common optimal movement pattern).

This idea was illustrated in research that simulated a sub-phase of rugby union designed to involve the least number of players (i.e. the ubiquitous 1 v 1 situation near the tryline). In this sub-phase, an attacker needs to run beyond a defender to score a try, whereas a defender needs to keep the attacker and ball in front of him/her. The experimental task was performed on a field of 5 m width by 10 m depth and two digital video cameras were used to record player trajectory motion. To study the interpersonal dynamics of decision-making and action in this sub-phase, a collective variable was identified to describe dyadic system behaviour captured by a vector connecting each individual in the dyad. The values for this collective variable were calculated from the angle between the defender–attacker vector and an imaginary horizontal line parallel to the tryline with its origin in the defender's position. This analysis method resulted in an angle close to +90 degrees before the attacker reached the defender and close to –90 degrees if the attacker successfully

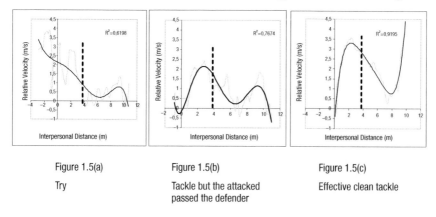

Figure 1.5(a)

Try

Figure 1.5(b)

Tackle but the attacked
passed the defender

Figure 1.5(c)

Effective clean tackle

Figure 1.5 Collective variable analysis in attacker–defender dyads.

passed the defender, with a zero crossing point emerging precisely when the attacker reached the defender (see Figures 1.5(a), 1.5(b) and 1.5(c)).

As a result of player interactions, the defender–attacker vector changed over time, with values of this angular relationship providing a potential collective variable to capture dyadic system behaviour. In addition, the first derivative of the collective variable over time was calculated, in order to analyze the rate of change of the relative positioning between an attacker and defender in a dyadic system. When an attacker achieves greater relative velocity of movement than a defender, the first derivative values of the collective variable will increase with the distance to the minimum (i.e. zero). Alternatively, when a defender's relative velocity is greater than an attacker's, the first derivative values tend towards the minimum. When there are no differences between the players' relative positions, the first derivative values tend towards zero.

Our results suggested how decision-making in attacker–defender dyads near the try area may be characterized as an emergent process. The approach phase was characterized by maintenance of defender–attacker horizontal angle values, since attacking players kept their running lines straight. A decrease in interpersonal distance between attackers and defenders led to some changes in running line, with the attacker aiming to avoid contact with the defender and using technical skills to explore the subsystem's stability, provoking some fluctuations in angle values. These changes in running line can be construed as evidence of perturbations within the dyadic system due to local interpersonal interactions. This is an emergent process constrained by the information field created by a decrease in interpersonal distance between the attacker and defender.

A continuous decrease in defender–attacker horizontal angle values after a zero crossing signified that a try occurred. Fluctuations in angle values signified that contact between the players took place. This interpretation was sustained by the assumption that the attacker (after a zero crossing) followed a straight line trajectory as the fastest way to reach the try area, a decision that led to angle values close to –90 degrees. However, when a defender's actions put an attacker on the floor, the angle value usually remained close to –50 degrees. In effective tackles, the horizontal angle never reached 0 degrees, signifying that the attacker never passed the defender. Despite the individual trajectories of each player in a dyad, the system always converged to one of very few states. For example, initially a defender is closer to the target area than an attacker. If a dribbling/running attacker manages to pass the defender with the ball, a structural change in system organization occurs. If contact occurs between the players an effective interception/tackle may take place and system stability is maintained by the defender.

The implication of this research is that practice task constraints should be designed to encourage opportunities for players to learn how to maintain or dissolve system stability in sub-phases of team games. In team games as complex systems, due to the dynamic, emergent nature of information supporting decision-making and action, it is too difficult to predict or prescribe large sequences of behaviour in advance. For this reason learning design should encourage the emergence of decision-making from the adaptive inter-individual interactions that occur during sub-phase performance, captured in small-sided practice games (Passos et al., 2008).

Conclusion

A constraints-led approach has been proposed as a theoretical framework for understanding learning design in sport pedagogy and physical education. Practitioners need to understand how important constraints, such as information available during practice, the structure of practice tasks and the skill level of the learner, interact to facilitate learning. This chapter examined how artificial aids during practice, e.g. use of a ball machine, might be implemented by pedagogists. Research showed how small-sided games (e.g. 1 v 1 or 3 v 3) might enhance players' skills in maintaining and dissolving stability in game sub-phases. It was also shown how the manipulation of augmented feedback to athletes and directing the search towards movement effects (i.e. an emphasis on developing an *image of achievement*) provides better opportunities to constrain the learners' search for emergent task solutions during discovery learning. It appears that directing learners' searches to movement effects during practice might prevent interference with self-organization processes in movement system dynamics as athletes explore the tasks. These, and many other issues, could form the basis of a non-linear pedagogy of relevance to physical educators and sport pedagogists (Chow et al., 2006).

References

Araújo, D., Davids, K., Bennett, S. J., Button, C. & Chapman, G. (2004). Emergence of Sport Skills under Constraint. In A. M. Williams & N. J. Hodges (eds), *Skill Acquisition in Sport: Research, Theory and Practice*, London: Routledge, pp. 409–433.

Bernstein, N. A. (1967). *The Control and Regulation of Movements*. London: Pergamon Press.

Bootsma, R. J. (1989). Accuracy of Perceptual Processes Subserving Different Perception-Action Systems. *Quarterly Journal of Experimental Psychology*, *41A*, 489–500.

Chow, J. Y., Davids, K., Button, C., Shuttleworth, R., Renshaw, I. & Araújo, D. (2006). Nonlinear Pedagogy: A Constraints-Led Framework to Understanding Emergence of Game Play and Skills. *Nonlinear Dynamics, Psychology, and Life Sciences*, *10*(1), 71–103.

Davids, K., Button, C., & Bennett, S. J. (2008). *Dynamics of Skill Acquisition: A Constraints-led Approach*. Champaign, Illinois: Human Kinetics.

Davids, K., Williams, A. M., Button, C. & Court, M. (2001). An Integrative Modeling Approach to the Study of Intentional Movement Behaviour. In R. N. Singer, H. Hausenblas & C. Jannelle (eds), *Handbook of Sport Psychology*, 2nd edn, New York: John Wiley & Sons, pp. 144–173.

Gibbs, R. (2006). *Embodiment and Cognitive Science*. Cambridge, UK: Cambridge University Press.

Gibson, J. J. (1979). *The Ecological Approach to Visual Perception*. Hillsdale, NJ: Lawrence Erlbaum Associates.

Guerin, S. & Kunkle, D. (2004). Emergence of Constraint in Self-Organized Systems. *Nonlinear Dynamics, Psychology and Life Sciences*, *8*, 131–146.

Jacobs, D. M. & Michaels, C. F. (2002). On the Apparent Paradox of Learning and Realism. *Ecological Psychology*, *14*, 127–139.

Kauffman, S. A. (1995). *At Home in the Universe: The Search for Laws of Complexity*. London: Viking.

Kugler, P. N. & Turvey, M. T. (1987). *Information, Natural Law, and the Self-assembly of Rhythmic Movement*. Hillsdale, NJ: Lawrence Erlbaum Associates.

McGarry, T. & Franks, I. (2007). System Approach to Games and Competitive Playing: Reply to Lebed (2006). *European Journal of Sport Science*, *7*(1), 47–53.

Montagne, G., Cornus, S., Glize, D., Quaine, F. & Laurent, M. (2000). A Perception-Action Coupling Type of Control in Long Jumping. *Journal of Motor Behavior*, *32*, 37–43.

Newell, K. M. (1985). Coordination, control and skill. In D. Goodman, R. B. Wilberg & I. M. Franks (eds), *Differing Perspectives in Motor Learning, Memory, and Control*. Amsterdam, North Holland: Elsevier, pp. 295–317.

Newell, K. M. (1986). Constraints on the development of coordination. In M. G. Wade & H. T. A. Whiting (eds), *Motor Development in Children: Aspects of Coordination and Control*. Dordrecht, Netherlands: Martinus Nijhoff, pp. 341–360.

Newell, K. M., Broderick, M. P., Deutsch, K. M. & Slifkin, A. B. (2003). Task Constraints and Change in Degrees of Freedom with Motor Learning. *Journal of Experimental Psychology: Human Perception and Performance*, *29*, 379–387.

Passos, P., Araújo, D., Davids, K., Gouveia, L. & Serpa, S. (2006). Interpersonal Dynamics in Sport: The Role of Artificial Neural Networks and Three-Dimensional Analysis. *Behavior and Research Methods*, *38*, 683–691.

Passos, P., Araújo, D., Davids, K. & Shuttleworth, R. (2008). Manipulating Constraints to Train Decision Making in Rugby Union. *International Journal of Sport Science & Coaching*, *3*(1), 125–140.

Renshaw, I., & Fairweather, M. M. (2000). Cricket Bowling Deliveries and the Discrimination Ability of Professional and Amateur Batters. *Journal of Sport Sciences*, *18*, 951–957.

Renshaw, I., Oldham, T., Davids, K. & Golds, T. (2007). Changing Ecological Constraints of Practice Alters Coordination of Dynamic Interceptive Actions. *European Journal of Sports Science*, *7*, 157–167.

Savelsbergh, G. J. P. & van der Kamp, J. G. (2000). Information in Learning to Co-ordinate and Control Movements: Is There a Need for Specificity of Practice? *International Journal of Sport Psychology*, *31*, 467–484.

Schmidt, R. C., O'Brien, B. & Sysko, R. (1999). Self-organization of Between-persons Co-operative Tasks and Possible Applications to Sport. *International Journal of Sport Psychology*, *30*, 558–579.

Warren, W. H. (1990). The Perception-Action Coupling. In H. Bloch & B. I. Bertenthal (eds), *Sensory-Motor Organizations and Development in Infancy and Early Childhood*. Dordecht: Kluwer Academic Publishers, 23–37.

Warren, W. (2006). The Dynamics of Perception and Action. *Psychological Review*, *113*, 358–389.

2 Instructions as constraints in motor skill acquisition

Karl M. Newell and Rajiv Ranganathan

Instructions as constraints in motor skill acquisition

One of the major roles of teachers and coaches in physical activity and sport is to convey information to the performer so as to enhance performance, learning and skill level. The role of instructional strategies in physical activity and sport has been the source of considerable study in the field of motor skill acquisition (e.g. Holding, 1965; Singer, 1975; Williams & Hodges, 2004; Wulf, 2007). Instructional strategies are interventions by an instructor in the motor learning of an individual or group that are presumed to facilitate the process of motor skill acquisition.

In this paper we focus on *one* aspect of instructional strategies; namely, the strategic role of instructions in learning and performing motor skills. The Wikipedia encyclopedia (as of August 21, 2008) provides a useful definition when it lists an instruction as a form of communicated information that is both command and explanation for how an action, behavior, method, or task is to be begun, completed, conducted, or executed. In this sense then, information from instructions is a forward-looking category of task-relevant information (i.e. directed at future performance) for the learner compared to the well-studied category of information feedback, which by definition provides information about some aspect of the past movement and behavior (Annett, 1969; Newell, 1996). Here we emphasize the role of instructions as constraints in channeling the search for task relevant solutions in motor learning.

It should be noted that there are several ways in which instructional information can be communicated to the learner. The primary modes or media of instructions include the spoken and written word although aspects of the same information can be conveyed in the visual presentation of a live or artificial representation of a movement sequence, such as in a demonstration or a video presentation, respectively, although there are other, less-used instructional strategies (Holding, 1965; Singer, 1975). In this paper, we emphasize the role of information through the spoken word of instructions because in practice this is perhaps the most common strategy of teachers and coaches to communicate information. The role of instructions in theory and practice will be discussed from within the general framework of this book: namely, the role of the constraints approach to practice and motor skill acquisition (see also Davids, Chapter 1; Davids *et al.*, 2008; Davis & Broadhead, 2007; Newell, 1986, 1996).

A caveat as background is the recognition that it is difficult to consider a particular instructional strategy in isolation of other instructional strategies. Thus, for example, instructions cannot be considered independent of demonstrations which often are used to convey the *same* information. Furthermore, instructions, and specifically the information to be conveyed through the instructions, cannot be considered independently of *what* is to be learned, the particular practice strategy in place (e.g. distribution of practice), the motor skill at hand (e.g. tennis forehand), and the skill level of the learner/performer.

Constraints on movement in physical activity

One way to consider the context in which an individual learns and performs a motor skill is to characterize the constraints to action (Newell, 1986; Davids, Chapter 1). In this view (see Figure 2.1), there are three general categories of constraints to movement in physical activity: those of the environment, the individual performer and the task. The environment reflects the constraints at the many levels of analysis external to the individual, the constraints of the performer reflect all of the structural and functional biological constraints of the body, while the task specifies the goal of the action and, in some cases, boundaries on the movement pattern that can be performed to realize the task goal. It is the confluence of these three categories of constraints that channels the organization of movement in physical activity and the emergent performance outcome. The collective of constraints on action, though of different categories, substance and

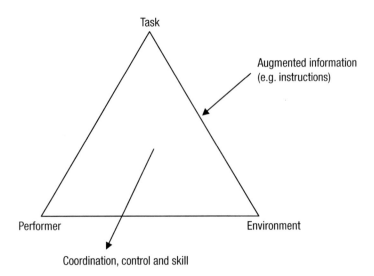

Figure 2.1 A schematic of the confluence of constraints to action (after Newell, 1986) with the addition of the role of the instructor.

influence, can be described in the same unifying language of dynamics (McGinnis & Newell, 1982; Newell & Jordan, 2007).

All past and present theories of motor skill learning have recognized the importance of the interaction of the individual and the environment, although they give different emphases to the relative contribution of these sources of influence (e.g. Development – Gesell, 1929; Schema theory – Schmidt, 1975; Learning theory – Thorndike, 1932; Behaviorism – Watson, 1930). A significant feature of the triangle of constraints approach to motor skill learning is that it gives emphasis to the role of the task in learning and performance and the interactive influence of the three categories of constraints on movement and performance. In effect, task goals and movement-related constraints are specifying boundary conditions on the interaction of the individual with the environment in the realization of the action goal.

The arrow external to the triangle in Figure 2.1 is highlighting the particular constraint of the instructions from the instructor that could relate to the environment or task, or both. It follows that the constraint of the intervention strategy adds to the confluence of the constraints to action that are present when the learner performs the task in the direct or immediate absence of instructor influence. This is consistent with the proposition that instructional strategies are not operating in isolation in the acquisition of motor skills but rather in concert with the other categories of constraints to action. The need is for the instructional strategy to exploit the potential for change in the dynamics of the performer/environment interaction and the learner's pursuit of the task goal and enhance learning and performance beyond that which would be achieved without an instructor (Vereijken & Whiting, 1990).

Instructions as a constraint

The general idea of a constraint is that it is a boundary condition to the dynamics of the system under consideration. Constraints can be essentially static and, thus, spatial and geometrical in nature, like the walls and doors of a room that have a very small (and usually imperceptible) rate of change. In addition, constraints can be time varying (to various degrees) as is the case with many physiological levels of analysis of the human system and the open, unpredictable environments of many physical activities and sport. It is against this background that Kugler *et al.* (1980, p. 9) proposed that the order in biological and physiological processes is primarily due to dynamics and the constraints that arise. Furthermore, they noted that both anatomical and functional constraints serve only to channel and guide dynamics; it is not that actions are *caused* by constraints, it is, rather, that some actions are *excluded* by them.

The idea of constraints is typically construed as a physical entity in nonliving systems but here we explore the concept in the context of instructions and human motor skill acquisition. In particular, we examine the role of instructions as a constraint that channels the emergence of the task-relevant co-ordination solution. The Wikipedia definition of instructions provided earlier holds them to be not only a constraint, as in setting a boundary to the movement pattern, but also prescriptive in conveying information about the movement pattern that should be produced. Interestingly, these contrasting interpretations of the role of information in instructions hold parallels to the theoretical divide about the prescriptions of motor programs and the role of constraints in the emergence of the dynamics of movement patterns (Kugler *et al.*, 1980).

Many of the constraints to action that are implicitly represented at the three corners of the triangle in Figure 2.1 are physical, in the sense that they have or reflect some form of property of the individual and/or environment. For example, the anatomy of the shoulder joint provides a constraint on the ways the arm can move. In contrast, the constraints of instructions can be considered as non-physical in that they are information about the boundary spatial and temporal properties of the to-be-performed movement pattern. This distinction, in and of itself, does not necessarily mean that the principles organizing the influence of physical and information constraints are any different to the organization of movement in action. Indeed, here we consider them in the same framework and language of the constraints to movement and action (McGinnis & Newell, 1982; Newell & Jordan, 2007).

The information in instructions

Although instructions are used frequently in the context of teaching and coaching motor skills there has been little analysis of the primary categories of information typically conveyed to the learner through instructions (although see Hodges & Franks, 2004). In this paper we outline working ideas from the perspective of contemporary theories on motor learning and control and look at the kinds of task-relevant information contained in instructions (Newell, 1996). In general, we view instructions as forward-looking with respect to what movement patterns or aspects of the action the learner or performer needs to produce or focus on in future practice trials.

The learning of a motor skill can be viewed as a search by the learner for a task-relevant co-ordination and control solution (Krinskii & Shik, 1964; Fowler & Turvey, 1978; Newell *et al.*, 1989). Therefore, rather than attempting to impose a movement pattern on the learner, the instructor, through interventions of augmented information and changes in the physical environment, attempts to facilitate this search process by the learner over practice trials. Thus, in this theoretical framework we focus on the ways in which the information conveyed by instructions could facilitate learning through searching. This approach places instructions beyond the role of merely providing a description of the task goal and the associated movement boundary conditions to potentially being part of founda-tional guidelines for the development of learning strategies – that is, strategies that effect change in the learning process. Below we outline instructional guidelines, giving examples of the kinds of information provided by instructions.

We would like to emphasize that the optimal strategies to enhance the learn-ing of a skill will to some degree be specific to the task and the individual. In this context, an important concept to consider during the learning process is the idea of an individual's "intrinsic dynamics" (Kelso, 1995), which are the co-ordination tendencies that are present in an individual even prior to learning the skill. From this viewpoint, learning does not involve *acquiring* new co-ordination patterns, but rather it involves adapting already existing co-ordination tendencies to achieve the task goal. These co-ordination tendencies will differ from person to person and as a function of skill level and prior experience.

Consider, for example, a badminton player attempting to learn to play tennis. This situation often poses some difficulty because the badminton player has a preferred co-ordination pattern of the arm (involving more wrist motion) that interferes with learning the pattern required for playing tennis. The learning problem faced by the badminton player is, therefore, qualitatively different from a complete novice trying to learn to play tennis. As a result, the strategies and instructions used must take into account both the co-ordination required for the task, and how the co-ordination tendencies of the individual can be exploited to achieve the goal.

There are several categories of movement information where instructions are typically given by teachers and coaches in practice and the challenge is to understand what movement property the learner needs information about from an instruction at a particular phase of learning a motor skill. Thus, the most central question is that of *what* information should be conveyed to the learner at a given level of skill for a particular task. It follows then that a major goal of the instructor is to understand what task-relevant information should be communicated to the learner via instructions.

To help structure our discussion about the role of instructions in motor skill acquisition we have identified two categories of information: information about the desired task outcome, and information about the desired movement pattern. In addition, we discuss aspects of the dynamical systems perspective that provide a basis for the role of information in creating changes in the co-ordination pattern. It is proposed that each of these types of information offers different levels of constraint to channel the search of the learner for the task-relevant co-ordination and control solution (Newell, 1996) and, therefore, should be used differentially as a function of task and skill level.

Categories of information in instructions

Information about task outcome

Perhaps the fundamental information conveyed by instructions is the goal of the task. Task goals are often defined in terms of outcome that is measurable, for example, in goals scored, height jumped, and time to complete the activity. When the task goal is a particular movement form, as in gymnastics or high-board diving, the relevant information to be conveyed is less clear and/or more difficult to convey than that of the discrete outcome of most tasks.

The information about desired task outcome is one of the most important instructions that serve as the reference of correctness (e.g. "hit the center of the target" in archery). In many learning situations, however, the learner knows the desired task outcome through prior experience and thus information about the task outcome does not have to be necessarily conveyed by the teacher through instructions. On the other hand, in whole-part-whole (i.e. when breaking a skill down to individual components) or progressive stages of learning, the desired outcome of a sub or part task is probably less well known to the learner and the teacher or coach may employ the same instructional approach to the part task goal as for the whole task goal.

The challenge of effectively transmitting task goal information, while seemingly straightforward, is well revealed in Polanyi's (1966) classic example of the rule governing bicycle riding: namely, "in order to compensate for a given angle of imbalance α, we must take a curve on the side of the imbalance, of which the radius (r) should be proportionate to the square of velocity (v) over the imbalance: $r \sim v^2/\alpha$" (p. 6–7). Clearly, cyclists, even experienced riders, do not know in the sense of declarative knowledge that this is the rule for the riding of a bicycle even though they are following this regularity in the movement dynamics of controlling the bicycle. Similarly, it seems reasonable to propose that instructional information in the form of the equation for juggling, as given by Shannon's theorem (Shannon, 1993): (F+D)H=(V+D)N, where F is the time a ball spends in the air, D is the time a ball spends in a hand, V is the time a hand is vacant, N is the number of balls juggled, and H is the number of hands, is unlikely to facilitate either the learning or teaching of juggling.

These examples demonstrate the point that while knowledge of the task goal is essential to performing the task, knowledge of the rule that produces success in terms of the task goal may not necessarily help an individual learn a motor skill or enable instructors to teach the learning of a skill any better. And, even if this information does facilitate learning to some greater or lesser degree in certain motor tasks, there are other categories of information that instructions can provide and that may be more effective in facilitating learning (Newell, 1996).

In addition, instructions about the task goal can also include general background knowledge as an explanation of how or why a particular movement form is appropriate for the task demand. For example, there have been studies of the effects of educating learners about the physics of the action to be learned (Wulf & Weigelt, 1997) and also information about the psychology or physiology of a task. The evidence in support of the success of this general explanation-type information in motor skill learning is very limited and is a topic that would benefit from systematic experimental study.

Information about movement pattern

Instructions can also be focused toward the desired movement pattern to be produced. Some motor tasks have an outcome goal that has to be realized within some additional boundary constraints on how the movement pattern is performed. Sport has many activity examples in this category, including those of swimming and track and field. In swimming, each stroke has particular constraints or rules about how the arms and legs are to move while a swimmer covers the set distance. In addition, there are some motor skills like gymnastics where the movement pattern itself is the outcome. In these cases, the teacher or coach has the significant challenge of trying to convey information to the learner about the intended movement pattern because there is little known about the principles of instructional information for creation of task-relevant movement pattern dynamics.

An important caveat here is the assumption that the instructor *knows* what the appropriate co-ordination pattern is that needs to be learned. As we have noted, this is specified as a constraint in some tasks (e.g. a 3½ somersault) but in most cases, there is a traditional champion's view of what the desired co-ordination pattern is that should be learned. That is, the assumption is made that the expert or champion of a given task performs with a certain co-ordination pattern and, therefore, by example, this is the co-ordination pattern that a learner needs to aspire to. This is similar to approaches in rehabilitation of movement disorders where movements of the typical population are considered to be the desired movement pattern (for additional criticisms of this approach, see Latash & Anson, 1996). It should be noted that a limit of the champions' model approach to determining the task-relevant movement pattern is that in a number of tasks there can be more than one movement pattern that is dynamically stable and that can reliably produce the task goal. Given that the constraints on the performer also differ from person to person, the appropriateness of the champions' model approach should not be taken for granted at face value.

The difficulties of using the spoken word to transmit information about a movement pattern leads naturally to the idea that a demonstration of the movement pattern of the to-be-learned skill is a more useful media to convey the information but there is very little research on the relative effects of instructions versus demonstrations in motor skill acquisition. In our view demonstrations provide information about the end-state dynamics to be produced by the learner (Newell, 1996) and evidence for their beneficial effects in skill learning is influenced by the task and skill level. This end-state information can be useful to some degree to a learner in searching for a task-relevant solution, however, it should be recognized that it does not convey information directly about how to change an evolving movement co-ordination pattern over practice trials. For example, Roberton *et al.* (1997) found that providing visual or verbal cues about the hopping pattern did not enable five-year-olds to produce the required pattern. Thus, in many motor skill contexts, this information needs to be supplemented, as appropriate, with related feedback and feed-forward information to facilitate effective and efficient learning through searching.

A framework for creating qualitative changes in co-ordination

So far, we have focused on the information in instructions with regard to task goal and movement patterns. However, as we have stressed earlier, the challenge of the instructor is to go beyond a description of the task goal and the movement pattern and to create conditions for facilitating the search process for a co-ordination solution in the learner. In this section, we discuss certain aspects of co-ordination, the concept of order and control parameters, and the implications they have for instructions.

Order parameters

Our knowledge of the principles that drive the learning of new patterns of co-ordination is very limited, including the acquisition of the fundamental motor sequence in infancy. Indeed, there are many aspects to this sequential and long-term process of change that require substantial research effort. One important need is the development of the facility to describe the collective co-ordination state of the to-be-learned movement pattern in a lower dimensional description than that of the complete motions of each biomechanical degree of freedom in the movement pattern.

One way to describe the co-ordination pattern is through what has been called the collective variable or order parameter for the task (Kelso, 1995). The order parameter is that which captures the collective organization of the degrees of freedom in part because it reveals when there is a change in the pattern of co-ordination. In the co-ordination task of oscillating two fingers (or other effectors) either in-phase (both effectors move up and down together) or anti-phase (one effector moves up while the other moves down), the relative phase between the respective effectors is the order parameter. Thus, the order parameter is 0 degrees in the in-phase motion and 180 degrees in the anti-phase motion.

The majority of physical activities in context involve the use of multiple body segments where the co-ordination of the many biomechanical degrees of freedom is required. A potential solution to this degrees of freedom problem (Bernstein, 1967) involves creating constraints between them so that the number of functional degrees of freedom is reduced (coordinative structures or synergies, Tuller et al., 1982). This is similar to a car having four wheels (biomechanical degrees of freedom) being controlled by a single steering wheel because of the constraints between the wheels.

What implications does this "low-dimensional nature of control" have for instructional strategies? Imagine the case of a driving instructor who does not recognize the structural constraints of the four wheels of the car trying to explain how to make a left turn. This would have to include instructions on the angle and the rate at which each wheel needs to be turned. This situation is not unlike the coach trying to teach a tennis serve by instructing the movement of the legs, the rotation of the hips, the position of the elbow, and so on. Not only does this approach create an "information-overload", it ignores the linkages between the different degrees of freedom. In contrast, the driving instructor and coach who understand the constraints underlying the system can give instructions that are both concise and effective by focusing (as useful) their attention toward the order parameter of the system.

The order parameters are expected to vary as a function of both the task and

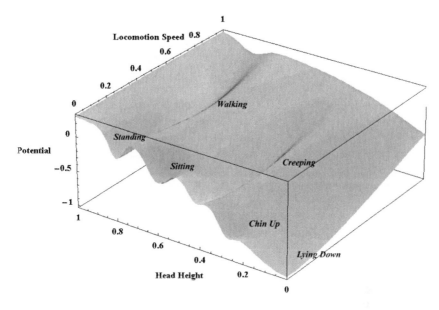

Figure 2.2 Order parameter example. The attractor landscape dynamics of the development of infant prone progression as organized by the scaling of two order
parameters – height of the head from the ground and locomotion velocity.
Adapted from Figure 6A of Newell *et al.* (2003) with permission.

skill level of the performer. However, apart from the relative phase parameter
that has been identified for bimanual co-ordination, there has been little effort
to try to identify the order parameter for the broad classes of motor skills, even
in the fundamental phylogenetic movement tasks, such as walking and running.
Newell *et al.* (2003) postulated that head height and movement speed were two
order parameters for the development by infants of the different modes of postural
control in locomotion, and these were variables that do not relate directly to the
individual effector degrees of freedom. This is shown in Figure 2.2, where each
combination of the order parameters of head height and movement speed corresponds to a different movement pattern such as creeping, walking or running.

The search for the identification of order parameters is one of the fundamental
issues in building the foundation for instructional guidelines. The key experimental strategy in searching for order parameters involves creating the conditions
to get a spontaneous change in the co-ordination mode (Kelso, 1995). Expert
coaches and physical education teachers probably have an intuitive understanding
of these "steering wheels" in the motor system and the instructions required to
change co-ordination patterns. However, the challenge for both researchers and
practitioners will be to characterize these order parameters and identify commo-
nalities to create a framework for providing information to bring about changes
in the co-ordination.

Control parameters

Closely related to the concept of the order parameter is the control parameter. A control parameter moves the system through its dynamical states even though it contains no specific information about the organization of the system (Kelso, 1995). Part of the instructions about the movement pattern may be directed toward bringing about a change to realize a new co-ordination pattern. In this situation, instructions (like feedback information) act as a control parameter, but the information is directed toward future performance (instead of some aspect of past performance as in feedback).

Thus, the relevant instructional information for learning can be considered in the unified context of order and control parameters. For example, in throwing, one of the control parameters is throwing velocity. Southard (2002) showed that as the velocity of the throw is increased, the co-ordination pattern changed significantly and the nature of the changes depended on the skill level of the thrower. This fits in well with the common observation that even elite baseball pitchers show significant changes in movement patterns when they have to throw the ball a very short distance with low velocity (see Figure 2.3).

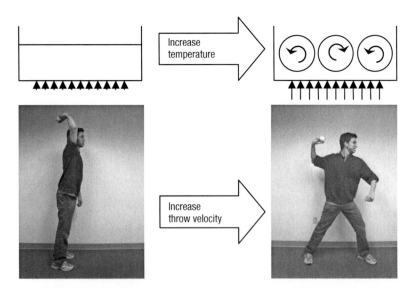

Figure 2.3 Control parameters and mode transitions. The top panels show the Rayleigh-Benard convection (adapted from Kelso, 1995). When the liquid is only lightly heated, there is no motion observed in the liquid. However, when the control parameter, i.e. the temperature, is increased beyond a certain point, convection rolls develop in the fluid. Arrows indicate the direction of rolling. The bottom panels demonstrate a similar idea in throwing. When the throwing velocity (the control parameter) is low (e.g. when throwing to a nearby target), a movement pattern without any stepping or hip rotations is used. However, when the throwing velocity is increased, a different movement pattern involving stepping and rotation of the hips and shoulders is observed.

An example of an instructional control parameter that is useful for changing the organization of a movement co-ordination pattern is transition information. The notion of transition information was presented in Newell *et al.* (1985) who proposed this information category as that which relates directly to the change in the co-ordination and control solutions that should occur in the future of the ongoing to next trial. Transition information is not prescriptive in the sense of dictating the specific movement dynamics that need to be produced. Rather, it is a direct form of feedback about the change required in future practice sessions to produce successful results. This may not be part of the resultant movement co-ordination pattern. Kernodle and Carlton (1992) have provided evidence for the relative effectiveness of transition information (in contrast to knowledge of results and videotape feedback) in the learning of an overhand throwing pattern with the non-dominant limb. Examples of transition information in this experiment were instructions such as "lag the movement of the hand behind the upper arm and elbow" and "release the ball later in the movement". As mentioned earlier, this information needs to be specific to the individual and may be especially critical to prevent the learner in the early stages of learning from settling into unhelpful co-ordination solutions that could have a detrimental effect on their skills in the long term (Knapp, 1964).

Identifying control parameters becomes critical to creating a qualitative change in the movement pattern. While control parameters usually have no information about the co-ordination pattern (e.g. velocity, distance or force), instructions related to the movement may also create the change (e.g. stand sideways to the target when throwing). A characteristic of these changes is that there is not a gradual progression from one movement pattern to the other; instead these periods are accompanied by high variability in performance followed by a spontaneous change in the pattern. Facilitating conditions for these changes to occur and providing relevant instructions during these periods of instability provide the greatest opportunity for instructors to guide the search process in the learner.

Presenting instructions

Apart from the informational content of instructions, a second critical factor is the presentation of instructions. This is of particular importance when providing instructions to novices or children who may not have task-relevant knowledge.

Providing an appropriate "concept"

An important aspect to instructions is to provide informational context to properties of the movement that is easily grasped by the learner. This has been found to be particularly important in learning new rhythms or space-time relations for bimanual co-ordination (Swinnen & Wenderoth, 2002). Franz *et al.* (2001) showed that when the two limbs are drawing semicircles, an easy conceptual pattern (i.e. producing the two semicircles so that they touched at the ends forming a circle) was much easier to produce than a more abstract pattern (i.e. producing the semicircles so that they touched in the middle forming a curved x pattern). Similarly, in the time-domain, when producing polyrhythms, experts seem to integrate the rhythms of each hand into a single complex polyrhythm (Deutsch, 1983; Summers, 2002) instead of trying to play two independent rhythms. For example, a common strategy that novice drummers use in producing a 2:3 polyrhythm is to tap their hands to the rhythm of the phrase "ring out the bells" (Moore, 1996), with the two hands simultaneously tapping for the first syllable and then alternating for the subsequent syllables. Klapp et al. (1998) have shown that this integrated method of instructing the 2:3 pattern using a phrase ("not difficult") is more effective than instructing the pattern of each hand independently.

In a similar vein, in teaching gymnastics to first grade students, Masser (1993) found that the cues such as "shoulders over knuckles" for doing a handstand, and "forehead on your knees" for doing a forward roll were effective in facilitating these behaviors. Additionally, the use of metaphors or analogies to facilitate this conceptualization (e.g. "pull the rings right into your hip" in gymnastics – Griffey et al., 1985, p. 134) may be an important tool for the instructor (Housner & Griffey, 1994; for a similar idea, see "image of achievement" – Whiting & den Brinker, 1982). Liao & Masters (2001) also showed that learning the topspin forehand in table tennis was more effective under an instruction using an analogy ("strike the ball while bringing the bat up along the hypotenuse of a right triangle") compared to when they were given a set of techniques from coaching manuals on how to hit topspin. Griffey et al. (1985) concluded that the use of metaphors not only make the instructions more concise, but also more image-evoking than discursive language (p. 136).

The findings from these studies demonstrate that the conceptualization of the task may be an important factor governing the stability and change of the co-ordination pattern. It follows that instructions that provide a simpler or focused task-relevant conceptualization may be more effective in getting the performers to produce the appropriate movement pattern.

Focus of attention

As mentioned in Chapter 1, another important part of an instruction is the focus of the performer's attention in the execution and learning of the movement skill (Wulf, 2007). This directly relates to the "frame of reference" problem – i.e. in terms of what variables should the instructions be phrased? In this regard, Wulf (2007) and others have shown that an external focus (i.e. attending to the effects of the movement) is more beneficial in the learning and retention of a skill than an internal focus (i.e. attending to the movement itself). For example, Wulf et al. (1999) showed that participants were more accurate in learning a golf shot when instructions were directed toward an external focus (e.g. paying attention to the club) than when the instructions were directed toward an internal focus (e.g. paying attention to the arm swing). In addition, Wulf et al. (2000) found that paying attention to the effects of the movement was also more beneficial than not paying attention to the movement at all. However, this effect seems to be mediated by skill level, where experts have been shown to benefit from an external focus whereas novices benefit from an internal focus (Perkins-Ceccato *et al.*, 2003).

The degree to which a directive of external focus of attention is general across tasks and skill level awaits systematic research. In the theory of an ecological approach to perception and action, Gibson (1968) viewed perceptual learning as the pick-up of higher order informational invariants and attention as the means to detect this information as, for example, in the optic array. Indeed, in this theoretical framework, attentional focus can constrain the movement organization so that perceptual learning can influence and enhance the learning of a motor skill. Instructions to attend to certain properties of the environment might be especially important in providing timing information to initiate and regulate movement sequences. For example, expert baseball batters have been found to use the information from the movement pattern of the pitcher to regulate their stepping patterns (Ranganathan & Carlton, 2007).

Concluding comments

An understanding of the role of instructional information in the acquisition of motor skills can only be sought more generally through theory development about the interface of symbolic information and dynamics in human learning and development. This is the longstanding philosophical problem of the relation between knowing how (procedural knowledge) and knowing that (declarative knowledge) (Ryle, 1984). Instructions are, in effect, the conveyance by an instructor of task-relevant information through the symbols of language to try to enhance the movement dynamics and action outcome of another individual, the learner.

In this paper we have outlined preliminary ideas on the primary categories of instructional information that appear most relevant to the learner. The most common use of instructions is about the task goal and a description to varying levels of detail about the movement dynamics that are most likely to realize the desired outcome and skill level. Another category of instructional information we have emphasized that is beyond the category of task description, is that which relates directly to the issue of bringing about change in the movement dynamics to improve performance.

Our knowledge of the principles of change in movement dynamics, particularly those for the qualitative change in co-ordination modes, is very limited (Newell, 1985, 1996). This is largely due to the study of motor learning being dominated by single degree of freedom laboratory tasks where the role of information feedback is very powerful. This lack of knowledge about the principles of change in whole body actions makes the application of the relevant instructional information in practice and theory more intuitive than formal. Our suspicion too is that a picture (demonstration) may, as the adage goes, be worth a thousand words, there are potential limits to facilitating the search processes of learning through end-state dynamics information alone. The uniqueness and potential power of instructions in practice is the forward-looking constraint on directly changing the qualitative and quantitative properties of a movement co-ordination pattern.

We anticipate that experienced and skilled coaches and physical education teachers have considerable local knowledge in their chosen domain about the task-relevant information for behavioral change that would be relevant to develop a formal theory of the instructional information for learning in movement and action. It seems likely that a central part of the theory and practice of instructions will be principles for determining the relevant dimensions of instructional information.

Acknowledgement

This work was supported by NSF 0518845. We would like to thank Inez Rovegno and the reviewers for helpful comments on an earlier version of the chapter.

References

Annett, J. (1969). *Feedback and Human Behavior*. Baltimore: Penguin.

Bernstein, N. A. (1967). *The Co-ordination and Regulation of Movements*. Oxford: Pergamon Press.

Davids, K. (2010). The Constraints-based Approach to Motor Learning: Implications for a Non-linear Pedagogy in Sport and Physical Education. In I. Renshaw, K. Davids & G. J. P. Savelsbergh (eds), *Motor Learning in Practice*. London: Routledge.

Davids, K., Button, C. & Bennett, S. (2008). *Dynamics of Skill Acquisition: A Constraints-led Approach*. Champaign, Illinois: Human Kinetics.

Davis, W. E. & Broadhead, G. D. (2007). *Ecological Analysis and Movement*. Champaign, Illinois: Human Kinetics.

Deutsch, D. (1983). The Generation of Two Isochronous Sequences in Parallel. *Perception and Psychophysics, 34,* 331–337.

Fowler, C. A. & Turvey, M. T. (1978). Skill Acquisition: An Event Approach with Special Reference to Searching for the Optimum of a Function of Several Variables. In G. E. Stelmach (ed.), *Information Processing in Motor Control and Learning*. New York: Academic Press, pp. 1–40.

Franz, E. A., Zelaznik, H. N., Swinnen, S. & Walter, C. (2001). Spatial Conceptual Influences on the Co-ordination of Bi-manual Actions: When a Dual Task Becomes a Single Task. *Journal of Motor Behavior, 33,* 103–112.

Gesell, A. (1929). *Infancy and Human Growth*. New York: Macmillan.

Griffey, D. C., Housner, L. D. & Williams, D. (1985). Coaches' Use of Non-literal Language: Metaphor as a Means of Effective Teaching. In M. Pieron & G. Graham (eds), *Sport Pedagogy*. Proceedings of the 1984 Olympic Scientific Congress. Champaign, Illinois: Human Kinetics, pp.131–137.

Hodges, N. J. & Franks, I. A. (2004). Instructions, Demonstrations and the Learning Process: Creating and Constraining Movement Options. In A. M. Williams and N. J. Hodges (eds), *Skill Acquisition in Sport: Research, Theory and Practice*. London: Routledge, pp. 145–174.

Holding, D. H. (1965). *Principles of Training*. Oxford: Pergamon.

Housner, L. D. & Griffey, D. C. (1994). Wax On, Wax Off: Pedagogical Content Knowledge in Motor Skill Instruction. *Journal of Physical Education, Recreation & Dance, 65,* 63–68.

Kelso, J. A. S. (1995). *Dynamic Patterns: The Self-Organization of Brain and Behaviour.* Cambridge, MA: MIT Press.

Kernodle, M. W. & Carlton, L. G. (1992). Information Feedback and the Learning of Multiple Degree of Freedom Activities. *Journal of Motor Behaviour, 24,* 187–196.

Klapp, S. T., Nelson, J. N. & Jagacinski, R. J. (1998). Can People Tap Concurrent Bi-manual Rhythms Independently? *Journal of Motor Behaviour, 30,* 311–329.

Knapp, B. (1964). *Skill in Sport: The Attainment of Proficiency.* London: Routledge & Kegan Paul.

Kugler, P. N., Kelso, J. A. S. & Turvey, M. T. (1980). On the Concept of Co-ordinative Structures as Dissipative Structures: I. Theoretical Lines of Convergence. In G. E. Stelmach & J. Requin (eds), *Tutorials in Motor Behaviour.* New York: North-Holland, pp. 1–49.

Krinskii, V. I. & Shik, M. L. (1964). A Simple Motor Task. *Biophysics, 9,* 661–666.

Latash, M. L. & Anson, J. G. (1996). What are Normal Movements in Atypical Populations? *Behavioral and Brain Sciences, 19,* 55–106.

Liao, C. M. & Masters, R. S. W. (2001). Analogy Learning: A Means to Implicit Motor Learning. *Journal of Sports Sciences, 19,* 307–319.

Masser, L. S. (1993). Critical Cues Help First-grade Students' Achievement in Handstands and Forward Rolls. *Journal of Teaching in Physical Education, 12,* 301–312.

Moore, J. M. (1996). A System for Understanding Polyrhythms. *Percussive Notes, 34,* 48–50.

McGinnis, P. M. & Newell, K. M. (1982). Topological Dynamics: A Framework for Describing Movement and its Constraints. *Human Movement Science, 1,* 289–305.

Newell, K. M. (1985). Coordination, Control and Skill. In D. Goodman, I. Franks & R. Wilberg (eds), *Differing Perspectives in Motor Learning, Memory and Control.* Amsterdam: North-Holland, pp. 295–317.

Newell, K. M. (1986). Constraints on the Development of Co-ordination. In M. G. Wade & H. T. A. Whiting (eds), *Motor Skill Acquisition in Children: Aspects of Co-ordination and Control.* Amsterdam: Martinies NIJHOS, pp. 341–360.

Newell, K. M. (1996). Change in Movement and Skill: Learning, Retention, and Transfer. In M. L. Latash & M. T. Turvey (eds), *Dexterity and its Development.* Hillsdale, NJ: Erlbaum, pp. 393–429.

Newell, K. M. & Jordan, K. (2007). Task Constraints and Movement Organization: A Common Language. In W. E. Davis (ed), *An Ecological Approach to Human Movement: Linking Theory, Research and Practice.* Champaign, Illinois: Human Kinetics, pp. 5–23.

Newell, K. M., Liu, Y-T. & Mayer-Kress, G. (2003). A Dynamical Systems Interpretation of Epigenetic Landscapes for Infant Motor Development. *Infant Development and Behavior, 26,* 449–472.

Newell, K. M., Morris, L. R. & Scully, D. M. (1985). Augmented Information and the Acquisition of Skill in Physical Activity. In R. L. Terjung (ed.), *Exercise and Sport Sciences Reviews Vol. 13,* Lexington, MA: Collamore Press, pp. 235–261.

Newell, K. M., Kugler, P. N., van Emmerik, R. E. A. & McDonald, P. V. (1989). Search Strategies and the Acquisition of Co-ordination. In S. A. Wallace (ed.), *Perspectives on Co-ordination.* Amsterdam: North-Holland, pp. 86–122.

Perkins-Ceccato, N., Passmore, S. R. & Lee, T. D. (2003). Effects of Focus of Attention Depend on Golfer's Skill. *Journal of Sports Sciences, 21,* 593–600.

Polanyi, M. (1966). The Logic of Tacit Inference. *Philosophy, 41,* 1–18.

Ranganathan, R. & Carlton, L. G. (2007). Perception-action Coupling and Anticipatory Performance in Baseball Batting. *Journal of Motor Behavior, 39,.* 369–380.

Roberton, M. A., Halverson, L. E. & Harper, C. J. (1997). Visual/verbal Modeling as a Function of Children's Developmental Levels in Hopping. In J. E. Clark & J. H. Humphrey (eds), *Motor Development Research and Reviews Vol. 1*, Reston, VA: National Association for Sport and Physical Education, pp. 122–147.

Ryle, G. (1984). *The Concept of Mind*. Chicago: Chicago University Press.

Schmidt, R. A. (1975). A Schema Theory of Discrete Motor Skill Learning. *Psychological Review*, 82, 225–260.

Shannon, C. E. (1993). Scientific Aspects of Juggling. In N. Sloane and A. Wyner (eds), *Claude Elwood Shannon: Collected Papers*. New York: IEEE Press, pp. 850–864.

Singer, R. N. (1975). *Motor Learning and Human Performance: An Application to Physical Education Skills*. New York: Macmillan.

Southard, D. (2002). Change in Throwing Pattern: Critical Values for Control Parameter of Velocity. *Research Quarterly for Exercise and Sport*, 73, 396–407.

Summers, J. (2002). Practice and Training in Bi-manual Coordination Tasks: Strategies and Constraints. *Brain and Cognition*, 48, 166–178.

Swinnen, S. P. & Wenderoth, N. (2004). Two Hands, One Brain: Cognitive Neuroscience of Bi-manual Skill. *Trends in Cognitive Sciences*, 8, 18–25.

Thorndike, E. L. (1932). *The Fundamentals of Learning*. New York: Teachers College, Columbia University.

Tuller, B., Turvey, M. T. & Fitch, H. L. (1982). The Bernstein Perspective II: The Concept of Muscle Linkage or Co-ordinative Structure. In J. A. S. Kelso (ed.), *Human Motor Behavior: An Introduction*. Hillsdale, NJ: Erlbaum, pp. 253–270.

Vereijken, B. & Whiting, H. T. A. (1990). In Defence of Discovery Learning. *Canadian Journal of Sports Science*, 15, 99–106.

Watson, J. B. (1930). *Behaviorism* (rev. edn). New York: Norton.

Whiting, H. T. A. & den Brinker, B. P. L. M. (1982). Image of the Act. In J. P. Das, R. F. Mulachy and A. E. Wall (eds), *Theory and Research in Learning Disabilities*. New York: Plenum, pp. 223–241.

Williams, A. M. & Hodges, N. J. (eds) (2004). *Skill Acquisition in Sport: Research, Theory and Practice*. London: Routledge, pp. 145–174.

Wulf, G. (2007). *Attention and Motor Skill Learning*. Champaign, Illinois: Human Kinetics.

Wulf, G., Lauterbach, B. & Toole, T. (1999). The Learning Advantages of an External Focus of Attention in Golf. *Research Quarterly for Exercise and Sport*, 70, 120–126.

Wulf, G., McNevin, N. H., Fuchs, T., Ritter, F. & Toole, T. (2000). Attentional Focus in Complex Motor Skill Learning. *Research Quarterly for Exercise and Sport*, 71, 229–239.

Wulf, G. & Weigelt, C. (1997). Instructions about Physical Principles in Learning a Complex Motor Skill: To Tell or Not to Tell. *Research Quarterly for Exercise and Sport*, 68, 362–367.

3 Building the foundations

Skill acquisition in children

Ian Renshaw

Introduction: why we need to base childrens' sport and physical education on the principles of dynamical systems theory and ecological psychology

As the childhood years are crucial for developing many physical skills as well as establishing the groundwork leading to lifelong participation in sport and physical activities, (Orlick & Botterill, 1977, p. 11) it is essential to examine current practice to make sure it is meeting the needs of children. In recent papers (e.g. Renshaw *et al.*, 2009; Renshaw *et al.*, 2010; Chow *et al.*, 2009) we have highlighted that a guiding theoretical framework is needed to provide a principled approach to teaching and coaching and that the approach must be evidence-based and focused on mechanism and not just on operational issues such as practice, competition and programme management (Lyle, 2002). There is a need to demonstrate how non-linear pedagogy underpins teaching and coaching practice for children given that some of the current approaches underpinning children's sport and P.E. may not be leading to optimal results. For example, little time is spent undertaking physical activities (Tinning, 2006) and much of this practice is not representative of the competition demands of the performance environment (Kirk & McPhail, 2002; Renshaw *et al.*, 2008). Proponents of a non-linear pedagogy advocate the design of practice by applying key concepts such as the mutuality of the performer and environment, the tight coupling of perception and action, and the emergence of movement solutions due to self-organisation under constraints (see Renshaw *et al.*, 2009). As skills are shaped by the unique interacting individual, task and environmental constraints in these learning environments, small changes to individual structural (e.g. factors such as height or limb length) or functional constraints (e.g. factors such as motivation, perceptual skills, strength that can be acquired), task rules, equipment, or environmental constraints can lead to dramatic changes in movement patterns adopted by learners to solve performance problems.

The aim of this chapter is to provide real-life examples for teachers and coaches who wish to adopt the ideas of non-linear pedagogy in their practice. Specifically, I will provide examples related to specific issues related to individual constraints in children and in particular the unique challenges facing coaches when individual constraints are changing due to growth and development. Part II focuses on understanding how cultural environmental constraints impact on children's sport. This is an area that has received very little attention but plays a very important part in the long-term development of sporting expertise. Finally, I will look at how coaches can manipulate task constraints to create effective learning environments for young children.

Focus on the individual

Although most teaching and coaching of children requires engagement with groups, a key tenet of non-linear pedagogy is a focus on the individual. This can be problematic as each member of a group will have unique intrinsic dynamics; each individual brings with him/her a set of movement capabilities when learning a new skill (Thelen, 1995). These capabilities are shaped by genetic factors, previous experiences and both physical and cultural environmental influences (Davids et al., 2003). For many teachers and coaches individualising practice sessions is problematic because individuals do not show homogeneity in the way that they develop (Adolph & Berger, 2006) and the acquisition of skills is not linear and is typified by sudden jumps and regressions (Davids et al., 2008). This means that at any point in time each child in a group possesses different action capabilities and additionally, functional and/or structural constraints change over short- and long-term timescales as a result of coaching interventions or due to growth and development. The impact on childrens' performance due to changes in intrinsic dynamics as a result of growth and how teachers and coaches can meet the needs of individuals will be discussed more in the following sections.

Changes in intrinsic dynamics and affordances

Coaching children is particularly challenging because changes in affordances for children are not only a result of changes in functional constraints (e.g. strength, perceptual skills) brought about by training, but are also due to changes in structural constraints caused by growth. Traditionally, growth in children has been modeled as an "S" shaped curve. However, recent findings have shown that growth curves do not represent the biological process of growth itself, but are a function of measurement methods (see Adolph & Berger, 2006). In fact, individuals demonstrate different developmental trajectories and human growth is typified by pulsatile biological processes, where increases in body dimensions occur in brief rapid bursts that punctuate a stable growth-free background during which most of development occurs (Lampl & Johnson, 1993) (see Figure 3.1). Additionally, specific parts, tissues, and organs have different growth rates. These changes are individually specific and therefore it becomes difficult to model coaching processes on a generalist approach to understanding growth. The implication for coaches is that changes in segment lengths as well as height and weight should be monitored on a regular basis during adolescence in order to take into account changes in body-scaled and action-scaled affordances (Fajen et al., 2009). For coaches, the main consideration is that structural changes lead to new affordances for individuals. For example, the span of a young child's hand may mean he/she has to shoot the basketball in two hands. As the child grows and the hand span increases, the ball can be set on one hand and the shooting technique can be more reflective of the champion's model (Newell & Rangathan, Chapter 2). From this example, it is clear that changes in both anatomical and functional constraints mean that key constraints that act to channel dynamics will change over time, leading to emergent movement solutions (Guerin & Kunkle, 2004).

For practitioners, a particularly challenging task is designing learning environments for children who are going through growth spurts, where the pulsatile processes are occurring at closer time intervals, leading to elevated velocity curves. In motor learning, the general advice provided to coaches who are coaching adolescents is that growth spurts lead to a decrease in the ability to learn new skills and conversely, learning takes place more easily during more stable phases of development (Pangrazi, 2004). However, it is worth noting that even in periods of no growth there is a need for athletes to continually retune and re-calibrate as

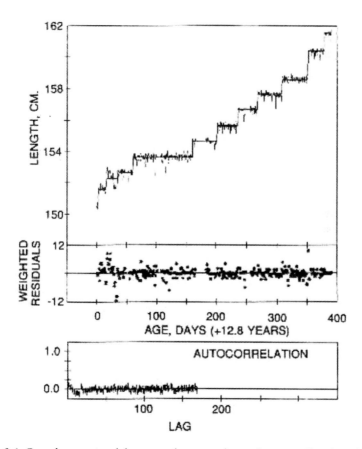

Figure 3.1 Growth spurts in adolescent males are made up of a series of brief rapid bursts that punctuate a stable growth-free background (Lampl & Johnson, 1993).

athlete's action capabilities change due to training and experience. For example, improvements in strength may provide new opportunities for action for the games player. An interesting question is to ask why changes in intrinsic dynamics due to growth would be treated differently to changes that are brought about by training. It may be that actually practicing regularly would lead to less disruption in co-ordination as re-calibration appears to occur quickly in terms of affordances (Mark, 1987). Additionally, examining the problem from a dynamical systems perspective would suggest that changing technique may well be easier during periods of instability as very stable movement patterns are more resistant to change (as evidenced by the challenges coaches face when trying to change the well-established techniques of veteran or elite players). Of course, the intrinsic demands of growing require the utilisation of energy and metabolic resources and the coach should be aware that physiological performance may be reduced during these periods. For talent identification processes, awareness that temporary reductions in available resources may be a contributory factor in performance has important implications and highlights the need to monitor performers over longer time spans of 2–3 months not via single snapshot trials (Hoare & Warr, 2000). Currently these proposed ideas need to be evaluated by empirical work to explore how growth spurts lead to changes in the (re-)organisation of information-movement couplings.

Individualising coaching in a group environment

The previous section highlighted the importance of individualising the coaching process. However, as any experienced coach knows only too well, a typical group will include individuals with below-average, average or above-average abilities. Essential to the effective design of learning opportunities for all individuals in a training group is the provision of learning tasks that facilitate success and lead to increased intrinsic motivation. A good tool for the coach would be to categorise the group using the three levels in Newell's model of learning (e.g. co-ordination, control and skill) to guide group membership (see Davids, Chapter 1). The use of these categories would help coaches to create different levels of challenge by using a differentiated learning approach (see Mosston & Ashworth, 2002). For example, when teaching net/court games indoors, three different games could be created by manipulating the task constraints of net height (low for faster games/high for slower); ball type (slower/faster or harder/softer), court size (long/thin or short/wide) and racket type (shorter handle/bigger head). Although teachers could allocate players to each game-type dependent on their level in Newell's stages of learning (see Davids et al., 2008), an alternative approach would be to allow individuals to choose which game they wanted to play. Allowing children to choose promotes autonomy, increases opportunities to feel competent and hence leads to enhanced intrinsic motivation (Ryan & Deci, 2000).

Cultural environmental constraints

Early days: why childrens' sports experiences should be multi-dimensional to develop expertise

Cultural environmental constraints are an important factor in the development of effective learning for all children regardless of whether their ambition is to be a champion or simply to play for the friendship and fun that sport can bring. In the first instance, parents are the key decision-makers in determining whether their child plays sport and then in choosing which particular sport(s) they play. A crucial decision for parents is to decide whether to enrol children in one or more sports. Should we be encouraging parents to promote the early specialisation in one sport model along the lines of the great champions of sport such as Tiger Woods, the Williams sisters or Sachin Tendulkar, or should we be encouraging participation in different sports, leaving specialisation until a much later stage of development? The issue of early specialisation or multi-dimensional development is currently a hot topic (for example, the *International Journal of Sport Psychology* produced a special issue on the topic (volume 38, 2008)) in the expertise literature with both the early specialisation and multi-dimensional development approaches having their respective champions. Much of the support for early specialisation comes as a result of the initial work of Ericsson and Smith (1991) that developed a descriptive theoretical framework to explain the expert performance approach by examining the contribution to expertise of specific practice environments. Their ongoing investigation of the role of deliberate practice in expert skill acquisition has become popular in the sport performance literature and has highlighted the importance of structured activities involving goal-directed skill learning, which require effort and concentration. It was estimated that experts typically spend about 10 years or 10,000 hours in deliberate practice to attain exceptional performance, which has found some support within the sports domain (Hodges & Starkes, 1996). Other researchers have provided support for Ericsson's approach by highlighting the lack of transfer between sporting tasks and indicate that sports-specific practice is essential to develop the perceptual and anticipatory skills displayed by experts in many different sports (see Renshaw & Fairweather, 2000; Wood & Abernethy, 1997).

However, although the evidence in support of early specialisation to become an expert cannot be denied, particularly in individual sports such as gymnastics (Laws *et al.*, 2007), there are some inherent risks attached to an early focus on one sport. Work over recent years by Côté and colleagues has highlighted that "getting serious" too soon can lead to performers who never experience the enjoyment associated with playing a wider range of sports and may lead to reduced physical health (Law *et al.*, 2007) and earlier drop out (Wall & Côté, 2006). In essence, these findings suggest that early sports experience (up to 12 years of age) should involve *sampling* a wide range of sports (Bloom, 1985) with high levels of *deliberate play* (Côté *et al.*, 2007). Sampling and deliberate play in these early stages of sporting careers is likely to lead to more enjoyment and fewer physical ailments such as overuse injuries from repetitive tasks. Importantly, for the aim of promoting lifelong involvement in participation or performance sport, the intrinsic motivation promoted by play-type activities is likely to lead to a lower likelihood of dropping out in youth sport, indirectly contributing to the attainment of adult expert-level performance (Wall & Côté, 2006).

The importance of early play experiences in the development of sports performance should not be underestimated and is valued by many current experts who attribute much of their success to the backyard pick-up games they played as youngsters (see Chappell, 2004). In these less-structured environments children are free to be inventive and creative without the fear of condemnation by over-zealous parents and coaches. Additionally, it seems that for invasion games, playing a wide range of sports can lead to enhanced decision-making skills further down the line (Abernethy et al., 2002; Berry et al., 2008).

These findings have important implications for parents, teachers and coaches in light of the fears of many adults in terms of allowing children to play in parks and streets. One solution would be for local authorities, sports clubs and schools to promote more hands-off approaches to early learning by providing deliberate play opportunities alongside, or perhaps instead of, a highly structured competition programme that may be actually limiting children's development and levels of enjoyment (Berry et al., 2008). While some traditionalists may baulk at the thought of "non-competitive" sport for children, some current research in the development of expertise in soccer has highlighted that those players who had taken part in a greater amount of playful football activity between 6–12 years of age were more likely to be awarded an academy contract with English professional clubs (Ford et al., 2006). Additionally, the testimony of experts clearly highlights that these "non-competitive" games are anything but as Chappell (2004) says "after playing in backyard games with my brother and his friends, test cricket was easy".

The previous discussion provides some support for the view that, during early childhood (6–12 years) participation should include a wide range of sporting activities, a position now advocated by the International Society of Sport Psychologists (see Côté et al., 2009). A multi-dimensional approach to sporting development enables individuals to become more rounded athletes and enhances their chances of finding a sport that they both enjoy and demonstrate aptitude in. Participation at this stage should not neglect the development of skills, but an underlying principle would be that whenever possible, skill should be allowed to emerge via deliberate play or well-designed games that are matched to the intrinsic dynamics of the children. At the end of the sampling phase, children (and their mentors) may make a decision to simply carry on playing at a recreational level for enjoyment and health. Alternately, the child, in conjunction with parents and coaches, may feel that he/she has some potential in a specific sport(s) and may choose to move into a more specialising phase. A decision to specialise means that the number of sports participated in is reduced to one or two (possibly a winter and summer sport), with much more time and effort being put into reaching high performance levels in this specialist area.

In summary, a non-linear approach to talent development highlights the importance of promoting a culture where multi-dimensional participation is encouraged in activities that are initially less structured. For those who may wish to have a single sports focus a compromise might be to encourage participation in sports with similar elements to the targeted sport (e.g. sports with similar perceptual skills, conceptual, movements or physical conditioning elements – see Schmidt & Wrisberg, 2008). This may ultimately lead to benefits for the individual in the chosen specialist sport as well as enhancing the adaptability of performers (Berry, 2008). Additionally, there should be an acknowledgement that there are likely to be multiple pathways to developing sporting expertise (Phillips *et al.*, 2010). Although there is evidence to support both specialisation and multi-dimensional development, a more multi-dimensional development route may be better from both a psychological and physiological viewpoint.

Manipulating task constraints to create effective learning environments for young children

When designing development programmes for children, perhaps sport administrators should take a leaf out of the book of those people they are trying to help, that is, the children themselves. When children engage in creative play they often design representative practice tasks that are suited to their own level of performance. Unlike adults, children do not set standards and performance tasks that are at inappropriate levels for the majority of the group. Children understand that if they create environments where their friends fail, they become quickly discouraged (Orlick & Botterill, 1977). Children intuitively adapt tasks to suit the action capabilities of individuals. For example, they shorten pitches or balance teams to make the games even.

Administrators and practitioners need to take more notice of the informal games that children design for themselves. At young ages (prior to 10 or 11 years of age), children should be given opportunities to learn new skills by a de-emphasis on formal, highly structured competition and the promotion of innovative practice sessions with flexibility in competition structures. For example, if a team is not using the width of the pitch appropriately in an invasion game, "channels" running parallel to the touchline through which the ball must travel before a team can score could be added. If a competition game becomes too one-sided the coaches could stop the game, reorganise the sides and play the rest of the game with an even contest that is challenging for all players. A rigid, formal competition programme means that coaches do not have this flexibility and an opportunity to challenge players is missed. This approach does not mean that children should not play competitive sport or that coaches should "dumb down" by creating games to suit the lowest skill level, but emphasises the need for activities and games that are suited to performers of all levels. For example, in cricket a pair's game (8-a-side) where "out" results in loss of runs rather than ending participation may be more appropriate for some children, while other children may be ready for the "real" 11-a-side game where out means out. Similarly, spending time in games like netball, playing small-sided games across the court (in the "thirds") with scoring by getting the ball to a player on the end-line (sideline) creates maximal activity and provides more opportunities to learn passing and movement skills within the context of teammates and opponents. An additional bonus of this approach is that children can learn without the pressure of playing in front of parents and adults in "proper" games. When the full netball game is played (which of course would be introduced at the appropriate time) adapting the height or size of the ring may promote more opportunities to score, meaning that final scores may be more reflective of the adult game, rather than at present where scores are often typical of those seen in low-scoring soccer matches!

As highlighted previously, one pedagogical strategy that allows children to be set appropriate challenges that are matched to their developmental skill levels involves setting up a range of games with different rules, court sizes and equipment. Approaches such as differentiated teaching (see Mosston & Ashworth, 2002) fit this model and can be used to achieve these ends. Alternatively, coaches and teachers can set problems for children and ask them to design their own games and activities. The advantage of this approach is that it gives children the opportunity to be autonomous and set achievable goals that promote feelings of competence. It also develops relatedness by working with others to develop the appropriate games. Modifying rules in games is important because manipulating task constraints forces learners to search for more functional movement solutions and produces adaptable performers who show degeneracy in the ways they are able to solve game-related problems (Davids et al., 2008).

In summary, the search for new solutions by exploring practice environments will facilitate unconscious processes of learning rather than relying on instructional constraints that may limit access to key perceptual information on which to base movements (Newell and Ranganathan, Chapter 2). In this perspective, the role of the coach is not to instruct performers by imposing a movement pattern on the learner, but rather to create conditions for facilitating the search process for co-ordination solutions. This approach highlights the need for less instruction and use of demonstrations of the perfect technique and an increased emphasis on tasks designed to promote the natural self-organising processes inherent in human movers (Renshaw et al., 2009).

Developing technique using non-linear pedagogy

A common criticism of approaches such as the Teaching Games for Understanding approach or Play Practice (see Bunker & Thorpe, 1982; Launder, 2001) is that they fail to address the development of appropriate techniques that are both safe (do not lead to injury) and effective. Although, the constraint-led approach advocated in this book highlights that the champion model, as Newell and Ranganathan (Chapter 2) describe it, may not be appropriate for every performer, it is generally accepted that the biomechanical degrees of freedom of the human body allied to specific task demands mean that the number of available functional movement solutions is limited. As such, activities and tasks designed to facilitate the development of "good" technique are not rejected in non-linear pedagogy, but the teaching strategies used to develop it must still be based on the principles of ecological psychology and dynamical systems theory discussed earlier. For example, coaches should attempt to develop technical skills by matching intrinsic dynamics with practice tasks that allow the subconscious, self-organisation of movements under constraints. How this approach would work in practice can be demonstrated by looking at teaching overarm throwing in striking and fielding games and the push pass in the invasion game of hockey. The prevalence of shoulder injuries in throwing for striking and fielding games has been predicated on the thrower failing to have the elbow above the shoulder during the throwing action (www. thebaseballmechanic.com/Throwing_Mechanics.html). In order to encourage a greater trunk–arm angle the coach could create a one-versus-one game where opponents are required to throw at a target on the ground or at a shortened stump. Throwing "down" at a target means that the trunk–elbow angle will be greater than 90 degrees at ball release, as the throwing pathway would start "high" and finish "low", resulting in the development of a "safer" throwing technique. Matching the task dynamics to the intrinsic dynamics inherent in the biomechanical structures of the arm–shoulder unit is important as it allows co-operation rather than competition between the system dynamics. Learning to throw to hit targets via one-on-one games also allows maximal activity in a group setting and promotes the acquisition of complimentary interceptive catching skills. A common error for young players in hockey is that the push shot actually becomes a hit. A simple task constraint that could be introduced to help the learner with this problem could be to place the ball the width of the stick away from the bottom of the hockey goal boards. This constraint means that the player cannot lift his/her stick but must sweep the ball away (from the goal). Giving the player a target "goal" to hit towards would also allow the coach to encourage accuracy. The width and distance of the target could be varied depending on the size and ability level of the hitter. As he/she becomes more proficient this target could be made narrower to encourage increased accuracy or moved further away to encourage greater force production in the push.

In summary, these examples show how coaches can manipulate task constraints to facilitate the development of sound techniques with less recourse to verbal instruction and feedback typical of traditional technique work. It is incumbent on coaches in their own sports to design similar practice tasks that meet the needs of the individuals in their groups. The experienced coach is well placed to complete such tasks as they have vast amounts of sport-specific knowledge and information to draw upon.

Conclusion

In this chapter, I have demonstrated the importance of considering individual, task and environmental constraints at all levels. On a global level, the developmental programmes to which children are exposed should encourage multi-dimensional development with participation in a number of sports being advocated. In this approach, play activities are not seen as frivolous but are an important part of skill learning. The importance of coaches and administrators having flexibility in practice and competitive sports programmes is essential so that children can be challenged at levels that are appropriate to their development. At the level of the coach or teacher the planning of individual sessions should facilitate self-organisation through the manipulation of individual, task and environmental constraints. Finally, the importance of manipulating task constraints to facilitate the design of learning environments at appropriate levels for children is empha-sised. For both individual skill development and tactical understanding in team games, letting "the game be the teacher" is an important message as it allows per-formers to use self-organising processes to develop their skills implicitly. However, games should not be selected from a coaching recipe book, but should be carefully designed to match the intrinsic and task dynamics of the task. Designing represent-ative games allows children to find solutions to game-based problems by attuning to the affordances provided by the movements of teammates allied to the actions of opponents. When coaches choose not to prescribe solutions, children will intrinsi-cally find the most appropriate ways to play. This approach utilises mistakes as a normal part of the learning process as learners search for optimal solutions. The good coach will understand this and will carefully structure coaching interventions to facilitate the process of learning based on the principled understanding of the learner and learning process advocated in this paper.

References

Abernethy, B., Côté, J. & Baker, J. (2002). *Expert Decision Making in Team Sport. Report to the Australian Sports Commission*. Brisbane, Australia: University of Queensland.

Adolph, K. E. & Berger, S. A. (2006). Motor Development. In W. Damon & R. Lerner (eds), *Handbook of Child Psychology: Cognition, Perception, and Language*. 6th edn, Vol. 2. New York: Wiley, pp. 161–213.

Berry, J., Abernethy, B. & Côté, J. (2008). The Contribution of Structured Activity and Deliberate Play to the Development of Expert Perceptual and Decision-Making Skill. *Journal of Sport & Exercise Psychology*, 30(6), 685–708.

Bloom, B. S. (1985). *Developing Talent in Young People*. New York: Ballentine.

Bunker, D. & Thorpe, R. (1982). A Model for the Teaching of Games in the Secondary Schools. *The Bulletin of Physical Education*, pp. 5–8.

Chappell, G. (2004). *Cricket: The Making of Champions*. Melbourne: Lothian Books.

Chow, J., Davids, K., Button, C., Renshaw, I., Shuttleworth, R. & Uehara, L. (2009). Nonlinear Pedagogy: Implications for Teaching Games for Understanding (TGfU). In T. Hopper, J. Butler & B. Storey (eds), *TGfU ... Simply Good Pedagogy: Understanding a Complex Challenge*. Ottawa: Ottawa Physical Health Education Association, pp. 131–143

Côté, J., Lidor, R. & Hackfort, D. (2009). ISSP Position Stand: To Sample or to Specialize? Seven Postulates about Youth Sport Activities that Lead to Continued Participation and Elite Performance. *International Journal of Sport and Exercise Psychology*, 9, 7–17.

Côté, J., Baker, J. & Abernethy, B. (2007). Practice and Play in the Development of Sport Expertise. In G. Tenenbaum & R. C. Eklund (eds), *Handbook of Sport Psychology*. New Jersey: John Wiley & Sons, pp. 184–201.

Davids, K. (2010). The Constraints-based Approach to Motor Learning: Implications for a Non-linear Pedagogy in Sport and Physical Education. In I. Renshaw, K. Davids & G. J. P. Savelsbergh (eds), *Motor Learning in Practice*. London: Routledge.

Davids, K., Glazier, P., Araujo, D. & Bartlett, R. M. (2003). Movement Systems as Dynamical Systems: The Functional Role of Variability and its Implications for Sports Medicine. *Sports Medicine, 33*(4),245–260.

Davids, K., Button, C. & Bennett, S. J. (2008). *Dynamics of Skill Acquisition: A Constraints-Led Approach*. Champaign, Illinois: Human Kinetics.

Ericsson, K. A. & Smith, J. (1991). Prospects and limits of the empirical study of expertise: An Introduction. In K. A. Ericsson & J. Smith (eds), *Toward a General Theory of Expertise*. Cambridge: Cambridge University Press, pp. 1–38.

Ericsson, K. A., Krampe, R. T. & Tesch-Römer, C. (1993). The Role of Deliberate Practice in the Acquisition of Expert Performance. *Psychological Review, 100*, 363–406.

Fajen, B. R., Riley, M. A. & Turvey, M. T. (2009). Information, Affordances, and the Control of Action in Sport. *International Journal of Sport Psychology, 40*, 79–107.

Ford, P. R., Ward, P., Hodges, N. & Williams, A. M. (2006). Antecedents of Selection into Professional Soccer: The Roles of Play and Practice in Progression and Regression. *Journal of Sport & Exercise Psychology, 28*, S68.

Guerin, S. & Kunkle, D. (2004). Emergence of Constraint in Self-organized Systems. *Nonlinear Dynamics, Psychology and Life Sciences, 8*, 131–146.

Hoare, D. G. & Warr, C. R. (2000). Talent Identification and Women's Soccer: An Australian Experience. *Journal of Sports Sciences, 18*, 751–758.

Hodges, N. & Starkes, J. (1996). Wrestling with the Nature of Expertise: A Sport Specific Test of Ericsson, Krampe, and Tesch-Romers' (1993) Theory of Deliberate Practice. *International Journal of Sport Psychology, 27*, 400–424.

Kirk, D. & McPhail, A. (2002). Teaching Games for Understanding and Situated Learning: Rethinking the Bunker-Thorpe Model. *Journal of Teaching in Physical Education, 21*, 177–192.

Lampl, M. & Johnson, M. L. (1993). A Case Study of Daily Growth during Adolescence: A Single Spurt or Changes in the Dynamics of Saltatory Growth? *Annals of Human Biology, 20*(6), 595–603.

Law, M. P., Côté, J. & Ericsson, K. A. (2007). Characteristics of Expert Development in Rhythmic Gymnastics: A Retrospective Study. *International Journal of Sport & Exercise Psychology, 5*, 82–103.

Launder, A. G. (2001). *Play Practice: The Games Approach to Teaching and Coaching Sports*. Champaign, Illinois: Human Kinetics.

Lyle, J. (2002). *Sports Coaching Concepts: A Framework for Coaches' Behaviour*. London: Routledge.

Mark, L. S. (1987). Eye-height Scaled Information about Affordances: A Study of Sitting and Stair Climbing. *Journal of Experimental Psychology: Human Perception and Performance, 13*, 360–370.

Mosston, M., & Ashworth, S. (2002). *Teaching Physical Education*. London: Benjamin Cummings.

Newell, K. M. & Ranganathan, R. (2010). Instructions as Constraints in Motor Skill Acquisition. In I. Renshaw, K. Davids & G. J. P. Savelsbergh (eds), *Motor Learning in Practice*. London: Routledge.

Orlick, T. & Botterill, C. (1977). *Every Kid Can Win*. Chicago: Nelson-Hall.

Pangrazi, R. P. (2004). *Dynamic Physical Education for Elementary School Children*. San Francisco: Pearson.

Phillips, E., Davids, K., Renshaw, I. & Portus, M. (2010). Expert Performance in Sport and the Dynamics of Talent Development. *Sports Medicine*, forthcoming.

Renshaw, I., Davids, K., Chow, J. W. & Hammond, J. (2010). A Constraints-led Perspective to Understanding Skill Acquisition and Game Play: A Basis for Integration of Motor Learning Theory and Physical Education Praxis? *P.E. & Sport Pedagogy*, forthcoming.

Renshaw, I., Davids, K., Chow, J. W. & Shuttleworth, R. (2009). Insights from Ecological Psychology and Dynamical Systems Theory can Underpin a Philosophy of Coaching. *International Journal of Sport Psychology*, 40, 580–602.

Renshaw, I. & Davids, K. (2008). *Implications of Nonlinear Pedagogy for Instruction, Practice, Organization, and Feedback*. Paper presented at the Fourth International Teaching Games for Understanding (TGfU) Conference, May 14–17th, BCU, Vancouver, Canada.

Renshaw, I. & Fairweather, M. M. (2000). Cricket Bowling Deliveries and the Discrimination Ability of Professional and Amateur Batters. *Journal of Sports Sciences*, 18, 951–957.

Ryan, R. M. & Deci, E. L. (2000). Self-determination Theory and the Facilitation of Intrinsic Motivation, Social Development, and Well-being. *American Psychologist*, 55, 68–78.

Schmidt, R. C. & Wrisberg, C. A. (2008). *Motor Learning and Performance: A Situation-based Learning Approach*, 4th edn. Champaign, Illinois: Human Kinetics.

Tinning, R. (2006). Thinking about Good Teaching in Physical Education. In R. Tinning, L. McCuaig & L. Hunter (eds), *Teaching Health and Physical Education in Australian Schools*. Frenchs Forest: Pearson Education Australia, pp. 232–239.

The Baseball Mechanic (2009). Throwing Mechanics ... the Right Way Goes a Long Way. Available online at: www.thebaseballmechanic.com/Throwing_Mechanics.html (accessed 21 July 2009).

Thelen, E. (1995). Motor Development: A New Synthesis. *American Psychologist*, 50(2), 79–95.

Wall, M. (2007). Developmental Activities that Lead to Dropout and Investment in Sport. *Physical Education and Sport Pedagogy*, 12,(1), 77–87.

Wall, M. & Côté, J. (2007). Developmental Activities that Lead to Dropout and Investment in Sport. *Physical Education and Sport Pedagogy*, 12(1), 77–87.

Williams, A. M. & Grant, A. (1999). Training Perceptual Skill in Sport. *International Journal of Sport Psychology*, 30 (2), 194–220.

Williams, A. M. & Ward, P. (2007). Anticipation and Decision Making: Exploring new horizons. In G. Tenenbaum & Eklund, R. C. (eds), *Handbook of Sport Psychology*. New Jersey: Wiley.

Wood, J. M. & Abernethy, B. (1997). An Assessment of the Efficacy of Sports Vision Training Programs. *Optometry and Vision Science*, 74, 646–659.

Part II

4 Perceptual training for basketball shooting

Raôul R. D. Oudejans and Johan M. Koedijker

Introduction

Playing basketball successfully requires many skills, such as dribbling and passing (either stationary or while running), jumping and rebounding, and defending. One of the most important skills is shooting as this is the only way to actually score points. The long-distance jump shot, and most notably the three-point shot, have become more and more important over the last few decades. Achieving a jump shot in basketball is an amazing accomplishment. Unlike in other far-aiming tasks (e.g. rifle shooting, pistol shooting, basketball free throw shooting, billiards) the body is in full motion and the distance to the target is never exactly the same from one shot to the next. The player is required to display multi-dimensional attention, simultaneously computing data on fast-moving fellow players and opponents as well as variables unique to each shot, before releasing an accurate shot (Oudejans *et al.*, 2002; Oudejans *et al.*, 2005; Ripoll *et al.*, 1986). Even more so, this difficult task has to be done in a very short time-window, following from the simple fact that the jump provides only limited time to make the shot before a traveling violation is made. How do expert shooters do that? When and for how long should a player look at the rim for an optimal shot? And the main question in this chapter: How can a player be trained to do this?

In general, practice in sports is often directed at physical constraints (conditioning), technical constraints (improving technical skills), and game tactics. The training of perceptual aspects of performance is not often a consistent element in training and preparation (see Abernethy, 1996; Williams & Ward, 2003). Yet, in the sport science literature there are more and more indications that perceptual expertise is an important characteristic of expertise in many sports (for overviews, see Abernethy *et al.*, 1998; Williams & Grant, 1999; Williams & Ward, 2007). Furthermore, several studies have shown that specific perceptual training holds much promise for further improvement of skill in sports (see Adolphe *et al.*, 1997; Oudejans *et al.*, 2005). Moreover, perceptual training often involves manipulations of the task constraints (e.g. with temporal or spatial occlusion) to force athletes to (learn to) use specific information at a specific time. In that sense, perceptual training originates from and often provides typical examples of the constraints-led perspective (Davids, Chapter 1; Davids *et al.*, 2008). The focus of the current chapter is on the visual control and possibilities for perceptual training in basketball shooting. As visual control of basketball shooting is dependent on shooting style, we will first discuss the two most relevant shooting styles used for the long-distance (jump) shot. Second, we will discuss the most relevant literature on the visual control of basketball shooting. Finally, we will discuss several ways to practice basketball shooting following the constraints-led perspective.

Basketball shooting styles

Basketball contains many different kinds of shots, such as the lay-up and the dunk, which are shots from very close by. Here we focus on the regular long-distance shot. There is a good deal of literature on this type of shot, most of it concerning the kinematics, biomechanics and physics of free throw and jump shooting (see Brancazio, 1981; Elliott, 1992; Elliott & White, 1989; Hay, 1993; Hudson, 1985; Kirby & Roberts, 1985; Knudson, 1993; Miller & Bartlett, 1993, 1996; Penrose & Blanksby, 1976). In the search for the determining factors of success, the role of variables such as release height, angle and speed were discussed and investigated, sometimes together with biomechanical variables such as shoulder angle and trunk inclination. Only rarely has the link been made between vision and shooting style whilst, in fact, different shooting styles can have very different consequences for the visual control of the shot, as will become apparent in this chapter. Note that with shooting style we refer to the movements that are made with the hands and the ball, not to what the feet do, as these could remain set on the floor (as in the set shot or free throw) or jump up (as in a jump shot). Descriptions in the literature make clear that the arm techniques used in the set shot and the jump shot are essentially the same (Hay, 1993; Kirby & Roberts, 1985).

Broadly speaking, two shooting styles have been reported. The first is the overhead-back spin style (see Hay, 1993; Hamilton & Reinschmidt, 1997; Kirby & Roberts, 1985) with which the ball is elevated high overhead to the shooting position and subsequently projected with a quick and forceful extension of the dominant elbow and flexion of the wrist (Hay, 1993; see Figure 4.1). Advantages of this style are that it allows backspin and a relative high point of release, both of which are critical for performance (Brancazio, 1981; Hamilton & Reinschmidt, 1997; Hudson, 1985). Moreover, with this high style the shooter can look at the basket from underneath the ball when it is held in the overhead shooting position (Hay, 1993; Kirby & Roberts, 1985; Penrose & Blanksby, 1976).

A lower pushing style is also reported (see Elliott, 1992; Kreighbaum & Barthels, 1981; Miller & Bartlett, 1996; Vickers, 1996a, b) during which the ball and hands remain below or at eye level for almost the entire shooting action. During the final extension, ball and hands are largely in front of the face and, hence, in the field of view (see Figure 4.1). An advantage of this low style is that more force can be applied compared to the high style. Generally, it seems that many expert male basketball players use a high style while many expert female players use the low style (with notable exceptions in either group). This is also apparent from the styles of participants in basketball studies (see de Oliveira *et al.*, 2006, 2008, 2009;

Figure 4.1 Examples of the high (left) and low (right) shooting style.

de Oliveira *et al.*, 2007; Oudejans *et al.*, 2002, 2005; Vickers, 1996 a, b). Still, style may also vary over shooting distance with lower styles for farther distances (see Miller & Bartlett, 1993, 1996).

In sum, in basketball two major shooting styles can be identified – a high and a low style – the main difference being whether or not the shooter can look at the basket from underneath the ball during the final shooting movements until ball release. Therefore, the two different styles also bring about differences in when a shooter can look at the hoop to pick up information about its location.

Visual control in basketball jump shooting

One of the earliest studies into the relation between vision and shooting accuracy in basketball was the study by Ripoll *et al.* (1986). They investigated eye-head co-ordination in the dynamic task of basketball jump shooting by expert, intermediate and beginning shooters. They monitored eye and head movements during the execution of jump shots and found that eye-head stabilization toward the target is critical in the dynamic situation of taking jump shots. The duration of head stabilization and eye-head stabilization toward the target was longer for successful shots than for misses.

Vickers (1996a, b) also investigated the relation between vision and basketball shooting. She examined free throw shooting performance by elite female basketball players (low style) and she collected detailed information about where and when, relative to the shooting movements, shooters fixated their gaze. She found that experts fixated their gaze at the hoop for a relatively longer period before initiating the final shooting movements, resulting in a long duration of final fixation on the target (between 800 and 1000 ms). Near-experts, who were found to miss more often, had shorter final fixation times (between 300 and 400 ms). This final fixation is called quiet eye (QE) and it appears that experts fixate their gaze on the target for a relatively longer period before and during the final movements (for an overview see Vickers, 2007).

A longer QE duration appears to be a characteristic of higher levels of skill in sport, not only in basketball shooting, but also in other far-aiming tasks, such as rifle shooting and dart throwing (Vickers, 2007). Furthermore, the temporal offset of QE relative to the phase of the aiming movement, and thus, the timing of QE, also appears to be crucial (Vickers et al., 2000). Fixating the target too soon or too late does not lead to the same level of accuracy as looking at the optimal moment and allowing the data collected visually to guide the aiming movements.

Empirical support for the relevance of the timing of QE was provided by Oudejans et al. (2002; Oudejans & Coolen, 2003) who investigated the visual control of expert male basketball players taking jump shots with a high style while wearing Plato liquid crystal (LC) goggles (see Figure 4.2) to manipulate vision. LC goggles were opened or shut instantaneously at specific moments coupled to the shooter's movements (see Oudejans & Coolen, 2003). In line with the possibility for late viewing with the high shooting style, Oudejans et al. demonstrated that with this style, late vision provided necessary and sufficient information for expert shooters to visually control their shooting. Specifically, expert shooters taking jump shots could detect sufficient information for accurate shooting during the period that the ball was above their line of sight until ball release, a period that only lasts about 350 ms. Moreover, it appeared that long and early looking (but without vision during the final 350 ms) had disastrous effects on shooting accuracy. In a follow-up study, de Oliveira et al. (2006) demonstrated that expert basketball shooters, high style and low style alike, prefer to use information from the rim as late as possible given their shooting style. For high-style shooters, this concerns the final period of about 350 ms before ball release (when ball and hands are above the line of sight). For low-style shooters, this concerns the period just before ball and hands enter the line of sight hereby blocking further vision of the basket.

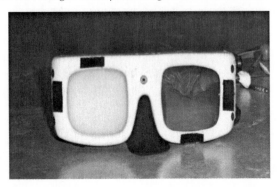

Figure 4.2 Plato LC goggles that can be opened and closed instantaneously.

In short, looking late seems to be essential for both low- and high-style expert shooting, because late viewing ensures the detection of the most optimal and updated information about the relative distance between the shooter and the basket.

Several follow-up studies by de Oliveira and colleagues (de Oliveira *et al.*, 2007, 2008) further substantiated these ideas. De Oliveira *et al.* (2007) showed that performance quickly deteriorated when the final shooting movement was even briefly delayed relative to visual information detection, implying that accurate shots actually need online detection of the most updated information about the target relative to the shooter's changing point of observation. Finally, de Oliveira *et al.* (2008) found patterns of gaze behaviour for experts taking free throws and jump shots consistent with the notion that accurate shooting requires online use of visual information that is detected as late as shooting style allows.

Thus, when it comes to the visual control of basketball shooting empirical results point to the importance of online detection of information as late as possible, that is, as late as a particular style allows. By detecting late information it is possible to adjust movement kinematics most appropriately to the situation close to ball release, so that forces applied fit best with the actual distance that the ball has to travel.

Perceptual training for high-style shooters

The studies discussed above make clear that an optimal timing and duration in information detection is essential for accurate shooting. One of the reasons why some *near-expert* shooters have lower shooting percentages than real expert shooters may be that they do not yet exhibit an optimal timing and duration of information pickup, that is, they pick up information either too early (before the final period), too briefly, or a combination of both. Research with basketball free throws and volleyball serve reception has shown that near-experts may exhibit sub-optimal gaze behavior during the execution of the task (Vickers, 1996a; Vickers & Adolphe, 1997). The question that was central in the study by Oudejans *et al.* (2005) was whether the timing and duration of the pickup of information of the basketball jump shot could be improved with specifically designed perceptual training and whether this would result in an improvement in shooting performance.

Oudejans *et al.* (2005) investigated the effects of an eight-week visual control training program on jump shooting performance of expert, young male (16–19 years) basketball players shooting with a high style. The training aimed to improve the pickup of information during the final period of a shot, just before ball release, by providing vision only during this period while wearing LC goggles as well as by having participants shoot from behind a screen (see Figure 4.3). These procedures imposed constraints on vision that made visual information for shooting available only after ball and hands had passed the line of sight. Under the assumption that sub-optimal performance would normally entail information detection that would be either too early (before the final period) or too brief during the final period, it was expected that by excluding all vision prior to the final

Figure 4.3 Picture of the screen used in the study by Oudejans *et al.* (2005).

Figure 4.4 Dribbling specs (left), a special ball (middle) and The JumpShooter® (right).

period, players' attention would be educated to the use of information available in this period. It was found that after late-vision training, game shooting percentages of these near-expert players indeed showed marked improvements (from 46% to 54% to 61%, prior to, during, and after intervention). The constraints imposed on vision during the training apparently forced players to use the more crucial data that was available during the final moments before ball release, thereby improving their actual in-game shooting performance. This shows that specific manipulations of the constraints on vision hold great promise for performance improvement in sports practice in general and in basketball (shooting) practice in particular. Other examples of perceptual training in basketball would be dribbling while occluding vision from the hands (see Figure 4.3), or passing and catching from behind a screen or after quickly turning around. For each skill it is a challenge for practice to design drills in which the relevant constraints are manipulated.

Case Study: Perceptual training for basketball shooting: Playing with constraints

Diagnostic

Players do not use the most useful perceptual information during shooting, that is, as late as possible given their shooting style.

Possible cause

This is not yet optimally developed, perceptual learning is not yet complete.

Constraints

Needless to say, as a coach there are various general ways to play with the constraints in shooting drills. First, note that there are already several official rules that prescribe different constraints for men, women and children. For example, the official size of a ball in women's basketball is smaller than a ball in men's basketball. Furthermore, especially for young children, there are constraints that can be adapted in practice, such as basket height and ball size – children below 12 years of age can play with a lower basket and a smaller, lighter ball (see Chase *et al.*, 1994). With these constraints the forces needed to reach the rim are reduced, allowing for a proper shooting technique not restricted by a lack of force. Second, variations in distance, one of the most important constraints in shooting, are crucial in learning to shoot a basketball and discovering the relations between different forces applied from different distances and the results of the shots. Young children should begin close to the basket when developing the proper shooting techniques. Only gradually should shooting distance be increased, following the gradual development of the skill and increases in strength as children mature. In addition, there are all kinds of shooting aids on the market to adjust important constraints for the shooting action, such as rim enlargers and reducers, specific balls with stripes (to emphasize spin) and drawings of hands (to emphasize proper hand positioning; see Figure 4.4, middle), and even shooting arm braces to force specific angular movements. Most relevant in light of the literature discussed so far, there is a device on the market with which screen training can be easily implemented, the Jumpshooter® (Figure 4.4 right).

This brings us to the most relevant visual control training for high-style shooters, that is, shooting from behind a screen (as in Figure 4.3 or 4.4, right) that only allows vision during the final instances before ball release when the shooter is close to the peak jump height during the shot. This training can easily be implemented in basketball practice by including a rebounder to return the ball to the shooter behind the screen. It is important to adjust the height of the screen as well as the distance between the shooter and the screen in such a way that the basket cannot be seen when the player is on the ground (just before the jump) but can only be seen when the shooter is in the air. The possible disadvantage that a player cannot see the end result of a shot from behind the screen, may easily be resolved by providing feedback (e.g. verbally) about whether the shot was a hit or a miss, or too long or too short, or too much to the left or right. This could be done by the rebounder or the coach. Furthermore, the screen training should, of course, not replace all regular shooting practice. Instead it should be used as a supplement to regular practice.

Just as effective, although more technologically advanced, is the method of manipulating vision using LC goggles in the same manner as that used during the studies by Oudejans et al. (2002, 2005). The goggles could be remotely controlled by the coach who may then provide the shooters with vision at any moment that he or she would prefer. It is advisable to adjust availability to the shooting style of the shooter. In all cases, the idea is to constrain vision in such a way that the shooter is forced to detect the most updated visual information so as to improve shooting performance.

Following the same principle it should be possible to manipulate the visual constraints of low-style shooters (that could be able bodied men or women as well as wheelchair basketball players) to improve shooting accuracy. Possibilities that would be worth pursuing are shooting after quickly turning around to face the basket, or stepping from behind a screen that first blocks vision, or riding (wheelchair) underneath a screen that blocks vision until it is cleared so that the basket can only be seen during the final instances just before ball release. In all these cases players are forced to use the latest, most updated and therefore most useful information. Preliminary data from our own lab in which expert wheelchair basketball players received the perceptual training intervention just described are promising. Using remotely controlled LC goggles, it is possible to open and close the goggles in such a way that vision is only allowed at those moments that are most appropriate for information detection for that shooting style. Again, extending manipulations of constraints on vision to other skills can be easily achieved, as long as one strives to organize the training environment in such a way that players are forced to rely on crucial information for task execution.

References

Adolphe, R. M., Vickers, J. N. & Laplante, G. (1997). The Effects of Training Visual Attention on Gaze Behaviour and Accuracy: A Pilot Study. *International Journal of Sports Vision, 4*, 28–33.

Brancazio, P. J. (1981). Physics of Basketball. *American Journal of Physics, 49*, 356–365.

Chase, M. A., Ewing, M. E., Lirgg, C. D. & George, T. R., (1994). The Effects of Equipment Modification on Children's Self-efficacy and Basketball Shooting Performance. *Research Quarterly for Exercise and Sport, 65*, 159–168.

Davids, K. (2010). The Constraints-based Approach to Motor Learning: Implications for a Non-linear Pedagogy in Sport and Physical Education. In K. Davids, I. Renshaw & G. J. P. Savelsbergh (eds), *Motor Learning in Practice*. London: Routledge.

Davids, K., Button, C. & Bennett, S. (2008). *Dynamics of Skill Acquisition: A Constraints-led Approach*. Champaign, Illinois: Human Kinetics.

de Oliveira, R. F., Huys, R., Oudejans, R. R. D., van de Langenberg, R. & Beek, P. J. (2007).

Basketball Jump Shooting is Controlled Online by Vision. *Experimental Psychology*, 54, 180–186.

de Oliveira, R. F., Oudejans, R. R. D. & Beek, P. J. (2006). Late Information Pick-up is Preferred in Basketball Jump Shooting. *Journal of Sports Sciences*, 24, 933–940.

de Oliveira, R. F., Oudejans, R. R. D. & Beek, P. J. (2008). Gaze Behaviour in Basketball Shooting: Further Evidence for Online Visual Control. *Research Quarterly for Sport and Exercise*, 79, 399–404.

de Oliveira, R. F., Oudejans, R. R. D. & Beek, P. J. (2009). Experienced Players Appear to Use Angle of Elevation Information in Basketball Shooting. *Journal of Experimental Psychology: Human Perception and Performance*, 35, 750–761.

Elliott, B. (1992). A Kinematic Comparison of the Male and Female Two-point and Three-point Jump Shots in Basketball. *The Australian Journal of Science and Medicine in Sport*, 24, 111–118.

Elliott, B. C. & White, E. (1989). A Kinematic and Kinetic Analysis of the Female Two-point and Three-point Jump Shots in Basketball. *Australian Journal of Science and Medicine in Sport*, 21, 7–11.

Hamilton, G. R. & Reinschmidt, C. (1997). Optimal Trajectory for the Basketball Free Throw. *Journal of Sports Sciences*, 15, 491–504.

Hay, J. G. (1993). *The Biomechanics of Sports Techniques*, 4th edn. Englewood Cliffs, NJ: Prentice Hall.

Hudson, J. L. (1985). Prediction of Basketball Skill Using Biomechanical Variables. *Research Quarterly for Exercise and Sport*, 56, 115–121.

Janelle, C. M., Hillman, C. H., Apparies, R. J., Murray, N. P., Meili, L., Fallon, E. A. & Hatfield, B. D. (2000). Expertise Differences in Cortical Activation and Gaze Behavior during Rifle Shooting. *Journal of Sport & Exercise Psychology*, 22, 167–182.

Kirby, R. & Roberts, J. A. (1985). *Introductory Biomechanics*. Ithaca, NY: Mouvement Publications.

Knudson, D. (1993). Biomechanics of the Basketball Jump Shot – Six Key Teaching Points. *Journal of Physical Education, Recreation, and Dance*, 64, 67–73.

Kreighbaum, E. & Barthels, K. M. (1981). *Biomechanics: A Qualitative Approach for Studying Human Movement*. Minneapolis, Minnesota: Burgess Publishing Company.

Miller, S. & Bartlett, R. M. (1993). The Effects of Shooting Distance in the Basketball Jump Shot. *Journal of Sports Sciences*, 11, 285–293.

Miller, S. & Bartlett, R. M. (1996). The Relationship between Basketball Shooting Kinematics, Distance and Playing Position. *Journal of Sports Sciences*, 14, 243–253.

Oudejans, R. R. D. & Coolen, H. (2003). Human Kinematics and Event Control: On-line Movement Registration as a Means for Experimental Manipulation. *Journal of Sports Sciences*, 21, 567–576.

Oudejans, R. R. D., Koedijker, J., Bleijendaal, I. & Bakker, F. C. (2005). The Education of Attention in Aiming at a Far Target: Training Visual Control in Basketball Jump Shooting. *International Journal of Sport and Exercise Psychology*, 3, 197–221.

Oudejans, R. R. D., van de Langenberg, R. W. & Hutter, R. I. (2002). Aiming at a Far Target Under Different Viewing Conditions: Visual Control in Basketball Jump Shooting. *Human Movement Science*, 21, 457–480.

Penrose, T. & Blanksby, B. (1976). Two Methods of Basketball Jump Shooting Techniques by Two Groups of Different Ability. *Australian Journal of Health, Physical Education and Recreation*, 71, 14–23.

Ripoll, H., Bard, C. & Paillard, J. (1986). Stabilization of Head and Eyes on Target as a Factor in Successful Basketball Shooting. *Human Movement Science*, 5, 47–58.

Vickers, J. N. (1996a). Visual Control when Aiming at a Far Target. *Journal of Experimental Psychology: Human Perception and Performance*, 22, 342–354.

Vickers, J. N. (1996b). Control of Visual Attention during the Basketball Free Throw. *American Journal of Sports Medicine*, 24, S93-S97.

Vickers, J. & Adolphe, R. M. (1997). Gaze Behaviour during a Ball Tracking and Aiming Skill. *International Journal of Sports Vision*, 4, 18–27.

Vickers, J. N., Rodrigues, S. T. & Edworthy, G. (2000). Quiet Eye and Accuracy in the Dart Throw. *International Journal of Sports Vision*, 6, 30–36.

5 Saving penalties, scoring penalties

Geert J. P. Savelsbergh, Olav Versloot,
Rich Masters and John van der Kamp

Introducing the penalty kick

The penalty kick was introduced as a direct cause of the following incident in the 1891 FA Cup semi-final between Notts County and Stoke City. One of the Notts County defenders prevented a goal by pushing the ball out of the goal mouth with his hand. The subsequent direct free kick, which was the standard sentence in those days, did not result in an equalizer for Stoke City. This was considered an outrageous injustice. More severe punishment of such ungentlemanly offences was called for, and so the penalty kick was introduced (Miller, 1998). The regulations for a penalty kick have been adjusted several times since 1891, but its composition has remained the same; a player takes a free kick to the goal from 11 m (i.e. 12 yards), facing only the opposing goalkeeper.

In this chapter, we discuss the penalty kick from both the perspective of the goalkeeper and the penalty taker. For the goalkeepers, we explain the role of visual perception and discuss recent evidence that shows that perceptual training can improve anticipation of penalty kick direction. We also discuss evidence that goalkeepers can present barely perceptible information cues to penalty kickers, which influence their kicking behaviour. We conclude by suggesting some rules of thumb for both penalty takers and goalkeepers.

The goalkeeper: perceiving the penalty taker's intentions

Skilled visual perception is part and parcel of expertise in sport. Of course, in stopping penalty kicks, professional goalkeepers exhibit levels of motor behaviour that require years of practice at diving to intercept the ball. An important component of goalkeeping is the use of visual information to perceive the penalty taker's intentions (e.g. decide where the ball will go) and to continuously guide the ensuing interceptive actions of the goalkeeper (Van der Kamp et al., 2008). In a penalty kick, the ball flight time is usually less than the time the goalkeeper needs to initiate and execute a dive for the ball. Hence, a goalkeeper who waits for the ball to be kicked (because ball motion provides the most reliable information) before deciding where to dive is very likely to arrive too late to intercept the ball. This rigorous time-constraint can be reduced by predicting to which side the ball will be directed and at what height, by using sources of information that are available before the penalty taker contacts the ball. In other words, the goalkeeper must use advance information generated by the penalty taker's actions during the run up to and the actual kick of the ball. It has been established for a large variety of time-constrained sports that experts and novices differ in the way that they use temporal and spatial aspects of information to anticipate future events and decide the most appropriate counter-action. High-skilled players show more effective visual search strategies and are able to pick up and use the most useful sources of information more quickly than their less-skilled counterparts. This enables high-skilled performers to anticipate the actions of an opponent and hence to reduce their response times.

Kuhn (1988) identified two strategies that allow a goalkeeper to save a penalty kick. In the first strategy, the goalkeeper decides in advance where to dive without taking the penalty taker's actions into account. In this strategy, the goalkeeper may guess where to dive or use prior knowledge of, for instance, the side to which the penalty taker prefers to kick the ball. In the second, kicker-dependent strategy, the goalkeeper anticipates the direction of the ball using early visual information of the penalty taker's actions. An important question is what is the nature of the early visual information that goalkeepers use to anticipate and when does it become available?

One attempt to characterise the visual information that goalkeepers use to anticipate a penalty kick was a study by Franks and Harvey (1997) analysing video images; they correlated the penalty taker's movements and posture with the direction of the shot. This analysis identified the non-kicking leg as an early and relatively reliable source of information. In 80% of the kicks the final positioning of the foot of the non-kicking leg next to the ball pointed in the direction of the shot. There are more reliable sources of information (e.g. the positioning of the kicking leg at foot–ball contact, 98%), but the positioning of the non-kicking leg occurs approximately 200–250 ms before foot–ball contact, which, unlike the more reliable sources, leaves the goalkeeper sufficient time to initiate and execute an interception.

The analyses of Franks and Harvey (1997) only provided evidence of the kind of information that is available for anticipation. Savelsbergh et al. (2002) used gaze recordings to address this confusion. Unskilled participants and skilled goalkeepers (i.e. from the highest amateur leagues in the Netherlands) were required to move a joystick to one of six areas (3 height × 2 sides) of a rectangle (representing the goal) in response to video clips of penalty kicks presented on a large screen. The penalty kick recordings were taken from a goalkeeper's perspective at eye-height. Each film showed the penalty taker's approach to the ball, actions before and during ball contact and the first portion of the ball's flight. Participants had to anticipate the direction of each penalty kick by moving the joystick as if to intercept the ball. Thus, in contrast to previous work, participants were actually producing an action in response to the penalty kick. The joystick allowed for an online or synchronised response to the events in the clip. The penalty kick was considered to be saved if the joystick was positioned in the correct location before or at the moment that the ball would have crossed the goal line. The skilled goalkeepers stopped more penalties than the unskilled goalkeepers (i.e. 36% versus 26%). The skilled goalkeepers were also more accurate at predicting the direction of the penalty kick, waited longer before initiating a response (i.e. approximately 300 ms versus 500 ms before foot–ball contact) and made fewer corrective movements with the joystick compared to unskilled goalkeepers. Visual search behaviour was analysed to identify the areas which were fixated most in preparation for a response. The skilled goalkeepers spent more time fixating the penalty taker's head, the ball and both the kicking and non-kicking leg, whereas the unskilled participants spent more time fixating the arm, trunk and hips. It also appeared that the viewing preferences of the unskilled participants were less pronounced, suggesting that their gazes wandered around the stimulus array without selectively attending to specific sources of information. In contrast, the skilled goalkeepers seemed to have learned to attend to a more narrow range of more informative areas.

Savelsbergh *et al.* (2002) compared two groups of participants distinguished by skill level. Yet a skilled goalkeeper is not by default a skilled penalty saver. Hence, Savelsbergh *et al.* (2005) examined the visual search behaviours of successful penalty savers and less successful penalty savers at the same skill level. A group of Dutch semi-professional goalkeepers was tested and classified as either successful or unsuccessful based on their penalty save performance in the film-based anticipation test. The more successful penalty savers were more accurate at predicting the direction and elevation of the penalty kick and waited longer before initiating a response. With respect to visual search this successful group distinguished themselves from the less successful penalty savers by spending longer periods of time fixating the non-kicking leg. Figure 5.1 presents the fixation percentages for the

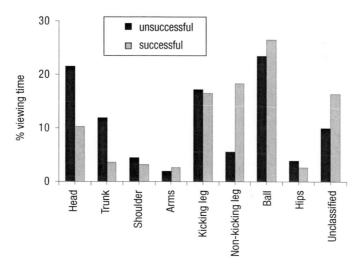

Figure 5.1 Percentage of fixation time for different areas for the most and least successful penalty saver in the study by Savelsbergh *et al.* (2005).

successful goalkeepers, and the unsuccessful goalkeepers, who performed at similar levels to the unskilled participants in Savelsbergh *et al.* (2002).

The successful penalty savers primarily fixated the kicking leg, the non-kicking leg, and the ball, while the unsuccessful penalty savers spent most time viewing the head, trunk, kicking leg and ball. As mentioned above, Franks & Harvey (1997) argued that just before foot–ball contact the non-kicking leg is most predictive of the direction of the penalty kick and at ball contact the kicking leg is most predictive, so it appears that the visual search of the successful penalty savers focused on these most informative areas. The unsuccessful penalty savers, however, showed a visual search pattern that resembled those of the unskilled participants examined by Savelsbergh *et al.* (2002). Better penalty savers distinguished themselves by focussing on the more reliable sources of information that are available shortly before contact (i.e. non-kicking, kicking leg). The exploitation of information available in the movements of the legs allows more accurate perception of the penalty taker's intentions. The key difference seems to be fixation of the non-kicking leg, although neither general goalkeeping skill, nor general differences in visual search patterns (e.g. number or duration of fixations) provided an explanation for expertise differences in penalty saving. Rather, expertise differences seem to be related to a combination of attention to the non-kicking leg just before ball contact and the moment at which the response is initiated.

Training perceptual anticipation in goalkeepers

Recently, Savelsbergh *et al.* (2009 in press) tested a strategy designed to improve perceptual anticipation of the penalty kick direction. They tried to optimise the goalkeeper's visual search behaviour. Savelsbergh *et al.* (2009) attempted to direct the goalkeeper's gaze in a systematic way to the most informative areas as they unfold in time during a penalty taker's run-up to the ball and actual kick. The gaze pattern most effective for an unskilled penalty saver to anticipate the direction of the ball was hypothesised to be: from the start of the penalty taker's run-up until foot–ball contact first look at the head, shift gaze to the hip region, and then the (lower) leg regions, paying special attention to the positioning of the non-kicking foot. Savelsbergh *et al.* (2009) examined whether perceptual training can establish such a gaze pattern and, if so, whether there is a consequent improvement in penalty-save performance.

Previous studies have demonstrated that anticipation can indeed be improved by perceptual learning by directing the performers attention to the more relevant sources of information (see Abernethy *et al.*, 1999). Savelsbergh *et al.* (2009), reasoned that perceptual learning is not exclusively a matter of learning to focus on the most useful information, but also involves learning to accurately couple attention to moments at which the most useful sources are available. In other words, not only are the specific sources of information important, but so is the way in which the sources unfold in time. Savelsbergh *et al.* (2009) used a moving highlight that was superimposed on a video clip of a penalty taker approaching and kicking a penalty (Figure 5.2). This approach enabled them to direct the

Figure 5.2 The highlight moved from the head, down through the upper body and hips towards the feet. These clips were shown to the training group (see Savelsbergh *et al.*, 2009).

goalkeeper's visual attention to the information-rich movements and postures of the penalty taker as they shift in time (i.e. from the head early in the run-up, to the hips, and then the legs just before ball contact). In this method it was not necessary to occlude information, thus maintaining the temporal relevance of the information sources as they became available in the penalty kick situation, and also the relative motion between informative areas. The participant goalkeepers, who were divided into three groups, responded to penalty kicks presented on a large screen by moving a joystick, as in the previous studies by Savelsbergh *et al.* (2002, 2005). A pre-test, training, post-test design was used.

The guided perceptual training group practiced with video clips (Figure 5.2) that were edited to highlight relevant information during the run-up and the kick. An unguided perceptual training group practiced with the same film clips but without the moving highlight. A control group performed only the pre-test and post-test. The results showed significant changes in the visual search behaviour of the guided perceptual training group. This was accompanied by an improvement in the initiation of the joystick movement, which after training coincided with the occurrence of the most important information source and led to better penalty-save performance than the other two groups. The results lend further support for the idea that sport-specific visual training programmes can lead to better anticipation of the outcomes of an opponent's actions (Farrow & Abernethy, 2002).

The penalty kicker: ignoring the goalkeeper's actions

The goalkeeper benefits from anticipating the actions of the penalty taker, so a performance advantage accrues from a kicker-dependent strategy. What about the penalty taker? As for the goalkeeper, two general strategies have been distinguished (Kuhn, 1988; Van der Kamp, 2006). In a keeper-independent strategy, the penalty taker chooses in advance (i.e. before the run-up) where to kick the penalty and does not take the actions of the goalkeeper into account. By contrast, in the keeper-dependent strategy the penalty taker leaves the final decision regarding where to aim the ball until the last moments before foot–ball contact. In doing so, the penalty taker tries to obtain information from the goalkeeper's posture and movements to anticipate the side to which the goalkeeper is going to dive. The penalty taker will then direct the ball to the side opposite to which the goalkeeper dives. Bootsma and Savelsbergh (1988) found that in 70% of the penalty kicks the ball is not directed to the side the goalkeeper dives, suggesting that a substantial number of penalty takers employ the keeper-dependent strategy (see also Kuhn, 1988). This observation remains mute about whether the keeper-dependent strategy is indeed the most advantageous strategy for the penalty taker. Recent empirical work suggests that it is not and that the penalty taker may be better to ignore the goalkeeper's actions.

Yet, the closer the penalty taker gets to the ball, the more difficult it may become to successfully change a planned kick. The benefits of a keeper-dependent strategy may therefore depend on the time available to adjust shot direction. Establishing this "point of no return" is important, since expert penalty savers tend to move late. Van der Kamp (2006) evaluated field penalty-taking performance of intermediate-skilled football players under conditions that imposed keeper-independent and keeper-dependent strategies. Participants took penalty kicks on a FIFA regulation synthetic grass pitch. There were two target areas (0.6 m × 0.6 m) to the left and to the right of the middle of the goal. Two lights, placed next to each other in the middle of the goal, signalled to which of the two target areas the participant should kick the ball. Penalty kicks were taken in three conditions. In the keeper-independent condition, participants were told that the signalled target area would not change. Hence, the decision on which side to kick to was defined before the start of the run-up. In addition, two keeper-dependent conditions were imposed. In the keeper-dependent-unaltered condition participants were informed that the signalled target may or may not change during the run-up. In fact, it did not. In the keeper-dependent-changed condition participants were also informed that the signalled target may or may not change. The target did in fact change, when participants were at one of three different distances from the ball, 2.4 m (early), 1.6 m (middle) or 0.8 m (late). A clear effect of strategy on penalty-taking perform-ance was found. Participants placed significantly more shots to the wrong side in the keeper-dependent-changed condition than in the other two conditions. The percentage of direction errors was significantly larger when the change of target was signalled late as opposed to early or in the middle of the run-up. During the run-up, the percentage of errors increased when the time available to alter the direction of the kick decreased. Van der Kamp (2006) showed that the minimum time required for participants to alter kick direction successfully was approximately 400 ms prior to ball contact. In other words, with less than 400 ms available, participants were unable to successfully employ the keeper-dependent strategy.

These findings indicate that the keeper-dependent strategy is less than perfect, particularly when the penalty taker has to change direction within 400 ms before foot–ball contact. It is, however, quite improbable that goalkeepers start their final dive for the ball that early (see Savelsbergh *et al.*, 2002). Moreover, if the penalty taker managed to successfully redirect the ball, shot accuracy was sacrificed. Van der Kamp (2006) concluded that anticipating the movement of the goalkeeper may decrease penalty-taking performance, mainly because there is not enough time to modify the kicking action. A keeper-independent strategy would therefore be preferable.

A final observation was that even when kick direction remained unaltered during the keeper-dependent strategy, variability of accuracy was high relative to the keeper-independent strategy. Van der Kamp (2006) speculated that this was caused by visually attending to the lights (i.e. the "goalkeeper"). Research has shown that the spatial accuracy of a broad range of actions is significantly enhanced by looking at the target prior to movement execution (Land & Hayhoe, 2001). In other words, kicking accuracy may have deteriorated because in the keeper-dependent conditions participants focussed on the lights ("goalkeeper") rather than on the target areas. Evidence for this contention in penalty kicking can be found in a study by Bakker, Oudejans, Binsch & Van der Kamp (2006), in which participants were asked to perform a penalty kick to a stationary goalkeeper on a large screen. Penalty-kick accuracy and visual gaze behaviours were measured. Three instruction conditions were created in which participants were told to: (1) simply score a goal; (2) to score a goal and attend to the goalkeeper; and (3) to score a goal and attend to the target area (i.e. the areas to the left or right of the goalkeeper).

The gaze recordings showed that participants looked more frequently to the goalkeeper or target area dependent on the instruction. When they were only instructed to score a goal, fixations to the target area were more frequent

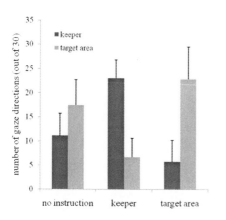 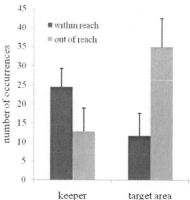

Figure 5.3 Gaze fixations to the goalkeeper and target area as a function of instruction (left panel), and penalty kick accuracy (i.e. the ball landing within and outside the keeper's reach) as a function of gaze fixations to the goalkeeper and target area (right panel) (see Bakker *et al.*, 2006).

(Figure 5.3). Further analyses demonstrated how gaze direction influenced the accuracy of the kick. Participants were more likely to kick the ball within reach of the goalkeeper when they fixated the goalkeeper than when they fixated the target area. In other words, looking at the goalkeeper impeded kicking accuracy.

It must be stressed, however, that there is one important limitation to this research: it does not include a goalkeeper that actually dives for the ball. It has been argued that prior to diving, a goalkeeper adopts movement strategies that are specific for the intended direction of the dive (Núñez Sànchez et al., 2005). In particular, there is extension of the knee on the side of the body that opposes the direction of dive, together with flexion of the other knee, which occurs 200 ms to 250 ms before the penalty taker kicks the ball (Sánchez et al., 2005). In a keeper-dependent strategy, the penalty taker may exploit these types of predictive information to anticipate the direction of the dive. The lack of predictive information in the previous studies (Bakker et al., 2006; Van der Kamp, 2006) may have caused an underestimation of the efficacy of the keeper-dependent strategy.

Back to the goalkeepers: how to implicitly influence the penalty taker

Another reason exists for why a penalty taker should consider choosing a keeper-independent strategy over a keeper-dependent strategy. The goalkeeper may, without the penalty taker being consciously aware that it happens, influence the penalty taker's perception of the goalkeeper and subsequently the penalty taker's decision about how and where to kick the ball. Van der Kamp and Masters (2008) examined the influence of goalkeeper posture on perception of goalkeeper size, and asked whether this would affect penalty kick performance.

In a first study, they showed that participants' perceptual judgment of the size (i.e. height) of a goalkeeper is influenced by the posture the goalkeeper assumes. Consistent with the well-known Müller-Lyer illusion, the goalkeeper with his arms raised to the sky was perceived to be taller than the goalkeeper with his arms pointing to the ground. To test whether goalkeeper posture actually influenced penalty taking,[1] van der Kamp and Masters presented the goalkeeper in the same variety of postures in a goal on a screen at 68% of life size (Figure 5.4). Handball players were told to score a goal by throwing the ball inside the posts but out of reach of the goalkeeper. They were informed that the goalkeeper could move but could not leave his position. Figure 5.4 shows the results of ten throws to each posture for one participant: the ball was thrown farther away from the goalkeeper's body when the arms were raised to the sky than in the other postures (although only the difference with arms-stretched to the side was statistically reliable). The magnitude of the difference in accuracy would have amounted to 14–15 cm in a real football penalty kick. Hence, goalkeeper posture appears to affect penalty-taking accuracy without the penalty taker knowing it.

A second example is perhaps even more intriguing. Masters, Van der Kamp and Jackson (2007) analysed approximately 200 video clips of penalty kicks from competitions such as the World Cup, Champions League and the English

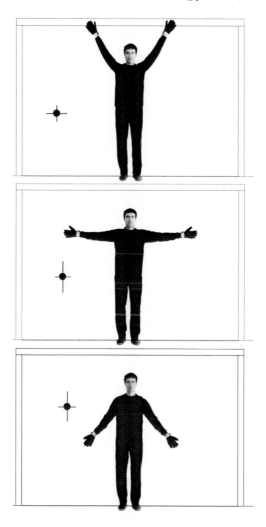

Figure 5.4 The mean (and standard error [SE]) landing location of penalty throws as a function of goalkeeper posture for one participant. The ball is thrown further from the goalkeeper with the arms raised up than with the arms pointing to the ground (Van der Kamp & Masters, 2008).

Premiership. They found that goalkeepers nearly always stand off-centre, although it was unclear why and goalkeepers did not dive more frequently to either side when they stood off-centre. Remarkably, the penalty kicks were more frequently directed to the side of the goalkeeper on which there was more space (i.e. mean 59 versus 41%). In subsequent laboratory experiments, Masters *et al.* (2007) demonstrated that a penalty taker is likely to be unaware that a goalkeeper is standing off-centre when the distances are 6 cm to 9 cm, but nevertheless can perceptually identify the side with more space and were more likely to direct the penalty kick to that side than to the other side. In one experiment, participants kicked a ball from a penalty spot situated 4.8 m from a screen on which an image of a goalkeeper was projected in a goal (i.e. the images were scaled to 44% of real life size). The goalkeeper's body axis was positioned at different distances to the left and right of the centre of the goal and participants were instructed to kick the ball to the side with more space and also to indicate their confidence that their judgment was correct. Even at the smallest distances (i.e. between ≈0.8 cm and ≈4.0 cm), participants correctly identified the side with more space above chance level. The accompanying confidence judgments, however, indicated that participants felt that they were guessing. Participants only reported increased confidence in their judgments when the goalkeeper was displaced by more than ≈4.0 cm. In a subsequent study, Masters et al. (2007) investigated whether penalty-kick direction was biased even when the penalty taker was not specifically trying to detect whether the goalkeeper was off centre. The set-up and stimuli remained the same but participants were instructed to only take a penalty kick when the goalkeeper was standing in the centre of the goal. They were told neither to kick to the side with more space, nor that the goalkeeper was always off-centre. At displacements ranging between approximately 2.5 cm and 4 cm, participants directed their kicks more frequently to the side with the more space, despite only kicking when they believed that the goalkeeper was positioned exactly in the middle of the goal. At greater displacements the number of penalty kicks dropped dramatically, indicating that for these distances participants were consciously aware that the goalkeeper was not positioned in the middle of the goal. In other words, these findings showed that the goalkeeper can influence which side of the goal a penalty kicker is likely to kick the ball (without the kicker knowing it) by standing off-centre by as little as 6 cm to 9 cm.

Rules of thumb for scoring and saving a penalty kick

Most professional football players adopt a goalkeeper-dependent strategy; they wait for the goalkeeper to move to a particular side and then shoot to the opposite side. However, van der Kamp (2006) revealed pitfalls in this strategy, especially when the goalkeeper deploys a kicker-dependent strategy. To avoid these pitfalls, it is advisable to deploy a goalkeeper-*independent* strategy: ignore the goalkeeper completely, pick the top (left or right, perhaps by the toss of a coin) and fire.

Some goalkeepers keep a list of penalty takers with their favourite side and height of penalty kick. This approach relies on penalty takers behaving consistently, which they do not. However, there are means by which a goalkeeper can influence the outcome of a penalty kick. Expert goalkeepers appear to pick up the information that they need during the penalty kicker's run to the ball. Savelsbergh et al. (2009) showed recently that visual search training can help unskilled goalkeepers to quickly learn to pick up this essential information by directing perceptual attention to the head of the penalty taker, then the hips and knees, and finally the foot of the non-kicking leg just before foot–ball contact. The result is faster initiation of movement and more penalty saves.

With a goalkeeper-dependent strategy, if the penalty taker delays too long before making a decision, the speed and accuracy of the penalty decreases, giving the goalkeeper a better opportunity to make a save. Consequently, a goalkeeper should wait until less than 400 ms before foot–ball contact before revealing where he/she will dive. In this way, the pressure is placed on the penalty taker, especially when the kicker is known to use a keeper-dependent strategy. The posture of the goalkeeper also seems to play a role in influencing the penalty taker. Both the position in the goal (Masters *et al.*, 2007) and the position of the arms (van der Kamp & Masters, 2008) can influence the direction of the penalty kick. By standing imperceptibly off-centre a goalkeeper can influence a penalty taker to direct the penalty more often to the side that has more space, without the penalty taker even realising that this is happening. The goalkeeper can then dive selectively to the side with more space, increasing the chances of making a save. Additionally, if the goalkeeper keeps his or her arms down, rather than up, it appears that kicks will pass closer to his or her body, further increasing the chances of making a save.

Note

1 In fact, the study required participants to perform a handball seven meter throw, which is the equivalent of a penalty kick in soccer. This task was chosen, because the (unskilled) participants were more accurate and less variable when throwing compared to kicking a ball at a target.

References

Abernethy, B., Wood, J. M. & Parks, S. (1999). Can the Anticipatory Skills of Experts be Learned by Novices? *Research Quarterly for Exercise and Sport*, 70, 313–318.
Bakker, F. C., Oudejans, R. R. D., Binsch, O. & van der Kamp, J. (2006) Penalty Shooting and Gaze Behavior: Unwanted Effects of the Wish Not to Miss. *International Journal of Sport Psychology*, 37, 265–280.
Bootsma, R. & Savelsbergh, G. J. P. (1988). Nooit Meer Tweede (Never Second Again). *Psychologie*, 6, 16–19.
Farrow, D. & Abernethy, B. (2002). Can Anticipatory Skills be Learned through Implicit Video-based Perceptual Training? *Journal of Sports Sciences*, 20, 471–485.
Franks, I. M. & Harvey, T. (1997). Cues for Goalkeepers: High-tech Methods used to Measure Penalty Shot Response. *Soccer Journal*, May, 30–33.
Kuhn, W. (1988). Penalty-kick Strategies for Shooters and Goalkeepers. In T. Reilly, A. Lees, K. Davids & W. J. Murphy (eds), *Science and football*. London: E & FN Spon, pp. 489–492.
Land, M. F. & Hayhoe, M. (2001). In What Ways do Eye Movements Contribute to Everyday Activities? *Vision Research*, 41, 3559–65.
Masters, R. S. W., van der Kamp, J. & Jackson, R. C. (2007). Imperceptibly Off-centre Goalkeepers Influence Penalty-kick Direction in Soccer. *Psychological Science*, 18, 222–3.
Miller, C. (1998). *He Always Puts it to the Right: A History of the Penalty Kick*. London: Orion Books.
Núñez Sànchez, F. J., Sicilia, A. O., Guerroro, A. B. & Pugniare, A. R. (2005). Anticipation

in Soccer Goalkeepers during Penalty Kicking. *International Journal of Sport Psychology*, 36, 284–98.

Savelsbergh, G. J. P., van Gastel, P. & van Kampen, P. (2009). Anticipation of Penalty Kicking Direction can be Improved by Directing Attention through Perceptual Learning. *International Journal of Sport Psychology*, (in press).

Savelsbergh, G. J. P., van der Kamp, J., Williams, A. M. & Ward, P. (2005). Anticipation and Visual Search Strategy in Expert Soccer Goalkeepers. *Ergonomics*, 48, 1686–1697.

Savelsbergh, G. J. P., Williams, A. M., van der Kamp, J. & Ward, P. (2002). Visual Search, Anticipation and Expertise in Soccer Goalkeepers. *Journal of Sports Sciences*, 20, 279–287.

Van der Kamp, J. (2006). A Field Simulation Study of the Effectiveness of Penalty Kick Strategies in Soccer: Late Alterations of Kick Direction Increase Errors and Reduce Accuracy. *Journal of Sports Sciences*, 24, 467–477.

Van der Kamp, J. & Masters, R. S. W. (2008). The Human Müller-Lyer Illusion in Goalkeeping. *Perception*, 37, 951–954.

Van der Kamp, J., Rivas, F., van Doorn, H. & Savelsbergh, G. (2008). Ventral and Dorsal Contributions in Visual Anticipation in Fast Ball Sports. *International Journal of Sport Psychology*, 39, 100–130.

6 Stochastic perturbations in athletics field events enhance skill acquisition

Wolfgang I. Schöllhorn, Hendrik Beckmann, Daniel Janssen and Jürgen Drepper

Introduction

The constraints-led perspective suggests three factors that form a basis for understanding complex phenomena in the training process. We will examine these in the context of three subsystems: the performer, the task and the environment. These three factors can provide basic variables for complex motor control and motor learning theories and can be used by coaches to improve performance by manipulating them during practice. However, we should always keep in mind that models for certain phenomena are simplified projections of reality (Stachowiak, 1973). In many cases the elements that were excluded during modeling are also neglected in the application phase. Therefore models can produce a new reality that is different from the original one. Specific problems that occur because of a separation of the performer and the environment can be seen in biomechanics and the psychology of perception, for example. In biomechanics, typically three types of forces that are assumed to cause movement are analyzed. While muscular and gravitational forces can clearly be assigned to either the performer or the environment, inertial forces can hardly be assigned to either. This seems to be even more important when we take into consideration the constant changes of the inertial tensors of all limbs in living systems that are caused by blood flow and breathing. These constant changes take care of involuntary variations in so-called movement repetitions, even if not intended by the performer. With respect to psychology of perception, the separation of performer and environment leads to similar problems. Depending on one's philosophy, the perception process is considered differently: (1) as a simple projection of the environment into the perception apparatus of the performer, allowing a clear separation of performer and environment; (2) as an active process of the performer that selects information from the environment based on his/her past experience; or (3) as dependent on the performer's activities not allowing a separation of the performer and the environment. Similar to the involuntary biomechanical changes of the inertial tensor, the perception process is also changing implicitly all the time due to the influence of previous perception processes. These changes of the performer and the environment and their interactions over time seem to be an essential characteristic of motor control and motor learning, especially in sports, and have been widely neglected in traditional models.

From this perspective, an approach that copes with all three subsystems, their interactions and their quantification in changing situations over time is suggested within the differential training approach.

The basis of the differential training approach

Differential training is mainly derived from the observation and essential influence of fluctuations in adaptive systems (Schöner et al., 1986). This fundamental influence of fluctuations can be observed in the early motor development of children (Thelen & Smith, 1994). During this period, children learn more rapidly than throughout their whole lifespan, which underlines the importance of the first two to five years of development for learning (Thelen & Smith, 1994). Fundamental characteristics of learning at this age seem to include a large variety of movements, a small amount of repetitions and only a small tendency to follow instructions, to parents' regret. During this period movement repetitions can only be identified at a very coarse level. If analyzed in detail, each repetition varies the previous movements, even after numerous trials. And these variations are endless during this most effective phase of learning. These variations are often interpreted as destructive noise or the inability to reproduce the same movement consistently by adults, rather than as a necessary stage in effective learning. In contrast, the differential training approach aims to enlarge the fluctuations or stochastic perturbations that occur in athletes' movement repetitions in order to provide additional information to the learner, not only from the movement itself, but also by creating a larger difference between two adjacent movement executions (Schöllhorn, 1999, 2000; Schöllhorn et al., 2006, 2009).

From a traditional point of view, at first glance, an increase in fluctuations could be considered as a new term for describing variable learning. Specifically, the differential training approach distinguishes itself from the variability of practice theory developed by Schmidt (1975) in the application of variability on different variables. While the variability of practice theory suggests varying key variable parameters in order to stabilize the invariants, the differential training approach pursues variations in the "invariant parameters" as well. The proposed variations include variations of joints involved, movement geometry, velocity, acceleration, time structure and rhythm, variations of "classical" movement errors, variations of equipment and environment, and combinations of all variations without any movement repetition. More specifically, the differential training approach adds stochastic perturbations to a "to-be-learned movement" with the intention to provide a larger potential solution space for an athlete, where he or she can react individually and more specifically in a shorter time. In comparison to traditional, more repetition-oriented training, in the differential training approach, a higher degree of stability in the "to-be-learned movement" is achieved by an increased instability during the acquisition process.

In comparison to team games, where there is ample opportunity for movement variation in a dynamic environment, track and field events attract a special interest because of the presence of many rule-governed restrictions on potential movement solutions. In this context the practical application and effectiveness of differential training in comparison to traditional, more repetition-oriented approaches, has been studied in several track and field disciplines for different levels and different ages. In the remainder of this chapter, we discuss some of the results of this program of work and their practical consequences in the context of hurdling.

A (track and) field study

In a differential training experiment in hurdling, 28 juvenile club athletes (13.2 ± 1.7 years) were assigned to a traditional and a differential training group after a 60 m hurdle race pre-test. Both groups received specific interventions for six weeks with 24 training sessions overall. Each training session lasted 90 minutes with 30 minutes on specific hurdle training. All other aspects of training were similar in both groups.

Training content of the traditional training group

The traditional group trained according to recommendations of the International Association of Athletics Federations (IAAF) mainly oriented towards the development of a relatively narrow ideal target movement derived from characteristics of world class hurdle sprinters (Jonath *et al.*, 1995). This training program is mainly characterized by approaching the target movement by means of exercises that display increasing similarity with the "to-be-learned movement" technique. This approach is supported by principles of coinciding kinematics and dynamics of the exercise with the target movement (Djatschkow, 1973). This training program typically involves numerous repetitions accompanied by feedback in the form of error descriptions and error corrections. In the majority of cases feedback was provided individually for every trial. All performers in this group were informed in advance about the technique by means of photographs and video recordings of world-class hurdle sprinters. Furthermore, all error corrections were conducted in line with IAAF recommended literature that is based on the performance of world class athletes, and which is oriented on the same movement model (Jonath *et al.*, 1995). A coarse impression of the traditional (T) exercises can be seen in Figure 6.7 (see Eastern Kentucky University Track and Cross Country Program, n.d.). All exercises $T_1 - T_i$ including the variations ($T_{k<variation>}$; <variation> = kind of variation) were performed at least three times. Figures 6.1 to 6.5 show exercises that are characteristic of traditional training and can be found in most track and field textbooks and coaching manuals (see Eastern Kentucky University Track and Cross Country Program, n.d.; Haberkorn & Plass, 1992; Jonath *et al.*, 1995).

- T_1: Walking over 4–6 m hurdles with a 6–8 m distance between the hurdles. During the hurdle step the lead leg starts with lifting up the bend knee (Figure 6.1(a)). When the thigh is horizontal the knee is extended and body weight is moved forward in order to cross the hurdle with the lead leg (Figure 6.1(b)). The trail leg is abducted with parallel external rotation whereby the knee is always higher than the ankle (Figure 6.1(c)). After passing the hurdle bar the knee of the trail leg is moved towards the breast (Figure 6.1(d)). When the thigh and calf of the rear leg is in movement direction, the foot is moved towards the ground by means of a hip extension (not illustrated).

- $T_{1\text{-}Arm}$: With and without arm movement.
- $T_{1\text{-}Side}$: Left and right leg.
- T_2: Comparable to T_1 but the hurdle step is executed by means of a short and flat jump and walking between the hurdles. The jump was accompanied with the following typical instruction: "During the downward movement of the lead leg after the hurdle bar the knee of the trail leg has to be moved up and towards the chest of the same body side (with knee bent) (Figure 6.2(b)–(c)).
- $T_{2\text{-}velocity}$: At slow running speed with at least seven steps between the hurdles.
- $T_{2\text{-}lead\ leg}$: Beside the hurdle, clearing the hurdle only with the lead leg.
- $T_{2\text{-}trail\ leg}$: Beside the hurdle, clearing the hurdle only with the trail leg.

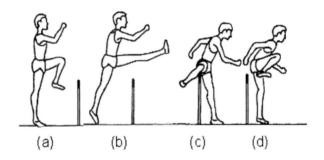

Figure 6.1 Traditional Exercise No. 1: "hurdle marching". (Meaning of letters (a)–(d) explained in the text; modified from Haberkorn & Plass, 1992, pp. 144, 147).

Figure 6.2 Traditional Exercise No. 2: "dynamic hurdle marching" (Meaning of letters (a)–(c) explained in the text; modified from Haberkorn & Plass, 1992, p. 144).

- $T_{2\text{-combinations}}$: Combinations of $T_{2\text{-velocity}}$ and $T_{2\text{-lead leg}}$ and $T_{2\text{-trail leg}}$ by arranging 6–8 hurdles at the left and right side of a line (for instance track marks). Athletes are running in a line, for instance in the order "lead leg – trail leg – trail leg – both legs ..."
  a With five steps between the hurdles.
  b With three steps between the hurdles.
- $T_{2\text{-supplementary exercises}}$:
  a Standing in front of the hurdles training only kicking the leading leg (Figure 6.3).
  b Placing a hurdle around 1 m in front of a wall. Standing beside the hurdle with the lead foot nearly 0.3 m behind the hurdle. Pushing the trail leg back (Figure 6.4(a)) and pulling it about the hurdle (Figure 6.4(b)) towards the chest (Figure 6.4(c)).
- T_3: running completely over the hurdles (Figure 6.5) with:
  a 7-step-rhythm interval between the hurdles (hurdle distances: women around 15 m and men around 17 m, according to stride length and performance level);

Figure 6.3 Supplementary exercise to Exercise No. 2: imitating the action of the lead leg (modified from Haberkorn & Plass, 1992, p. 145).

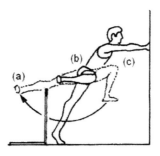

Figure 6.4 Supplementary exercises to Exercise No. 2: imitating the action of the trail leg (meaning of letters (a)–(c) explained in the text; modified from Haberkorn & Plass, 1992, p. 148).

Figure 6.5 Clearing the hurdle (modified from Haberkorn & Plass, 1992, p. 134).

    b   5-step-rhythm interval between the hurdles (hurdle distances: women around 11 m and men around 13 m); and

    c   3-step-rhythm interval between the hurdles (competition distances = target movement).

Training content for the differential training group

The training of the differential training group was mainly characterized by no repetition and no error correction in order to generate larger differences between adjacent movements and to allow athletes to find their own solution for the current movement task. In contrast to the traditional group, the differential training group was oriented towards the development of individual and situational solutions that regard deviations from an ideal model not as a source of error, but rather as necessary fluctuations, providing the basis for skill adaptations. This is claimed to be advantageous in situations that change frequently over time and is reflected in Bernstein's definition of practice as "repetition without repetition" (Bernstein, 1967). Instead of the production of typically identical and stable repetitions, every hurdle exercise was combined with a new instruction that was always related to the previous exercise but with an additional task. These additions are termed stochastic perturbations of the target movement in the classical understanding of ideal, person and situation-independent solutions. The term "noise" is avoided because of its common narrow associations with a white noise frequency spectrum that prerequisites equidistant measurement points, which cannot be assured in normal training. In the case of T1 in the traditional approach, the movement is just repeated several times with some instructive error corrections. In the differential training approach, already at the second hurdle a modification of the first hurdle task has to be performed. This modification can be a change in arm position (Figure 6.6(a)), in knee angle (Figure 6.6(b)) or position of the trunk (Figure 6.6(c)), for example. At the third hurdle this modification might be a more extended elbow angle, at the fourth hurdle it might be a modification of hip flexion velocity and so on.

While the traditional approach follows the first column downward in Figure 6.8

Figure 6.6 Example for a modification of traditional training exercises in the differential training approach by changing the geometry of the movement (modified from Haberkorn & Plass, 1992, p. 144).

exercise	variations in movement execution																							
	ankle (l/r)				knee (l/r)				hip (l/r)				shoulder (l/r)				elbow (l/r)				hand (l/r)			
	φ	ω	α	ρ	φ	ω	α	ρ	φ	ω	α	ρ	φ	ω	α	ρ	φ	ω	α	ρ	φ	ω	α	ρ
T_1																								
T_2																								

Figure 6.7 Suggestions for stochastic perturbations that are oriented on traditional methodical series of exercises. Legend: φ: joint angle; ω: joint angular velocity; α: joint angular acceleration; ρ: rhythm; T_i: traditional exercise.

with several mostly identical repetitions, the differential training approach always meanders along the lines with continuous modifications to the original traditional exercise. The modifications can vary every time at each joint and for each joint-related variable. Once the rhythm is modified, it can be related to a single joint as well as to several joints, for example, where a joint movement can be slow-fast-slow. If these variations are not limited to the hurdle step, but include the steps between hurdles, an additional amount of variations will occur. Obviously these variations differ enormously from the variations that are suggested by the variability-of-practice approach. The differential training approach also differs from the contextual interference approach (Shea & Morgan, 1979) due to the number of variations involved. While in the contextual interference approach variations are switched between two to four ideal target patterns in most cases, in the differential training approach no ideal target pattern exists and therefore an endless number of variations is available.

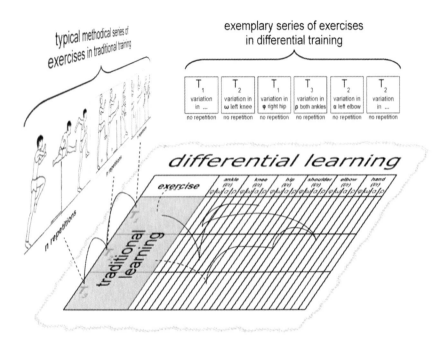

Figure 6.8 Suggestion for a systematic approach for stochastic perturbations in differential training using traditional methodical series of exercises (T_1) and possible changes in joint angles (ϕ), joint angular velocity (ω), joint angular acceleration (α) and internal rhythm (ρ).

Research outcomes

In order to ensure that results are not caused by enormous changes in performance of single individuals, the results are compared qualitatively in advance (Figure 6.9). When we compare individual performances during the pre- and post-tests of the traditional training group and the differential training group, a clear advantage for the differential training group is evident. Every individual of the differential training group can be matched to an individual in the traditional training group whose performance did not increase as much.

Analysis of group means showed no significant differences for both groups during the pre-test in which the traditional training group ran the 60 m hurdles on average in 11.76 sec and the differential training group in 11.70 sec. After six weeks of intervention both groups improved their performance significantly, by 0.33 sec (traditional group) and 0.64 sec (differential group). The differential group improved its performance significantly more than the traditional group, as Figure 6.10 illustrates.

In the traditional understanding of skill acquisition by means of drills in order to generate automated motor programs, the differential training approach at first glance seems to be counterintuitive. However, members of the differential

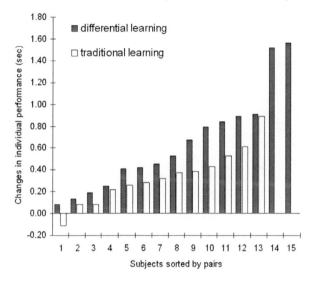

Figure 6.9 Changes in individual performances in a 60 m sprint hurdle race between traditional learning and differential learning group participants sorted into pairs.

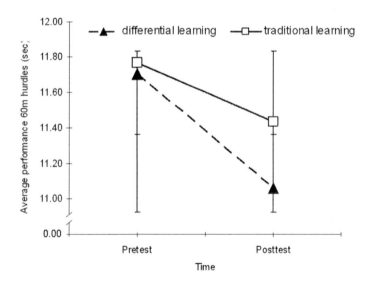

Figure 6.10 Average group performances for 60 m sprint hurdle race of the traditional and differential learning group at pre- and post-tests.

training group improved their hurdle sprint performance significantly more than the traditional drill-oriented group despite, or rather because of, errors in training. In accordance with the predictions made early in the development of the theory of differential training (see Schöllhorn, 1999), training with stochastic

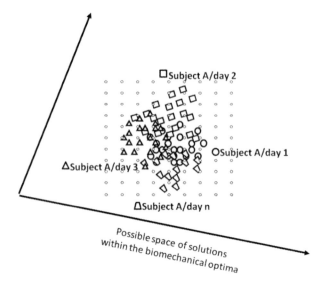

Figure 6.11   Schematic depiction of several training sessions of a single individual in the discus throw (day 1, 2, 3, ...n).

perturbations seems to enable the individual to adjust themselves towards individual and situational optimization. Overall the results verified previous findings in shot-put (Beckmann & Schöllhorn, 2003), soccer (Schöllhorn *et al.*, 2006), tennis (Humpert & Schöllhorn, 2006), and handball (Wagner & Müller, 2008) where similar advantages of the differential training approach could be identified, not only during the acquisition phase but also in subsequent retention phases.

Advantages of the differential training approach can be explained by the additional assumption that the system will change by itself over time (Schöllhorn *et al.*, 2009). In traditional approaches, the task and athlete are assumed to remain as constant and stable systems, while variations in the environment are assumed to cause necessary adaptations. In contrast, the differential training approach assumes that the athlete and the environment are a continuously changing subsystem. On the basis of this assumption, a stable task has to be adapted on different timescales to both these subsystems as well as to changes in their interactions.

Support for this assumption is provided by investigations of the stability/ variability of several training sequences (Bauer & Schöllhorn, 1997). Analysis of several throws of world-class discus athletes over a period of one year not only revealed individual throwing styles, but also day-dependent throwing patterns that were more similar within one day than between different days. In Figure 6.11 an explanatory schema for several training sessions of a single individual is displayed. Obviously, no throwing pattern within any training session is identical and all throwing patterns of a single training session cover a different area within the possible space of biomechanical solutions that only overlap in small areas. Although there is only a limited area of overlap, this covered space continuously forms the

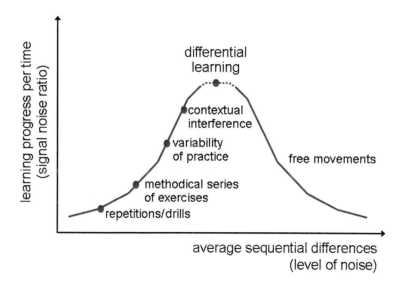

Figure 6.12 A framework for different motor learning approaches (Schöllhorn, Mayer-Kress, Newell & Michelbrink, 2009).

characteristics of the throwing patterns of each individual, which rarely overlap with throwing patterns of other individuals. However, the continuously growing area corresponds to the continuously changing subsystem (the athlete) and provides also an explanation for phenomena that occur after a longer break. During such a break the changes of the subsystem can be expected to be larger and probably lead to a movement pattern that is outside the area that has been covered by throws in previous training sessions. This characteristic can often lead to poorer performance. From a traditional point of view, the space of all possible movement solutions will be covered slowly by numerous repetitions and error corrections. Alternatively, the differential training approach, in accordance with the logics of artificial neural nets (Herz *et al.*, 1991), covers the whole possible space of solutions from the beginning with a coarse meshed net, relying on the system's ability to be able to interpolate well within the nodes of the net. Evidence for such an ability in humans is provided by our visual system, which constantly interpolates scene perception over our blind spot in which the visual nerve departs the eye towards the brain. As well as the explanation of several other phenomena, one advantage of this model is a more effective organization of the learning process by means of a smaller number of movement executions.

Keeping in mind the above described logics of artificial neural nets, another advantage can be seen in the assignment of other movement learning approaches to a more generalized learning model. In this model all motor learning theories can be considered as the application of nets with different mesh size or as applications of a different amount of noise (Schöllhorn *et al.*, 2009). In consequence, finding the optimum learning approach for an individual athlete corresponds to finding the optimum amount of stochastic perturbations for each individual in each situation. In these terms the repetition approach (Gentile, 1972) is associated with a small amount of noise but also corresponds with a small learning rate (learning progress/time). The methodical rows of exercise approach (Gaulhofer & Streicher, 1924), the variability of practice approach (Schmidt, 1975) and the contextual interference approach (Shea & Morgan, 1979) display an increasing amount of noise with increasing learning rates in this order. Figure 6.12 depicts the assumed influence of subsequent exercise differences on learning rate. The figure displays the information that can be derived from the change of noise, dependent on situational noise identification. When athletes, such as beginners or children, show large variability in their movement repetitions it is traditionally recommended to reduce the "noise" in training, whereas in more advanced training (when the movement repetitions become more stable) an increase in variations is required in order to approach the optimum "noise" of training contents. With respect to learning rate, the most effective amount of stochastic perturbations seems to be provided by the differential training approach (Schöllhorn, 1999, 2000) while a further increase would result in a decrease in learning rate. A further decrease could be associated with the additional training of other sports disciplines, for example, if a hurdler who competes in track and field events is practising basketball or swimming skills as well. Maybe this additional training will provide a broader basis for future development, but with respect to hurdle technique no essential support is expected. The reason a rather blurred maximum performance result is shown in Figure 6.11 is that there are several factors affecting these results. As well as individual movement patterns identified in previous studies, there is the individual's level of fatigue (Jäger et al., 2003), certain states of emotions and even the type of music an athlete is listening to during a movement (Janssen et al., 2008).

Conclusions

In the context of track and field practice, research brings into question the value of traditional repetition-oriented approaches with person-independent and time-stable movement patterns. Alternatively, the differential training approach suggests there is a significant advantage to be gained by allowing increasing fluctuations in exercises and performances in order to achieve more individual and more stable solutions. In hurdling this is accompanied by additional stochastic perturbations. In a traditional point of view these perturbations correspond to the execution of errors that counter-intuitively lead to an increase in performance during the acquisition phase. Verified by several other experiments, as in the shot-put (Beckmann & Schöllhorn, 2003), the same intervention is accompanied by additional advantages in the retention phase. Obviously, the differential training approach in track and field supports the exploratory character of a larger space of movement solutions that does not reduce the variations as learning progresses, but shifts the variations from more kinematic to dynamic and rhythmic variations.

References

Bauer, H. U. & Schöllhorn, W. I. (1997). Self-organizing Maps for the Analysis of Complex Movement Patterns. *Neural Processing Letters*, 5, 193–199.

Beckmann, H. & Schöllhorn, W. I. (2003). Differential Learning in Shot Put [Abstract]. In W. I. Schöllhorn, C. Bohn, J. M. Jäger, H. Schaper & M. Alichmann (eds), *1st European Workshop on Movement Science. Book of Abstracts.* Köln, Germany: Sport & Buch Strauß, p. 68.

Bernstein, N. (1967). *The Co-ordination and Regulation of Movement.* Oxford, Great Britain: Pergamon.

Djatschkow, V. M. (1973). Die Vervollkommnung der Technik der Sportler [Perfection of Athletes Technique]. *Theorie und Praxis der Körperkultur, Vol. 22.* Berlin: Sportverlag.

Eastern Kentucky University Track and Cross Country Program (n.d.), *Hurdle Technique.* Available online at: http://www.track.eku.edu/hurdle-technique.htm (accessed 3 March 2009).

Gaulhofer, K. & Streicher, M. (1924). *Grundzuege des oesterreichischen Schulturnens [Fundamentals of Austrian School Gymnastics].* Wien: Deutscher Verlag für Jugend und Volk.

Gentile, A. M. (1972). A Working Model of Skill Acquisition with Application to Teaching. *Quest, 17(1),* 3–23.

Haberkorn, C. & Plass, R. (1992). *Leichtathletik 1. Didaktische Grundlagen und Lauf [Track and Field, Vol. 1:* Fundamentals of Didactics and Running Events]. Frankfurt am Main, Germany: Diesterweg.

Hertz, J. A., Palmer, R. G. & Krogh, A. (1991). *Introduction to the Theory of Neural Computation.* Boulder, CO, United States: Westview.

Humpert, V. & Schöllhorn, W. I. (2006). Vergleich von Techniktrainingsansätzen zum Tennisaufschlag [Comparison of Technique Training-approaches by Means of Tennis Serve]. In A. Ferrauti & H. Remmert (eds), *Trainingswissenschaft im Freizeitsport,* Hamburg, Germany: Czwalina, pp. 121–124.

Jäger, J. M., Alichmann, M. & Schöllhorn, W. I. (2003). Erkennung von Ermüdungszuständen anhand von Bodenreaktionskräften mittels neuronaler Netze [Recognizing Fatigue in Ground Reaction Forces by Means of Artificial Neural Networks]. In G. P. Brüggemann & G. Morey-Klapsing (eds), *Biologische Systeme.* Hamburg, Germany: Czwalina, pp. 179–183.

Janssen, D., Schöllhorn, W. I., Lubienetzki, J., Fölling, K., Kokenge, H. & Davids, K. (2008). Recognition of Emotions in Gait Patterns by Means of Artificial Neural Nets. *Journal of Non-verbal Behavior, 32(2),* 79–92.

Jonath, U., Haag, E., Krempel, R. & Müller, H. (1995). *Leichtathletik 1: Laufen [Track and Field. Vol. 1: Running Events].* Reinbek, Germany: Rowohlt.

Schmidt, R. A. (1975). A Schema Theory of Discrete Motor Skill-learning. *Psychological Review, 82,* 225–260.

Schöllhorn, W. I. (1999). Individualität – ein vernachlässigter Parameter? [Individuality – a Neglected Parameter?] *Leistungssport, 29(2),* 5–12.

Schöllhorn, W. I. (2000). Applications of Systems Dynamic Principles to Technique and Strength Training. *Acta Academiae Olympiquae Estoniae, 8,* 67–85.

Schöllhorn, W. I., Mayer-Kress, G., Newell, K. M. & Michelbrink, M. (2009). Time Scales of Adaptive Behavior and Motor Learning in the Presence of Stochastic Perturbations. *Human Movement Science, 28(3),* 319–333.

Schöllhorn, W. I., Michelbrink, M., Beckmann, H., Trockel, M., Sechelmann, M. & Davids,

K. (2006). Does Noise Provide a Basis for the Unification of Motor Learning Theories? *International Journal of Sport Psychology*, 37(3/4), 34–42.

Schöner, G., Haken, H. & Kelso, J. A. S. (1986). A Stochastic Theory of Phase Transitions in Human Hand Movement. *Biological Cybernetics*, 53(4), 247–257.

Shea, J. & Morgan, R. (1979). Contextual Interference Effects of the Acquisition, Retention and Transfer of a Motor Skill. *Journal of Experimental Psychology: Human Learning and Memory*, 5, 179–187.

Stachowiak, H. (1973). *Allgemeine Modelltheorie [General model theory]*. Vienna: Springer.

Thelen, E. & Smith, L. B. (1994). *A Dynamic Systems Approach to the Development of Cognition and Action*. Cambridge, MA, United States: Bradford.

Wagner, H. & Müller, E. (2008). The Effects of Differential and Variable Training on the Quality Parameters of a Handball Throw. *Sports Biomechanics*, 7(1), 54–71.

7 Interacting constraints and inter-limb co-ordination in swimming

Ludovic Seifert, Chris Button and Tim Brazier

Introduction

Research into swimming skill has typically been concerned with performance improvement rather than the motor control or learning processes that are responsible for performance (Pelayo *et al.*, 2007; Seifert & Chollet, 2008). Swimming performance has been characterised by such biomechanical characteristics as the stroking parameters (velocity, stroke rate, stroke length and stroke index) (Hay, 2002; Pendergast *et al.*, 2006), active drag, power output and propelling efficiency (Pendergast *et al.*, 2005; Toussaint & Truijens, 2005; Toussaint *et al.*, 2000), as well as hand kinematics and kinetics during the underwater path (Schleihauf, 1979; Schleihauf *et al.*, 1988). Research has also considered the energetic characteristics of swimming, such as lactate production, oxygen consumption and heart rate variability (Lavoie & Montpetit, 1986; Pelayo *et al.*, 2007; Toussaint & Hollander, 1994). Whilst of great value, these classic performance variables provide an indirect indication of how humans co-ordinate limb movements to attain high performance and overcome different types of constraints. Therefore, this review presents recent findings on inter-limb co-ordination based on the constraints-led approach and their applications in training and learning.

Overview: the constraints-led approach in swimming

As documented throughout this book, Newell (1986) presented three types of constraints that influence co-ordination in movement. In the following subsections, we shall discuss examples of each type of constraint, and also acknowledge the confluence of constraints that act to shape a swimmer's co-ordination patterns.

Environmental constraints

In swimming, environmental constraints refer largely to water properties such as the density or temperature of the fluid, the direction of water flow, the underwater visibility, and waves on the surface of the water. Movement in the aquatic environment naturally imposes forward resistance (called drag force: D). A certain amount of propulsive force is needed to overcome this drag force. Drag force is a function of the swimming velocity squared: $D = K \bullet v^2$, where K is a constant of proportionality depending on body size and shape of the swimmer ($K = 0.5 \bullet Cx \bullet Ap \bullet \rho$, where Cx is the hydrodynamic coefficient, Ap the projected frontal area, ρ the density of water) (Pendergast *et al.*, 2005; Toussaint & Truijens, 2005; Toussaint *et al.*, 2000). The swimmer develops power to overcome drag force with the following formula: $P_d = D \bullet v$. However, the total mechanical power output (P_o) is greater than that needed to overcome active drag because part of it is wasted to accelerate the water away from the body (called kinetic power: P_k). Finally, $P_o = P_d + P_k$ (Toussaint & Truijens, 2005) suggests that the active drag is the product of interacting constraints (environmental and organismic) that have been broken down into pressure or form drag (approximately 55% of total drag), skin friction drag (20–25%) and wave drag (20–25%) (Pendergast *et al.*, 2005). The proportion of each component varies with changes in velocity, for example in front crawl, the wave drag becomes important above 1.5–1.6 m.s.$^{-1}$ (Toussaint & Truijens, 2005) representing 50% of the total drag at 2.2 m.s.$^{-1}$ (Vennell *et al.*, 2006). Therefore, changes in velocity directly influence the level of environmental constraint that is experienced by the swimmer.

Front crawl

Even though lower active drag more typically occurs during front crawl than other strokes (i.e. breaststroke), the challenge is to manage the transition between the underwater and aerial parts of the cycle, by adapting (1) the time allowed to glide with one arm stretched forward at the water surface while the second arm propels; and (2) the time devoted to the aerial arm recovery. Based on the degree of continuity between the propulsive actions, three theoretical modes of co-ordination exist: (i) when the Index of Co-ordination (IdC) = 0%, the mode is opposition; (ii) when IdC < 0%, the mode is catch-up; and (iii) when IdC > 0%, the mode is superposition (for further details, see Chollet *et al.*, 2000). When environmental constraints increase with swimming velocities of 1.47 to 1.92 m.s.$^{-1}$, the inter-arm co-ordination of elite males switches from a catch-up mode (IdC ~ –10±5%) to a superposition mode (IdC ~ 3±6%) (Seifert *et al.*, 2007b). In fact, when the velocity increases above a critical value (a velocity of approximately 1.8 m.s.$^{-1}$), only the superposition mode is observed (Seifert *et al.*, 2007b). Kolmogorov *et al.* (1997) showed a particularly large increase in active drag (up to 70N) and power (up to 150W) exists near 1.8 m.s.$^{-1}$, which would explain the transition in the arm co-ordination of elite males at about this speed. At higher velocities (>1.5 m.s.$^{-1}$) wave drag becomes even more important (wave drag amounts to up to 50% of total drag) (Toussaint & Truijens, 2005). Thus, similar to ships, the calculation of the "hull speed" for a swimmer with an arbitrary height of 2 m showed a value of 1.77 m.s.$^{-1}$ (Toussaint & Truijens, 2005). Hence, above a self-organised critical velocity (>1.7–1.8 m.s^{-1}), the environmental constraints elicit a superposition co-ordination of the arms. This would explain why increases in velocity conjointly lead to changes of drag force, power output and index of co-ordination (see Figures 7.1 and 7.2; Seifert *et al.*, 2008c).

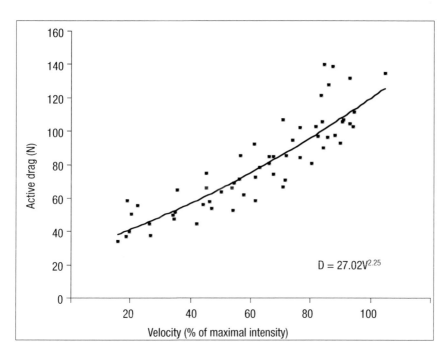

Figure 7.1 Relationship between index of co-ordination and swimming velocity.

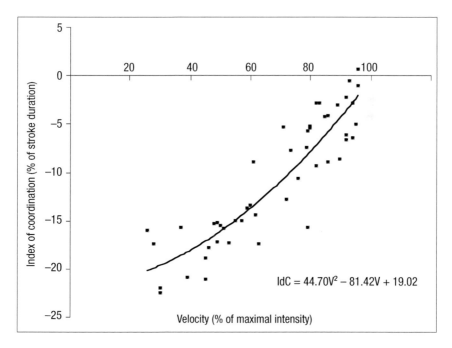

Figure 7.2 Relationship between active drag and swimming velocity.

Finally, wearing a wetsuit (task constraint) can artificially decrease the environmental constraint, notably the friction drag by 5% to 7.5%, which explains the greater glide duration and catch-up mode of inter-arm co-ordination of triathletes swimming at an 800 m race pace with a wetsuit (IdC = –11.7%) as opposed to without (IdC = –9.6%) (Hue *et al.*, 2003).

Breaststroke

The breaststroke technique is strictly controlled, and Fédération Internationale de Natation (FINA) rules (task constraints) impose that arm and leg recoveries must occur underwater explaining why the highest active drag levels are to be found during breaststroke (Kolmogorov *et al.*, 1997). For example, at a velocity of 1.25 m.s.$^{-1}$, active drag was close to 20 N in front crawl and 40 N in breaststroke, and at 1.45 m.s.$^{-1}$, active drag was close to 25 N in front crawl and 95 N in breaststroke (Kolmogorov *et al.*, 1997). Previously, Kent and Atha (1971) have studied the passive drag of the body position at five key points of the breaststroke cycle, showing that for a velocity of 1.5 m.s.$^{-1}$, the passive drag equalled 92 N in glide position, 165 N in breathing position, 222 N during the arm and leg recoveries position, 214 N when the legs begin their propulsion and 205 N when the legs finished their propulsion in extended position. These variations in resistance indicate the importance of organising the arm-leg co-ordination effectively in order to minimise the environmental constraints. Therefore, the first challenge of breaststroke swimmers is to monitor the duration of the glide time with the body fully extended between the leg propulsion and the arm propulsion. In particular, the swimmer must estimate when his instantaneous velocity decreases below his mean velocity to start the arm propulsion. For the second challenge, the imposed underwater recoveries require synchronised arm and leg recoveries to minimise active drag. Third, the swimmer should adopt a hydrodynamic position with one pair of limbs while the other pair of limbs is propelling.

Four time gaps (T1, T2, T3, T4) can be used to quantify the time lags between arm and leg actions (for further details, see Chollet *et al.*, 2004). T1 is the time difference between the end of leg propulsion and the beginning of arm propulsion (the glide duration). T2 is the time difference between the beginning of arm recovery and the beginning of leg recovery. T3 is the time difference between the end of arm recovery and the end of leg recovery; and T4 is the time difference between 90° arm flexion in arm recovery and 90° leg flexion in leg recovery. Finally, the total time gap (TTG) is defined as the sum of the absolute values of T1, T2, T3 and T4, and is used to assess the effectiveness of the global arm-leg co-ordination (Seifert & Chollet, 2009). The time gaps and TTG are expressed as the percentage of a complete cycle. When environmental constraints increase at higher swimming velocities (i.e. 1.2–1.3 m.s.$^{-1}$ to 1.5–1.6 m.s.$^{-1}$), the TTG of expert breaststrokers was shown to decrease from 60% to 20%. This higher degree of co-ordination is mainly due to the change of T1, i.e. the decrease of the glide duration from 30–40% to 0–10% (Chollet *et al.*, 2004; Seifert & Chollet, 2009; Takagi *et al.*, 2004), leading to better continuity between the legs and arms propulsion. Having a high degree of co-ordination does not automatically mean a decrease of each time lag to 0%; some superposition modes of co-ordination (partial superposition of arms and legs propulsion and/or partial superposition of arm recovery with leg propulsion) would be adequate for high environmental constraints (Seifert & Chollet, 2005; Seifert *et al.*, 2006).

Task constraints

Task constraints concern the goal of the activity and can be further classified into three categories (Newell, 1986): (1) the task goal inducing a co-ordination mode; (2) the rules or instructions imposed upon an activity; and (3) equipment. The rules or instructions that can serve to direct the learner towards a desired mode of co-ordination are discussed later in this chapter (see "Training and teaching using the constraint-led approach in swimming").

To test how variable a swimmer's co-ordination patterns are, a "scanning task" can be used where imposed race pace, stroke rate and number of strokes per 25 m lap (i.e. distance per stroke) are progressively increased from the minimal to the maximal value that could be sustained by the swimmer. This type of task goal explores the range of the swimmer's capabilities. For example, when the stroke rate increases above a critical value (a rate of 50 cycles per minute), only the superposition mode occurs (Seifert *et al.*, 2007b). An ambiguous task instruction may be to "swim at different race paces like slow, medium, and fast" and the co-ordination

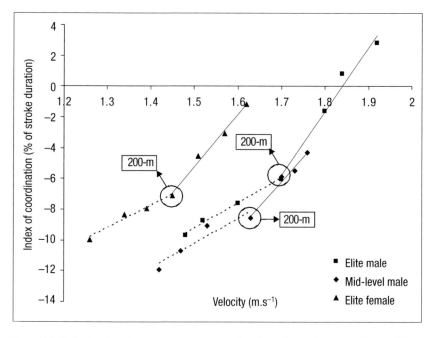

Figure 7.3 Relationships between race paces and index of co-ordination. Hatched line: slow pace, continued line: fast pace (adapted from Seifert *et al.*, 2007b).

adopted by the swimmer could then be analysed to determine the effective bandwidth of co-ordination variability. Seifert *et al.* (2004a, 2007b) asked elite and non-expert male and female swimmers to simulate seven race paces (1500 m, 800 m, 400 m, 200 m, 100 m, 50 m, maximal velocity) over 25 m (Figure 7.3). Interestingly, the results indicated that, whatever the expertise level or gender, the 200 m pace was the critical point for adapting co-ordination as it marked the separation between the mid and long-distance paces and the sprint paces.

A fatigue-inducing task constraint, like swimming at maximal velocity for a given distance (for the 100 m event, see Seifert *et al.* (2005a, 2007a); for the 200 m event, see Alberty *et al.* (2005); for the 400 m, see Schnitzler (2005); for the 800 m, see Delaplace (2004)), can be used to evaluate the stability of co-ordination. High expertise is revealed by relatively stable IdC values over the course of a race, whereas lower expertise and/or fatigue is indicated by an increase of IdC. An increase of IdC thus does not indicate greater propulsive efficiency but rather greater time spent in the pull and push phases due to lower hand velocity and thus smaller mechanical power output (Seifert *et al.*, 2007a; Toussaint *et al.*, 2006).

Another task constraint may be the requirement to swim at an imposed stroke rate as dictated by an instrument or device, such as a metronome (Alberty *et al.*, 2008; Potdevin *et al.*, 2003, 2006). For example, high variability in co-ordination modes is observed at low stroke rates because active drags are low, suggesting that several motor solutions are possible (Potdevin *et al.*, 2003). Swimming velocity can also be imposed by a luminous rail (Montpetit *et al.*, 1988), a system by which the subject's passing over each pylon (placed at every 10 m at the bottom of the pool) has to coincide with an underwater audio signal (Montpetit *et al.*, 1981), or a swimming flume (Monteil *et al.*, 1994). Alternatively, artificially applied resistance can be used with a tethered swimming system (Aujouannet *et al.*, 2006; Yeater *et al.*, 1981) or a parachute (Brazier, 2008; Llop *et al.*, 2006; Schnitzler *et al.*, 2008).

Organismic constraints

Organismic constraints refer to the swimmer's properties, notably anthropometric characteristics (like arm span, arm size, hand area, foot size, leg length and height), locomotor disabilities, passive drag and flotation parameters (hydrostatic lift, sinking force acting at the ankle), strength, endurance, and laterality (handedness and the preferred breathing side) which could be included in larger categories such as age, gender, expertise, confidence, and the swimmer's speciality (sprint vs mid-distance, swimmer vs triathlete).

Front crawl

Several studies have shown that organismic constraints affect the inter-arm co-ordination and the co-ordination symmetry in front crawl. For example, Seifert *et al.* (2004a) showed that females typically have less propulsive continuity between the propulsion of the two arms (Figure 7.3) than males because of their greater fat mass, a different distribution of this mass, lower arm strength, and greater difficulty in overcoming forward resistance. In breaststroke, notably in sprint paces, the females also exhibit less propulsive continuity between the arm and leg actions than males, because females tend to glide longer (mean time gap T1 equalled to 31.7% for females vs 27.4% for males) and are not able to superpose the end of the arm recovery with the beginning of the leg propulsion (mean time gap T3 equalled to 6.2% for females vs 2.7% for males) to maintain high mean velocity (Seifert & Chollet, 2005).

Moreover, it is reasonable to assume that a swimmer with large hands and/or feet will have bigger propulsive surfaces and thus a greater yield for every action, on condition that these actions are efficient. Thus, using fins or paddle, the instructor can artificially increase beginners' propulsive surfaces and induce new co-ordination, on condition that the quality of catch is monitored (Sidney *et al.*, 2001). Conversely, swimmers with locomotor disabilities, i.e. amputation, cerebral palsy, spinal cord injury or others, may have smaller propulsive surfaces than able-bodied swimmers or an unbalanced capacity for propulsion, both of which would influence their inter-arm co-ordination (Satkunskiene *et al.*, 2005). These authors showed that even if swimmers with locomotor disabilities vary the co-ordination mode in relation to their degree of impairment, correct co-ordination is fundamental to front crawl swimming, just as in able-bodied swimmers.

Moreover, breathing can bring about catch-up co-ordination because the time spent inhaling leads to a lag time in propulsion (Lerda *et al.*, 2001) on the preferential breathing side (Seifert *et al.*, 2005b, 2008a). Throughout a 100 m race, Seifert *et al.* (2005b) found that swimmers having unilateral breathing patterns (every 2, 4, or 6 arm strokes) showed an asymmetric co-ordination ("rickety swimming"), characterised in non-experts by a prolonged catch with the arms extended forward to facilitate head rotation during breathing and thus by catch-up to the breathing side. Conversely, swimmers with bilateral breathing patterns (breath every 3 or 5 arm strokes) tended to balance the arm co-ordination by distributing the asymmetries (Seifert *et al.*, 2005b). The control of breathing laterality would help to bring about efficient inter-arm co-ordination. Seifert *et al.* (2008a) manipulated breathing laterality by imposing seven breathing patterns (each trial was swum on 25 m to avoid fatigue), divided in two categories: unilateral patterns and bilateral patterns. The results indicated that breathing to the preferential side led to an asymmetry, in contrast to the other breathing patterns, and the asymmetry was even greater when the swimmer breathed to his non-preferential side. Moreover, co-ordination was symmetric in patterns with breathing that was bilateral, axed (as in breathing with a frontal snorkel) or removed (as in apnoea) (Seifert *et al.*, 2008a).

Finally, skill level or the capacity to swim fast appears to be the most influential organismic constraint. Because elite male swimmers develop higher drag force and higher power output than mid-level swimmers, they can overcome higher forward resistance (environmental constraint) leading them to switch to a superposition co-ordination mode (Seifert *et al.*, 2008c). Superposition co-ordination (high

IdC) is not the determinant of high velocity but emerges from the high active drag that swimmers must overcome to swim fast; in other words, the environmental constraint of swimming fast is the cause of co-ordination changes and not the consequence.

Breaststroke

In elite breaststroke, the propulsion of one set of limbs is performed while the other set is in hydrodynamic position (limbs extended in glide position) to ensure propulsive continuity. However, in sprint paces, some elite breaststrokers do not alternate the leg and arm propulsion but show a partial superposition between the end of the arm recovery and the beginning of the leg propulsion, which still allows them to reach high velocity (Leblanc *et al.*, 2005; Seifert & Chollet, 2005). Conversely, two superposition co-ordination modes are commonly observed in early breaststrokers, which do not typically translate to fast speeds (Leblanc *et al.*, 2009; Seifert *et al.*, 2008b). The beginner's co-ordination often forms a bistabile regime, which globally looks like an "accordion" and a "windscreen wiper" (Seifert & Chollet, 2008). Some beginners superpose two contradictory phases (leg propulsion during the arm recovery and arm propulsion during the leg recovery) in which no phase is effective because each propulsive action is thwarted by a recovery action. This accordion-like co-ordination pattern is generally linked to time lags in the cycle; for example, beginners regularly stop their hands at the chest at the end of arm propulsion, usually to take a long breath (Figure 7.4). By doing so, the arm recovery lags and overlaps with the leg push. In contrast to the beginner, the expert's hands do not stop at the chest because this position causes strong forward resistances.

Figure 7.4 "Accordion" co-ordination mode corresponding to superpose two contradictory phases (propulsion with recovery) (adapted from Seifert & Chollet, 2008).

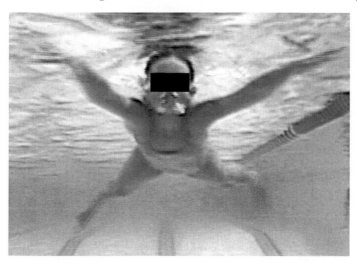

Figure 7.5 "Windscreen wipers" co-ordination mode corresponding to superpose two propulsive phases (propulsion of arms and legs) (adapted from Seifert & Chollet, 2008).

Other beginners superpose two propulsions: a complete superposition of the propulsive phases of the arms and legs resembles the movement of "windscreen wipers", while a partial superposition of the propulsions occurs with the body in an X position with arms and legs in complete extension (Figure 7. 5). This position can result from a lack of sensation in the forward-extended arms, with the beginner not performing a true catch but continuing the stroke by a lateral arm movement to maintain buoyancy.

In terms of performance, these superposition co-ordination modes are ineffective and may be considered by many as "technical errors". However, these co-ordination modes answer to a different functional goal than those of the elite breaststrokers, notably to sustain the body near the water surface rather than to go forward fast. In fact, these two attractors, which both often arise spontaneously, can be explained by mechanical principles. Accordion co-ordination is the least efficient but, mechanically, is the easiest to achieve, which explains its prevalence in beginners. Beginners synchronise the flexion movements of both arms and legs, as well as the extension movements. This control mode is based on the principle of iso-contraction of the non-homologous limbs, i.e. to the in-phase muscle contraction of the arms and legs (Baldissera *et al.*, 1982) (also called egocentric constraint, Swinnen *et al.*, 1997). Although this co-ordination mode appears to be the most stable and the easiest to perform in bimanual co-ordination (Kelso, 1984), hand-foot tasks (Jeka *et al.*, 1993; Kelso & Jeka, 1992) and walking-running (Diedrich & Warren, 1995), this arm to leg co-ordination is not as effective for breaststroke swimming because it entails a freezing of the degrees of freedom that superposes contradictory actions in term of propulsion. In the "windscreen wiper" mode of co-ordination, the flexion movement of one set of limbs occurs during the extension of the other set, following the principle of iso-direction, which consists of making movements in the same direction (e.g. arms and legs go forward or backward on the longitudinal axis) (also called "allocentric" constraint) without involving muscular iso-contraction (Baldissera *et al.*, 1982; Swinnen *et al.*, 1997). This type of behaviour is also inefficient in breaststroke because performing two propulsions simultaneously does not maximise the long propulsive time preferred by experts.

Training and teaching using the constraints-led approach in swimming

Practitioners can use the constraints-led approach to help them to identify and understand influential control parameters that bring about a desired co-ordination mode. As the following brief case studies illustrate, it is equally important to analyse the environmental context of practice, to prepare the task instructions, and to take into account the individual swimmer(s) that are to be trained.

Manipulating task constraints

As suggested previously, the organismic and the environmental constraints, which are perhaps less accessible to manipulation by a practitioner, could in fact be altered indirectly through task constraints in order to channel motor learning. For example, research has shown that varying a swimmer's breathing patterns can lead to different inter-arm co-ordination in front crawl than those used with preferred breathing side and rate (Seifert *et al.*, 2008a). The practical applications for the coach or the instructor could be: (1) to help children to determine their preferred side for unilateral breathing; (2) to use a variety of learning situations to encourage symmetric co-ordination, i.e. alternating task constraints with unilateral, bilateral and frontal snorkel breathing; and (3) to adapt the breathing rate to the swim distance by inserting "no breath" rules (especially in sprint, by allowing the swimmer to breathe only once or twice every 25 m). Alternately, an auditory metronome that prescribes breathing time could be set to coincide with alternating phases of a stroke at a consistent speed.

The desired mode of co-ordination could be further encouraged with the use of equipment or resistive devices. For example, many coaches advocate the use of swim paddles worn on the hands to develop propulsive forces so that the inter-arm co-ordination in front crawl would be modified (Sidney *et al.*, 2001). Indeed the use of specific resistance training methods for more advanced swimmers to develop power is quite common, however the change in stroke parameters are commonly only a secondary thought (see Case Study, p. 53). Using a tether to pull or hold back, or using a parachute to slow the swimmer can amplify the behaviour that reflects poor co-ordination or a lack of dissociation. For example, pulling the swimmer leads to velocity peaks, situations in which the breaststroke swimmer has to dissociate the actions of the arms and legs to optimise the glide. This strategy has been used to monitor the alternation between propulsion and glide times for the underwater part of the breaststroke start (Seifert *et al.*, 2007c). However, in using a half open resistance parachute there is an enhancement in the continuity of the propulsive phases between the two arms (i.e. increase of IdC) from a catch-up to a superposition mode of co-ordination in front crawl (Brazier, 2008). This is achieved through decreasing the catch phase and increasing the push phase duration. Superposition co-ordination is seen predominately in sprinters, but is believed to be more efficient than a traditional catch-up stroke as it provides a consistent application of power from the arms.

Using instructions to shape new response dynamics

Rules or instructions could be given by practitioners to guide learners towards effective co-ordination patterns (see Newell & Ranganathan, Chapter 2). This strategy is particularly effective amongst early learners when combined with the use of analogies that direct attention to the effects of their movements. For example, "make the water boil with your toes", "draw a keyhole shape with your hands", and "glide like a torpedo", are fun and motivating cues, but importantly they are also effective at inducing whole-body co-ordination changes. Whilst many coaches are seduced into using task "decomposition", for example to teach leg propulsion separately from the arm stroke in breaststroke or to break down the leg stroke phases (bend, separate, squeeze together), in fact more effective results can be induced with simple instructions such as "glide two seconds with the arm stretched forward", "do not stop the hand to the breast" or "make two kicks for every arm stroke" (see Case Study, p. 94). As discussed in Chapter 1, this kind of task "simplification" preserves important perception-action relationships whilst limiting the amount of complex information to be processed by the swimmer all at once.

Conclusion

The main purpose of this review was to explore how the constraints-led approach provides a better understanding of inter-limb co-ordination in swimming. In view of the three types of constraint developed by Newell (1986), it appears that there is no one co-ordination mode that is effective for everyone. Conversely, the effectiveness of a co-ordination mode will always be greatly impacted by the inter-acting constraints operating on the swimmer at that time. It is also important to be aware that a co-ordination mode that may be ineffective in terms of performance is not automatically a mistake, but could be a functional solution with regards to the constraints sustained by the swimmer. It is important to remind practitioners that the goal of beginners will usually be to maintain their body near the water surface rather than to swim fast. Therefore, the level of constraint involved in the training and teaching process should take into account the individual preferences of the swimmer. Modifying task constraints, possibly through the provision of simple instructions, is a powerful way to alter the learner swimmer's co-ordination dynamics.

Case Study: Parachute resistance training

As a coach of sub-elite swimmers, Rob decides to use parachute resisted swimming to add some variety to his training sessions. Rob asks his swimmers to perform six 25 m maximal efforts with full recovery, twice a week, over a six week block. Rob's intention is for the swimmers to create an association with superposition swimming, and enhance muscle fibre activation per stroke (i.e. power). Initially, Rob was concerned when he discovered that during the training sets, the swimmers' index of co-ordination (IdC) increased, and also that stroke length (SL), stroke rate (SR) and maximal velocity actually decreased. Fortunately, these training behaviours did not translate into consistently reduced performance. In fact, the swimmers reported a greater understanding and feeling for a superposition stroke when swimming without the parachute. Rob was relieved to find that after six weeks training with the drill, swimming-specific strength (elbow flexor and extensor strength) increased, with an improvement in 50 m sprint time. On reflection, it seems the swimmers may need more time to adapt their improved strength into a functional co-ordination pattern. Rob decides that this new training stimulus needs to be carefully integrated with training to allow the co-ordination pattern to 'settle' or stabilise under the influence of constraints.

Case Study: Manipulating arm and leg cycle co-ordination

The classic drills of performing two arm propulsions for one leg propulsion (2:1) or one arm propulsion for two leg propulsions (1:2) are well-founded to bring about improved co-ordination in breaststroke. This task goal requires dissociating the propulsive actions of the arms from those of the legs by integrating glide times. Initially, this is difficult for beginners because the lack of a sharp sensation of the catch causes them to omit the glide and instead focus on using their arms to maintain buoyancy. In fact, this drill has also proven effective with elite swimmers. It was adopted by the French national champion in 2004 for the 50 m, 100 m and 200 m breaststroke events to prepare the swimmer for the Athens 2004 Olympic Games (Seifert *et al.*, 2006). Initially, after practicing this drill his co-ordination showed deterioration, with an increase in the relative duration of the contradictory superposed movements (assessed by time gaps T2 and T3) that resulted in a shortened glide (assessed by time gap T1). This motor change was inefficient because, despite a new French record in the World Championship of July 2003, for the first time his performance in the finals was not as good as in the semi-finals. Therefore, technical sessions were held to focus on the dissociation of the arms and legs and then on the continuity of propulsive movements. The technical sessions were successful, leading to greater glide time (T1) and less superposition of negative arm and leg movements (T2 and T3), and thus a better degree of recovery co-ordination. Manipulating the arm and leg cycle co-ordination in training enabled this elite swimmer to achieve a higher velocity during the propulsive phases and to conserve this high velocity during the glide time (Seifert *et al.*, 2006).

Note

Sociocultural constraints such as the presence of other swimmers or an evaluative audience have received little attention in swimming research and are not considered further in this review.

Acknowledgements

The authors thank Didier Chollet for his advice and the interesting discussion about inter-limb co-ordination, which contributed greatly to the quality of this chapter.

References

Alberty, M., Potdevin, F., Dekerle, J., Pelayo, P., Gorce, P., Sidney, M. (2008). Changes in Swimming Technique during Time to Exhaustion at Freely-chosen and Controlled Stroke Rates. *Journal of Sports Sciences, 26*(11), 1191–1200.

Alberty, M., Sidney, M., Huot-Marchand, F., Hespel, J. M. & Pelayo. P. (2005). Intracyclic Velocity Variations and Arm Co-ordination during Exhaustive Exercise in Front Crawl Stroke. *International Journal of Sports Medicine, 26*, 471–475.

Aujouannet, Y., Bonifazi, M., Hintzy, F., Vuillerme, N., Rouard, A. H. Effects of a High-intensity Swim Test on Kinematic Parameters in High-level Athletes. *Appl Physiol Nutr Metab. 2006, 31*, 150–8.

Baldissera, F., Cavalleri, P. & Civaschi, P. (1982). Preferential Coupling between Voluntary Movements of Ipsilateral Limbs. *Neuroscience Letters, 74*, 95–100.

Brazier, T. (2008). Comparing the Kinetics and Kinematics of Parachute and Non-parachute Resisted Swimming, *Unpublished Master of Physical Education Thesis in Exercise and Sports Science*, Dunedin: University of Otago.

Chollet, D., Chalies, S. & Chatard J.C. (2000). A New Index of Co-ordination for the Crawl: Description and Usefulness. *International Journal of Sports Medicine, 21*, 54–59.

Chollet, D., Seifert, L., Leblanc, H., Boulesteix, L. & Carter M. (2004). Evaluation of the Arm-leg Co-ordination in Flat Breaststroke. *International Journal of Sport Medicine, 25*, 486–495.

Delaplace, C. (2004). Contribution à l'analyse du Crawl du Nageur Non-expert: Étude des Paramètres Spatio-temporels, des Parties Nagées et Non Nagées et de la Coordination de Nage en Fonction du Niveau d'expertise, de la Distance et du Genre [Front Crawl Analysis in the Non-expert Swimmer: Spatial-temporal Parameters, Swimming and Non-swimming Segments, and Co-ordination in Relation to Skill, Distance Swum and Gender], *Unpublished PhD Thesis*, France: University of Montpellier.

Diedrich, F. J. & Warren, W. H. (1995). Why Change Gaits? Dynamics of the Walk-run Transition. *Journal of Experimental Psychology: Human Perception and Performance, 21*, 183–202.

Hay J. G. (2002). Cycle Rate, Length, and Speed of Progression in Human Locomotion. *J Appl Biomech, 18*, 257–270.

Hue, O., Benavente, H. & Chollet, D. (2003). The Effect of Wet Suit Use by Triathletes: An Analysis of the Different Phases of Arm Movement. *Journal of Sports Sciences, 21*, 1025–1030.

Jeka, J. J., Kelso, J. A. S. & Kiemel, T. (1993). Spontaneous Transitions and Symmetry: Pattern Dynamics in Human Four-limb Co-ordination, *Human Movement Science, 12*, 627–651.

Kelso, J. A. S. (1984). Phase Transitions and Critical Behavior in Human Bi-manual Co-ordination. *American Journal of Physiology, Regulatory, Integrative and Comparative Physiology, 15,* R 1000–1004.

Kelso, J. A. S. & Jeka, J. J. (1992). Symmetry Breaking Dynamics of Human Multi-limb Co-ordination, *Journal of Experimental Psychology: Human Perception and Performance, 18,* 645–668.

Kent, M. & Atha, J. (1971). Selected Critical Transient Body Positions in Breast Stroke and their Influence upon Water Resistance. In L. Lewillie, J. P. Clarys (eds), *Swimming Science I,* Brussels: Université Libre de Bruxelles, pp. 119–126.

Kolmogorov, S. V., Rumyantseva, O. A., Gordon, B. J. & Cappaert, J. (1997). Hydrodynamic Characteristics of Competitve Swimmers of Different Genders and Performance Levels. *Journal of Applied Biomechanics, 13,* 88–97.

Lavoie, J. P. & Montpetit, R. R. (1986). Applied Physiology of Swimming. *Sports Medicine, 3*(3), 165–189.

Leblanc, H., Seifert, L., Baudry, L. & Chollet, D. (2005). Arm-leg Co-ordination in Flat Breaststroke: A Comparative Study between Elite and Non-elite Swimmers. *International Journal of Sports Medicine, 26,* 787–797.

Leblanc, H., Seifert, L., Chollet, D. (2009). Arm-leg Co-ordination in Recreational and Competitive Breaststroke Swimmers, *Journal of Science and Medicine in Sport, 12,* 352–35.

Lerda, R., Cardelli, C. & Chollet, D. (2001). Analysis of the Interactions between Breathing and Arm Actions in the Front Crawl. *Journal of Human Movement Studies, 40,* 129–144.

Llop, F., Tella, V., Colado, J. C., Diaz, G. & Navarro, F. (2006). Evolution of Butterfly Technique when Resisted Swimming with Parachute using Different Resistances. *Portuguese Journal of Sports Sciences, 6*(Supl. 2), 302–303.

Monteil, K. M., Rouard, A. H. & Troup, J. P. (1994). Etude des Paramètres Cinétiques du Nageur de Crawl au Cours d'un Exercice Maximal dans un Flume [Kinetic Parameters in Front Crawl Swimmers during Maximal Exercise in a Flume]. *Revue STAPS, 33,* 57–68.

Montpetit, R., Cazorla, G. & Lavoie, J. M. (1988). Energy Expenditure during Front Crawl Swimming: A Comparison between Males and Females. In B. E. Ungerechts, K. Wilke & K. Reischle (eds), *Swimming Science V.* Champaign, Illinois: Human Kinetics Publishers, pp. 229–235.

Montpetit, R., Léger, L. A., Lavoie, J. M. & Cazorla, G. (1981). VO2 Peak during Free Swimming using Backward Extrapolation of the O2 Recovery Curve. *European Journal of Applied Physiology, 47,* 385–91.

Newell, K. M. (1986). Constraints on the Development of Co-ordination. In M. G. Wade & H. T. A. Whiting (eds), *Motor Development in Children: Aspect of Co-ordination and Control.* Dordrecht: Nijhoff, pp. 341–360.

Pelayo, P., Alberty, M., Sidney, M., Potdevin, F. & Dekerle, J. (2007). Aerobic Potential, Stroke Parameters, and Co-ordination in Swimming Front Crawl Performance. *International Journal of Sports Physiology and Performance, 2,* 347–359.

Pendergast, D. R., Capelli, C., Craig, A. B., di Prampero, P. E., Minetti, A. E., Mollendorf, J., Termin, A. & Zamparo, P. (2006). Biophysics in Swimming. *Portuguese Journal of Sport Sciences, 6*(Supl. 2), 185–189.

Pendergast, D. R., Mollendorf, J., Zamparo, P., Termin, A., Bushnell, D. & Paschke, D. (2005). The Influence of Drag on Human Locomotion in Water. *Undersea and Hyperbaric Medicine, 32,* 45–58.

Potdevin, F., Bril, B., Sidney, M. & Pelayo, P. (2006). Stroke Frequency and Arm Co-ordination in Front Crawl Swimming. *International Journal of Sport Medicine*, 27, 193–198.

Potdevin, F., Delignières, D., Dekerle, J., Alberty, J., Sidney, M. & Pelayo, P. (2003). Does Stroke Frequency Determine Swimming Velocity Values and Co-ordination? In J. C. Chatard (ed), *Biomechanics and Medicine in Swimming IX*. Saint Etienne, France: University of Saint Etienne, pp. 163–167.

Satkunskiene, D., Schega, L., Kunze, K., Birzinyte, K. & Daly, D. (2005). Coordination in Arm Movements during Crawl Stroke in Elite Swimmers with a Loco-motor Disability. *Human Movement Science*, 24, 54–65.

Schleihauf, R. E. (1979). A Hydrodynamic Analysis of Swimming Propulsion. In J. Terauds & E. W. Bedingfield (eds), *Swimming Science III*. Baltimore: University Park Press, pp. 71–109.

Schleihauf, R. E., Higgins, J. R., Hinricks, R., Luedtke, D., Maglischo, C., Maglischo, E. W. & Thayer, A. (1988). Propulsive Techniques: Front Crawl Stroke, Butterfly, Backstroke and Breaststroke. In B. E. Ungerechts, K. Wilke & K. Reischle (eds), *Swimming Science V*. Champaign, Illinois: Human Kinetics Publishers, pp. 53–59.

Schnitzler, C. (2005). Vers l'intégration des Coordinations Motrices dans une Perspective d'analyse et d'optimisation de la Performance en Nage Libre. *Unpublished Ph.D. Thesis*, France: University of Rouen.

Schnitzler, C., Brazier, T., Button, C. & Chollet, D. (2008). Effect of Velocity and Added Resistance on Kinematical and Kinetical Parameters in Front Crawl. In T. Nomura & B. Ungerechts (eds) *1st International Scientific Conference of Aquatic Space Activities*, Tsukuba, Japan: University of Tsukuba, pp. 266–271.

Seifert, L., Boulesteix, L., Carter, M. & Chollet, D. (2005a). The Spatial-temporal and Co-ordinative Structure in Elite Men 100 m Front Crawl Swimmers. *International Journal of Sports Medicine*, 26, 286–293.

Seifert, L., Boulesteix, L. & Chollet, D. (2004a). Effect of Gender on the Adaptation of Arm Co-ordination in Front Crawl. *International Journal of Sport Medicine*, 25, 217–223.

Seifert, L., Chéhensse, A., Tourny-Chollet, C., Lemaitre, F. & Chollet, D. (2008a). Effect of Breathing Pattern on Arm Co-ordination Symmetry in Front Crawl. *Journal of Strength and Conditioning Research*, 22(5), 1670–1676.

Seifert, L. & Chollet, D. (2005). A New Index of Flat Breaststroke Propulsion: Comparison between Elite Men and Elite Women. *Journal of Sports Sciences*, 23, 309–320.

Seifert, L. & Chollet, D. (2008). Inter-limb Co-ordination and Constraints in Swimming: A Review. In N. P. Beaulieu (ed) *Physical Activity and Children: New Research*, Hauppauge, New York: Nova Science Publishers, pp. 65–93.

Seifert, L. & Chollet, D. (2009). Modelling Spatial-temporal and Co-ordinative Parameters in Swimming. *Journal of Science and Medicine in Sport*, 12, 495–499.

Seifert, L., Chollet, D. & Allard, P. (2005b). Arm Co-ordination Symmetry and Effect of Breathing in Front Crawl. *Human Movement Science*, 24, 234–256.

Seifert, L., Chollet, D. & Bardy, B. (2004b). Effect of Swimming Velocity on Arm Co-ordination in Front Crawl: A Dynamical Analysis. *Journal of Sports Sciences*, 22, 651–660.

Seifert, L., Chollet, D. & Chatard, J.C. (2007a). Changes in Co-ordination and Kinematics during a 100 m Front Crawl. *Medicine and Science in Sports and Exercise*, 39, 1784–1793.

Seifert, L., Chollet, D., Papparadopoulos, C., Guerniou, Y. & Binet, G. (2006). Longitudinal Evaluation of Breaststroke Spatial-temporal and Co-ordinative Parameters: Preparing of the 100 m Breaststroke Bronze Medallists of the Athena 2004 Olympic Games. *Portuguese Journal of Sport Sciences*, 6(*Supl. 2*), 260–262.

Seifert, L., Chollet, D. & Rouard, A. (2007b). Swimming Constraints and Arm Co-ordination. *Human Movement Science, 26*, 68–86.

Seifert, L., Leblanc, H. & Chollet, D. (2008b). Analysis of Inter-limb Co-ordination and its Variability in Swimming, *2nd International Congress of Complex Systems in Sport & 10th European Workshop of Ecological Psychology*, 4–8 November, Madeira, Funchal, p. 135.

Seifert, L., Toussaint, H., Schnitzler, C., Alberty, M., Chavallard, F., Lemaitre, F., Vantorre, J. & Chollet, D. (2008c). Effect of Velocity Increase on Arm Co-ordination, Active Drag and Intra-cyclic Velocity Variations in Front Crawl. In T. Nomura & B. Ungerechts (eds), *1st International Scientific Conference of Aquatic Space Activities*, Tsukuba, Japan: University of Tsukuba, pp. 254–259.

Seifert, L., Vantorre, J. & Chollet, D. (2007c). Biomechanical Analysis of the Breaststroke Start, *International Journal of Sports Medicine*, 28(11), 970–976.

Sidney, M., Paillette, S., Hespel, J. M., Chollet, D. & Pelayo, P. (2001). Effect of Swim Paddles on the Intra-cyclic Velocity Variations and on the Arm Co-ordination of Front Crawl Stroke. In J. R. Blackwell & R. H. Sanders (eds), *XIX International Symposium on Biomechanics in Sports*, San Francisco: ISBS, pp. 39–42.

Swinnen, S. P., Jardin, K., Meulenbroek, R., Douskaia, N. & Hofkens-Van Den Brandt, R. (1997). Egocentric and Allocentric Constraints in the Expression of Patterns of Inter-limb Co-ordination. *Journal of Cognitive Neuroscience, 9*, 348–377.

Takagi, H., Sugimoto, S., Nishijima, N. & Wilson, B. (2004). Differences in Stroke Phases, Arm-leg Co-ordination and Velocity Fluctuation due to Event, Gender and Performance Level in Breaststroke. *Sports Biomechanics, 3*, 15–27.

Toussaint, H. M., Carol, A., Kranenborg, H. & Truijens, M. (2006). Effect of Fatigue on Stroking Characteristics in an Arms-only 100m Front Crawl Race. *Medicine and Science in Sports and Exercise, 38*, 1635–1642.

Toussaint, H. M. & Truijens, M. (2005). Biomechanical Aspects of Peak Performance in Human Swimming. *Animal Biology, 55*, 17–40.

Toussaint, H. M. & Hollander, A. P. (1994). Energetics of Competitive Swimming. Implications for Training Programmes. *Sports Medicine, 18*(6), 384–405.

Toussaint, H. M., Hollander, A. P., van den Berg, C. & Vorontsov, A. (2000). Biomechanics in Swimming. In W. E. Garrett & D. T. Kirkendall (eds), *Exercise and Sport Science*, Philadelphia: Lippincott, Williams & Wilkins, pp. 639–660.

Vennell, R., Pease, D. & Wilson, B. (2006). Wave Drag on Human Swimmers. *Journal of Biomechanics, 39*, 664–671.

Yeater, R. A., Martin, R. B., White, M. K. & Gilson, K. H. (1981). Tethered Swimming Forces in the Crawl, Breast and Back Strokes and their Relationship to Competitive Performance. *Journal of Biomechanics, 14*, 527–537.

8 The changing face of practice for developing perception

Action skill in cricket

Ross Pinder

Introduction

The use of bowling machines is common practice in cricket. In an ideal world all batters would face real bowlers in practice sessions, but this is not always possible, for many reasons. The clear advantage of using bowling machines is that they alleviate the workload required from bowlers (Dennis *et al.*, 2005) and provide relatively consistent and accurate ball delivery, which may not be otherwise available to many young batters. Anecdotal evidence suggests that many if not most of the world's greatest players use these methods within their training schedules. For example, Australian internationals Michael Hussey and Matthew Hayden extensively used bowling machines (Hussey & Sygall, 2007). Bowling machines enable batsmen to practice for long periods, developing their endurance and concentration. However, despite these obvious benefits, in recent times the use of bowling machines has been questioned by sport scientists, coaches, ex-players and commentators. For example, Hussey's batting coach comments "...we never went near a bowling machine in [Michael's] first couple of years, I think there's something to that ..." (Hussey & Sygall, 2007, p. 119).

This chapter will discuss the efficacy of using bowling machines with reference to research findings, before reporting new evidence that provides support for an alternative, innovative and possibly more representative practice design. Finally, the chapter will provide advice for coaches on the implications of this research, including a case study approach to demonstrate the practical use of such a design.

Research on the use of bowling machines

As Davids helps to summarise in Chapter 1, the main criticism of the use of a bowling machine is that it leads to different movement patterns for both young semi-skilled and adult skilled batsmen compared to that seen when facing a bowler (Renshaw *et al.*, 2007: Pinder *et al.*, 2009). Practicing against machines appears to lead batsmen to search for informational variables which are in fact non-specifying; players search for and rely on environmental information that is irrelevant to a competitive performance environment (Pinder *et al.*, 2009; Renshaw *et al.*, 2007).

Essentially, players learn to "bat against the machine". In Pinder et al.'s study of young semi-skilled batsmen, data showed significant adaptations to movement timing and co-ordination for both a defensive and attacking stroke, with initiation of the backswings occurring after ball release (drive: 0.06 sec; defence: 0.06 sec) against the bowler, but significantly later against the bowling machine (drive: 0.15 sec; defence: 0.14 sec). In contrast, Renshaw et al. (2007) reported that when skilled batsmen faced a bowling machine, the point of backswing initiation varied greatly but occurred around the point of ball release.

Due to the lack of advanced information afforded by a bowling machine (e.g. no pre-delivery bowler information), these less-skilled developing batsmen demonstrated a prospective control strategy based on the emergence of ball flight information. This delayed movement initiation resulted in significantly lower peak backswing heights, and shorter step lengths in order to provide task success (e.g. hit the ball). These factors led to more "upright" final shot positions, with players tending to play the ball well in front of the pad, suggesting they were "pushing at the ball" in an attempt to reduce the distance between the pitch and point of contact. This movement response can be classified as a reduction in shot quality when facing the bowling machine, as general cricketing wisdom highlights the need to play the ball as late as possible (Woolmer et al., 2008).

Notably, Pinder et al. (2009) demonstrated that players at the control stage of learning achieved similar levels of coupling to the skilled batters of Renshaw et al. (2007) in relation to the two major components of the early stages of the batting action – the backswing initiation and front foot movement. At this control stage of learning, batsmen appear to have acquired the coordinative relationships between movement components, but still need to finely tune these to dynamic performance contexts (Davids et al., 2008). This finding highlights the importance of designing practice tasks for new batsmen which will allow them to learn to recognise the different variables possible in the performance environment. For example, learning to pick up cues early on from a bowler's action and translate that information into a successful shot. They then need to be able to reproduce this behaviour in a real performance environment (Jacobs & Michaels, 2002).

Perceptual skill in cricket: current thinking

Similar to other sports, research examining cricket batting has reported a relationship between skill level and anticipatory ability, with previous evidence proposing that only skilled batters have an ability to use advanced information afforded by the bowler's action (Weissensteiner et al., 2008; Müller et al., 2006). A recent re-evaluation of the occlusion paradigms on which much of the anticipation research is based has proposed that these findings may be the result of experimental design (for a review and critique see van der Kamp et al., 2008). Additionally, much of the research analysing perceptual skill in sport has compared experts with novices, and as such there was a need to re-examine these issues by targeting players in developmental stages via methodological strategies that examined perception and action in unison. In fact, as well as examining movement kinematics, the procedures adopted in Pinder *et al.* (2009) enabled us to demonstrate that players below expert level are in fact able to use information from a bowler's action at or before ball release.

The importance of the role that perceptual skill plays in sport has led to a large increase in research aimed at discovering the best methods to promote perceptual skill acquisition (Dicks *et al.*, 2008). Several researchers have stressed the importance of enhancing perceptual skills in cricket batters (Williams & McRobert, 2008; Weissensteiner *et al.*, 2008). There is, however, limited research on the most appropriate methods to use, which have been proposed to be more closely related to experience of large amounts of task-specific practice than simply maturation (Weissensteiner *et al.*, 2008). The key phrase in these proposals is "task specific". Given that research has now demonstrated that facing a bowling machine and facing a real bowler are both very different practice tasks (Pinder *et al.*, 2009; Renshaw *et al.*, 2007) it would seem that the only way to practice these skills is via game play or facing real bowlers so players can attune themselves to key informational variables reflective of the real performance or behavioural setting.

An interesting option worthy of further investigation is video-based training for cricket (Williams & McRobert, 2008). Although the use of video simulations for training perceptual skill in sport is receiving a lot of research attention there are still major doubts over the effectiveness of this type of training set-up. Questions raised regarding the difference in the task design and competitive context include: (1) dimensions of the display; (2) differences between viewing angle or players perspective; and (3) restrictions on information available for perceptual pick-up (Williams *et al.*, 1999; Williams *et al.*, 2005). Additionally, much of this research focuses on simple outcome measures as opposed to movement responses such as co-ordination and timing, with no researchers having yet examined the practical use of video simulation training in cricket batting (Williams & McRobert, 2008). Considering the previous findings, research was needed to develop innovative methods to allow batters to undertake the volume of task-specific practice required to develop perceptual skills (Weissensteiner *et al.*, 2008), while maintaining a greater level of representative task design (Brunswik, 1956; Dicks *et al.* 2008).

The changing face of practice: evidence for the use of video-based practice

Pinder *et al.* (2009) considered the previous concerns surrounding the current understandings of perceptual skill acquisition, and sought to investigate the movement responses and co-ordination for the forward defensive and drive strokes of semi-skilled batsmen under three different practice task constraints that were considered to provide differing levels of representativeness. The three conditions were: (1) facing real bowlers; (2) facing a bowling machine set to the same speed and release height; and (3) facing the same bowlers on a video screen/simulation. Video footage of four left-arm bowlers was filmed from a batsman's perspective from the popping (batting) crease, and set-up procedures followed those of Taliep *et al.* (2007) to create a realistic viewing angle of 7° and a virtual distance of

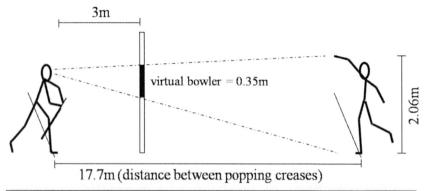

Figure 8.1 A view of the experimental set-up and the video screen training in action.

17.7 m (the distance between the popping creases: see Figure 8.1). The bowling speed (28.14 ± 0.56 m.s.$^{-1}$) and release height (2.06 ± 0.07 m) of the bowlers (n=4) were then replicated with the bowling machine to provide consistent conditions in all three practice tasks.

Results

Developing junior batsmen (n = 12, age = 15.6 ± 0.7 years) were chosen as the focus of the research, with the role of practice task constraints being proposed to be especially crucial during the early stages of the control stage of learning (Davids *et al.*, 2008). Movement initiations and responses, as well as upper- and lower-body kinematics were compared across all three practice tasks. Data on movement initiation times revealed some extremely interesting results, particularly relating to the information-movement coupling of the batsmen in the early phases of the batting action. Results are represented in seconds (mean ± standard deviation) before the impact (or virtual impact) of bat and ball, with ball release occurring 0.64 sec before impact. During the backswing phase, the movement of the bat was initiated significantly later against the bowling machine (drive: 0.50 ± 0.07 sec; defence: 0.49 ± 0.08 sec) than against both the bowler (drive: 0.58 ± 0.07 sec; defence: 0.58 ± 0.07 sec) and the video screen (drive: 0.59 ± 0.08 sec; defence: 0.59 ± 0.09 sec), for which there were no differences (see Figure 8.2). Related to this earlier initiation of backswing is peak bat height attained by the batters under the varying conditions. Batters attained similar bat heights in both bowler (drive: 1.52 ± 0.25 m; defence: 1.34 ± 0.29 m) and video screen conditions (drive: 1.52 ± 0.23 m; defence: 1.36 ± 0.21 m), however, when facing the bowling machine this height was significantly reduced (drive: 1.41 ± 0.26 m; defence: 1.27 ± 0.31 m). The delayed initiation of the backswing when facing the bowling machine afforded less time for the batters to complete their full backswing, leading to shorter backswing times and lower peak bat heights (see Figure 8.2). Different responses were seen for the front foot movement initiation and step lengths of the batters across the three conditions. The front foot movement occurred later when facing the bowling machine (drive: 0.41 ± 0.08 sec; defence: 0.39 ± 0.09 sec) when compared with the responses of the bowler (drive: 0.48 ± 0.08 sec; defence: 0.47 ± 0.11 sec) and video screen conditions (drive: 0.50 ± 0.08 sec; defence: 0.49 ± 0.09 sec). As a result of this delayed initiation, both the timing of front foot placement and total step length were affected, with significantly shorter step lengths and total movement times against the bowling machine. Supportive kinematic analysis confirmed the similarities between the bowler and video screen, and the differences with the bowling machine conditions. When comparing the bowler and video screen conditions there were no differences between the joint segment angles of the front and back elbows and front knee at backswing initiation, front foot movement and downswing initiation. However, there were significant differences across this entire period for both conditions when compared to the bowling machine responses for the upper body kinematics.

Importantly, the results also displayed marginally different downswing initiation times across all conditions, with changes to the upper body joint angles at the later phases (front foot placement and impact) of the shots. Due to the changes in the level of representativeness, and "quality" of ball flight information available (and the actions that preceded it) all three conditions demonstrated different final movement characteristics. As discussed by Pinder *et al.* (2009), the differences caused in the bowling machine condition were attributed to the delayed initiation of the shots due to the removal of advanced information from the bowlers' actions. However, when this information was present in the video condition, the differences could be attributed to the *intentionality* of the batsmen. A reduction in depth perception due to representing the action as a two-dimensional image, and the task not requiring the batter to physically intercept a ball led to a reduction in the perception-action link during the later stages of the action, and changes to the downswing initiation and joint kinematics (body position) at impact. It is proposed that the *contextualisation* of practice situations may go some way to counter these differences (see below); however research is required to further investigate these claims.

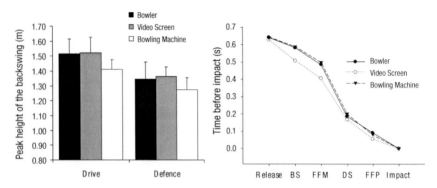

Figure 8.2 Evidence for the use of video-based training designs, including temporal responses of the forward drive (BS: backswing initiation; FFM: front foot movement; DS: downswing initiation; FFP: front foot placement) and peak bat heights across three different practice tasks.

Implications

A video screen afforded similar anticipatory and advanced information to the real task of batting against a bowler, with preparatory movement responses (backswing initiations and peak bat height, front foot movement initiation and step lengths) comparable for the video and bowler conditions. With the support of kinematic analysis, it was demonstrated that the players "coupled" movements to the same information sources when this advanced information was available for perceptual pick-up irrespective of whether it was provided from a real bowler or replicated on a video display. Although more research is needed, this study demonstrates that the use of video screen technology in cricket batting provides a more representative practice task than facing a bowling machine when relating to the pick-up of advanced or early ball flight information. The results provide tentative support for the use of video training against fast bowling in a safe environment, where the previous concerns surrounding achieving the required volume of task specific practice for advancing perceptual skill may be answered. Clearly, these suggestions require specific testing, with a focus on the implementation of a video-based training design, with particular emphasis on the transfer to the competitive practice task of facing real fast bowlers.

It must be clarified that this chapter is not intended to advocate the removal of bowling machines from practice. As outlined at the beginning of this chapter, there are situations when the use of a bowling machine becomes a necessity. It could also be suggested that bowling machines may play an important role in the early stages of skill acquisition, where a learner begins to establish the very basic relationships between dynamical movement components (Davids *et al.*, 2008). Using a bowling machine in this situation would enable consistent ball feeding to facilitate the emergence of basic co-ordination patterns, which are viewed as the fundamental starting block by most coaches. However, a coach should be aware of the limitations and possible hindrance of bowling machine practice to higher levels of perceptual skill acquisition.

Consider the following: If research has demonstrated that batting against a bowler and a bowling machine are different ecological practice tasks, what benefit do experts gain from using such practice methods? Do they simply get better at playing a bowling machine? How does this relate to facing a bowler? How could players of all skill levels use video-based practice methods to prepare for specific situations?

A coach should be aware of the benefits and limitations of different forms of practice tasks and that every practice situation holds some level of representativeness of the competitive environment (i.e. batting in a game). Regardless of the practice task employed (e.g. bowling machine, bowler or video screen), it is the role of the coach to use methods of contextualising practice in ways that may lead to a greater level of representativeness of a game situation. For example, while batting, players could be provided with various game scenarios, field settings and dynamic game changes (e.g. fall of wickets) simulating those they may face in real game situations.

Case Study: Maximising representativeness in practice

Identify the problem

Providing a large volume of representative practice for the development of perceptual skill in junior cricket batters.

Setting

Junior cricket team.

Constraints

Access to players, overuse of bowlers.

The coach of Seven Hills Cricket Club's U-15s, Scotty Turner, was aware of the importance of a large volume of practice for developing batters, and the emphasis placed on facing real bowlers in practice at an elite level. Scotty liked to keep up to date with new coaching ideas and scientific literature, and as a result had read a scientific report on the use of bowling machines with junior batters. His main concern for the upcoming winter training schedule was being able to provide his batters with quality bowling, so they would be prepared for the following summer season. However, a lot of the team had serious sporting commitments outside of cricket (e.g. AFL, Hockey) during the winter season, and it was always a challenge to get all players training at the same time. In addition to this, when the bowlers were available, Scotty was cautious of over bowling them at this developmental age, particularly his fast bowlers. The key problem therefore, was how to enable his batters to receive the volume of practice that he knew would be necessary for them to compete in the upcoming season, without relying on a bowling machine.

Before winter training began, Scotty decided to film all of his bowlers from the batters' perspective. Not only did he capture footage of his fast, medium-pace and slower spin bowlers, but he also saw the opportunity to be adventurous, and took video footage of the fast bowlers from Seven Hill's U-17s when the opportunity arose. With the committee requiring some convincing to release some club funds, Scotty initially hired a large screen and projector to help demonstrate his training design. Using simple maths he was able to provide a realistic image of the bowlers on the screen based on the height of the bowler and distance of the batsmen from the screen. Although this set-up seemed very foreign to the players, and caused much amusement to begin with, it soon became clear that the screen was giving an unexpected level of realism. "Ha-ha, no good looking back at us mate!" shouted Jack, as an embarrassed looking Lee quickly shot a glance behind him to see if a keeper was readying to take a delivery that he was sure he'd just nicked.

The committee released funds to buy the large screen and projector, and Scotty used the video screen extensively throughout the winter, in addition to letting his batters hit balls from real bowlers and a bowling machine on a regular basis. The key thing he found was that his batters were able to "face" the really quick U-17 bowlers on the screen, when they were not confident enough to face them in real life, or from balls delivered at the same pace from a bowling machine. Additionally, when "facing" the slower bowlers, batters were learning to pick types of deliveries from the wrist position at release. Will Springer was a promising batter, and a good all-round sportsman, but the previous summer he'd had a lot of trouble against quicker bowlers. "I've been practicing loads against the bowling machine, whenever I got the chance," admitted Will. Scotty felt that Will looked tentative when moving forward against the fast boys, and didn't appear to react quickly enough or have time to organise his responses. Scotty knew that to progress past this stage would take a considerable amount of time facing the bowlers and building up confidence, and saw this as an ideal opportunity to make use of the video screen footage. Will trained against the U-15 fast bowlers on the video screen and was developing a better base and ready position at release – ready to move either forward or back, but not getting "stuck on the back foot". Having built up confidence from repeatedly judging the length and line of deliveries, Will was then using this knowledge to face the real bowlers themselves and moving forward into deliveries and hitting well straight back down the ground. "Hey! What have you done with the real Will?" shouted Jack, as yet another ball whistled past him and he was left quizzically wondering how Will was suddenly so good at playing his bowling.

Through careful editing Scotty created training sets designed to replicate game situations. Importantly, for each set, he knew the landing points of each delivery and was able to assess if the batters were reacting accordingly. To further increase the representativeness of his practices, Scotty made the players bat in pairs just as they would in a game and game scenarios with appropriate field settings. The non-batting partner stood behind the batter and between them they adjudged the outcome of the delivery and linked it back to the game scenario and fielding set-up. The video training was always linked to regular net practice where batters were required to link these judgments (e.g. attempting to change the pace on the ball, or working the ball into specific gaps) and practice running between the wickets (see Renshaw & Holder, Chapter 9). A range of practice designs helped to counter the constraints that a coach like Scotty may face. Using a combination of game scenarios, field settings, innovative and imaginative practice tasks and an understanding committee, the Seven Hills U-15s were well prepared when the summer season rolled around.

References

Brunswik, E. (1956). *Perception and the Representative Design of Psychological Experiments*, 2nd edn. Berkeley, CA: University of California Press.

Davids, K., Button, C. & Bennett, S. (2008). *Dynamics of Skill Acquisition: A Constraints-led Approach*. Champaign, Illinois: Human Kinetics.

Dennis, R. J., Finch, C. F. & Farhart, P. J. (2005). Is Bowling Workload a Risk Factor for Injury to Australian Junior Cricket Fast Bowlers? *British Journal of Sports Medicine*, 39, 843–846.

Dicks, M., Davids, K. & Araújo, D. (2008). Ecological Psychology and Task Representativeness: Implications for the Design of Perceptual-motor Training Programmes in Sport. In Y. Hong & R. Bartlett (eds), *Handbook of Biomechanics and Human Movement Science*, New York: Routledge, pp. 129–139.

Hussey, M. & Sygall, D. (2007). *Mr Cricket: Driven to Succeed*. Victoria: Hardie Grant.

Jacobs, D. M. & Michaels, C. F. (2002). On the Paradox of Learning and Realism. *Ecological Psychology*, 14(3), 127–140.

Müller, S., Abernethy, B. & Farrow, D. (2006). How do World-class Cricket Batsmen Anticipate a Bowler's Intention? *The Quarterly Journal of Experimental Psychology*, 59, 2162–2186.

Pinder, R. A., Davids, K., & Renshaw, I. (2009). *The Use of Video Simulations in Cricket Batting*. Paper presented at the Evolution of the athlete coach education conference 2009.

Pinder, R. A., Renshaw, I. & Davids, K. (2009). Information–movement Coupling in Developing Cricketers under Changing Ecological Practice Constraints. *Human Movement Science*, 28, 468–479.

Renshaw, I., Oldham, A. R. H., Davids, K. & Golds, T. (2007). Changing Ecological Constraints of Practice Alters Co-ordination of Dynamic Interceptive Actions. *European Journal of Sport Science*, 7, 157–167.

Taliep, M. S., Galal, U. & Vaughan, C. L. (2007). The Position of the Head and Centre of Mass during the Front Foot Off-drive in Skilled and Less-skilled Cricket Batsmen. *Sports Biomechanics*, 6(3), 345–360.

van der Kamp, J., Rivas, F., van Doorn, H. & Savelsbergh, G. J. P. (2008). Ventral and Dorsal Contributions in Visual Anticipation in Fast Ball Sports. *International Journal of Sport Psychology*, 39, 100–130.

Weissensteiner, J., Abernethy, B., Farrow, D. & Müller, S. (2008). The Development of Anticipation: A Cross-sectional Examination of the Practice Experiences Contributing to Skill in Cricket Batting. *Journal of Motor Behavior*, 30, 663–684.

Williams, A. M., Davids, K., & Williams, J. G. (1999). *Visual Perception and Action in Sport*. London: E. & F. N. Spon.

Williams, A. M. & Ericsson, K.A. (2005). Perceptual-cognitive expertise in sport: Some considerations when applying the expert performance approach. *Human Movement Science*. 24 (3), 283–307.

Williams, A. M. & McRobert, A. (2008). Perceptual-cognitive Skill in Cricket Batting: From Testing to Training. In T. Reilly (ed.), *Science and Sports: Bridging the Gap*, World Commission of Science & Sports, pp. 122–134.

9 The "nurdle to leg" and other ways of winning cricket matches

Ian Renshaw and Darren Holder

Introduction

The emergence of Twenty20 cricket at the elite level has been marketed on the excitement of the big hitter, where it seems that winning is a result of the muscular batter hitting boundaries at will. This version of the game has captured the imagination of many young players, who all want to score runs with "big hits". However, in junior cricket, boundary hitting is often more difficult due to size limitations of children and games being played on outfields where the ball does not travel quickly. As a result, winning is often achieved via a less spectacular route – by scoring more singles than your opponents. However, most standard coaching texts only describe how to play boundary scoring shots (e.g. the drives, pulls, cuts and sweeps) and defensive shots to protect the wicket. Learning to bat appears to have been reduced to extremes of force production, i.e. maximal force production to hit boundaries or minimal force production to stop the ball from hitting the wicket. Initially, this is not a problem because the typical innings of a young player (<12 years) would be based on the concept of "block" or "bash" – they "block" the good balls and "bash" the short balls. This approach works because there are many opportunities to hit boundaries off the numerous inaccurate deliveries of novice bowlers. Most runs are scored behind the wicket by using the pace of the bowler's delivery to re-direct the ball, because the intrinsic dynamics (i.e. lack of strength) of most children means that they can only create sufficient power by playing shots where the whole body can contribute to force production. This method works well until the novice player comes up against more accurate bowling, when they find they have no way of scoring runs.

Once batters begin to face "good" bowlers, they have to learn to score runs via singles. In cricket coaching manuals (e.g. the English Cricket Board's *Cricket Coaches Manual*, n.d.), running between the wickets is treated as a separate task to batting, and the "basics" of running, such as how to "back-up", carry the bat, calling and turning and sliding the bat into the crease are "drilled" into players. This task decomposition strategy focusing on techniques is a common approach to skill acquisition in many highly traditional sports, typified in cricket by activities where players hit balls off tees and receive "throw-downs" from coaches. However, the relative usefulness of these approaches in the acquisition of sporting skills is increasingly being questioned (Pinder et al., 2009). We will discuss why this is the case in the next section.

Representative practice and coupling action to perception

As Renshaw highlights in Chapter 3, practice to improve performance is closely linked to the level of representativeness of the activities undertaken. Coaches need to design practice activities that replicate the real performance environment. Only activities that include the full range of information sources a player can expect to face in a real game will result in a transfer of skills from the practice to the game. For example, practicing by facing bowling machines at the expense of real bowlers prevents attunement to the key information sources (i.e. the bowlers' actions) and at the same time promotes the development of information-movement couplings that are different to those seen when facing real bowlers (Pinder et al., 2009; Renshaw et al., 2007). An alternative approach is to use task simplification where key information sources are preserved, enabling perception, decision-making and technique to be developed simultaneously. We will provide examples of task simplification later in the paper.

Affordances for action

A key reason why practice tasks must be representative of the competition environment is that this enables the player to become attuned to key affordances. An affordance is an environmental property that provides opportunities for action (Gibson, 1986). It is important to understand that the availability of an affordance is specific to the individual's ability to exploit it. For example, a 140 km/h^{-1} bouncer aimed at the batter's head affords a top player like Sachin Tendulkar a chance to hit the ball for six, while for less able players the same delivery simply affords an opportunity to duck out of the way of the ball (as quickly as possible!). An affordance for a batter looking to score a single could be a fielder standing 5 m too deep or a ball hit to the non-dominant side of the fielder. The process of education of attention (Beek et al., 2003) allows batters to become attuned to their own capabilities in relation to their environment. In ecological psychology, the environment is not just the physical environment but refers to teammates and opponents. As such, batters need to be attuned to the capabilities of their batting partner(s) (e.g. speed and agility) and opposition fielders (e.g. handedness) to determine the best placement of a shot. At a more advanced level, attunement to affordances offered by the physical environment (e.g. length of the grass, softness of the ground, wind direction) will influence shot selection.

Stability to instability and back again: from no runs to run-outs to runs

At the co-ordination level (see Davids et al., 2008) children will initially explore a number of solutions before settling on one movement pattern that is able to give them some success. For example, when batting against novice bowlers, the batter soon realises that if he defends the accurate balls it will not be long before the bowler bowls an inaccurate ball from which runs can be scored. In dynamical systems terms, the "system" becomes stable and the child does not search for any other solutions. As players move through developmental pathways they are soon faced with better bowlers who bowl few inaccurate balls. At this stage, the stable solution fails to work. For the knowledgeable coach this "failure" provides an opportunity to break the stability of the system by introducing practice tasks and coaching activities that can force players to find new solutions. The coach can deliberately create instability in the system by making the batters face accurate bowlers in simulated game situations. During this training phase individuals have opportunities to gather knowledge and information leading to the selection of appropriate new solutions. However, coaches need to be aware that during this time individuals will show high levels of variability in skill execution, and performance will be interspersed with periods of "success" and "failure".

Coaches should understand that increased variability and making mistakes is part of the normal process of learning and will precede the emergence of new "stable" solutions. This is an important point because if the coach is trying to improve the single-taking ability of batters, initially this can lead to more run-outs as players make poor decisions about the opportunities for taking singles. As such, coaches must carefully consider the timing of interventions, and trying to change behaviours just before a major tournament or important match would not be recommended! Intervention programmes need to be based on the needs of individual players and require the identification of key factors that limit the emergence of new solutions.

Rate limiters for running singles

A player's ability to take singles may be limited by any number of factors, but typically these will be technical, perceptual or mental. Technically, players may not have the hitting skill to deflect or vary the force of shots to manoeuvre good deliveries (e.g. good line and length) into spaces between fielders. On a more basic level, batters may not "back-up" when at the non-striker's end by moving down the pitch while the ball is in flight. Tactically, batters may not have the perceptual skills to recognise when a fielder is placed too deep to stop a single or if there is adequate "space" between fielders (i.e. they do not know how far away from a player a ball must be before there is a run scoring opportunity). At a more advanced level, the player may not know if the fielder is right- or left-handed and cannot take a run by hitting the ball to the non-dominant side of the fielder. A common issue for many coaches is that the mindset of young players is about "not getting out" and "me" rather than about scoring runs and "us". As such, they often do not look for run-scoring opportunities and are happy to simply wait for the bad ball. As we discussed above, this strategy has a very short lifespan and should be challenged as soon as possible.

Before designing any intervention strategy to improve the ability to score singles, a coach must identify the key factors that are acting as rate limiters. Coaches can choose from a range of strategies to search for this information, including: (1) observation of performance in matches and training activities; (2) the use of statistical analysis of performance; and (3) discussions with the players. In the next section we will provide examples of activities that will focus on how to develop performance for each of the technical, perceptual or mental rate limiters.

Practice tasks to solve rate limiters

Technical skills

Activity 1: Scoring singles

Learning to score singles requires the batter to be able to make controlled contact to direct the straight ball into run-scoring positions. This can be challenging for young players as often they will try to "flick" or "deflect" the ball into space. A technique that can be employed is to adjust the orientation of the lead shoulder, allowing the bat to swing along this line (see Figure 9.1). This means that more of the bat face is presented to the ball for a longer period and is therefore a much safer method. Additionally, this technique provides the batter with a range of timing options to make ball contact during the arc of the swing. An earlier contact will result in the ball being hit on a "straighter" line of travel, while a later contact will result in a "squarer" line of travel (see Figure 9.2). In order to build the batter's confidence in completing this challenging task, the coach should arrange cones 10 m apart on the 30 m circle (see Figure 9.3). At the start of the session the batter would be asked to simply hit the ball between the two blue cones (1), before moving on to hit between the blue and red (2)(alternately to the off and leg side), then red to yellow (3) and finally yellow to white (4). The coach could then randomise the choice of hitting zone. The task can be made competitive by awarding points for hitting the ball through the nominated zone and providing

Figure 9.1 A technique that can be employed to place the ball is to adjust the orientation of the lead shoulder, allowing the bat to swing along this line. This means that more of the bat face is presented to the ball for a longer time period resulting in a much safer method than "flicking" the ball.

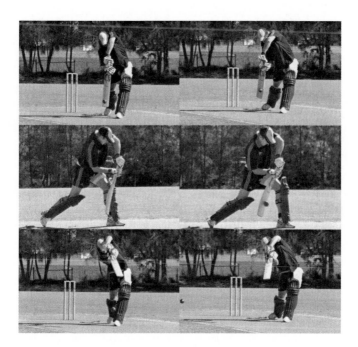

Figure 9.2 Allowing the bat swing to unfold along the line of the shoulders provides the batter with a range of timing options to make ball contact during the arc of the swing. An earlier contact will result in the ball being hit on a "straighter" line of travel (left column) while a later contact will result in a "squarer" line of travel (right column).

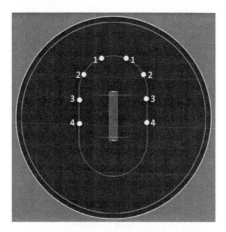

Figure 9.3 In order to build the batter's confidence in learning to place the ball by adjusting the line of the shoulders and hitting at earlier or later points of the swing, the coach should arrange cones 10 m apart on the 30 m circle. At the start of the session the batter would be asked to simply hit the ball between the two blue cones (1), before moving on to hit between the blue and red (2) (alternatively to the off and leg side), then red to yellow (3) and finally yellow to white (4).

Figure 9.4 Bat swing variability: Only by developing a full bat swing (top) can players learn to vary the level of force production (between hard to soft). This principle follows along the lines of the degrees of freedom argument of Bernstein in that the aim for young players should be to reach a level of co-ordination where the batter is able to complete a full bat swing. At this level of control (Newell, 1986), the batter is able to choose to swing with varying levels of force, or limit the length of the swing (middle and bottom).

records for each player. An extension of the task is to award more points for more difficult scoring areas as determined by the player or coach.

Activity 2: Changing the pace of shots

As discussed in the introduction, the typical approach is to teach young players to learn the shots for hitting boundaries and for defending their wicket. Force production is either maximal or minimal. However, in order to become a skilful batter, players need to be able to vary the amount of force with which they hit the ball. However, while we recognise that there are situations where young players should be encouraged to defend and/or hit the ball hard, we would suggest that it is only by developing a full bat swing (see Figure 9.4 (top)) that players can learn to vary the level of force production (between hard to soft). This principle follows along the lines of the degrees of freedom argument of Bernstein in that the aim for young players should be to reach a level of co-ordination where the batter is able to complete a full bat swing. At that level of control (Newell, 1986), the batter is able to choose to swing with varying levels of force, or limit the length of the swing (see Figure 9.4 (middle and bottom)). The coach can adapt the organisation of the previous task by placing cones in concentric circles at 5 m, 15 m, 30 m and 50 m. Similar to before, the player or coach nominates which circle the ball should finish in.

Activity 3: Games

The potential number of games for practicing hitting the ball into space is almost limitless. However, the coach should remember to devise games that are representative of the demands of the real game. For example, the coach could segment the field and require players to hit the ball between strategically placed fielders in the designated area(s). One simple game could involve the coach setting up a 40 m boundary and any ball hit over the boundary would not count as runs. It is worth noting that many coaches will use the 30 m circle used in one-day cricket as the boundary. However, we have found that this distance means that players can only hit the ball "in front" of fielders meaning that fielders can move in closer than they could in real games. It is important that batters are able to "place" and "pace" the ball into gaps between and/or beyond the fielders. This allows batsmen to score singles by utilising their new-found abilities of hitting the ball with different levels of force (i.e. pace) in order to direct the ball into the available space between fielders.

The role of the coach does not end once the game has been set up. In fact, the coach should encourage batters to search the environment for information that will enhance his/her ability to take singles. For example, the coach could stop the game and ask the batters to nominate the dominant hand of each fielder. Coaches can also deliberately manipulate tasks by requiring fielders to play a specific role (such as not walking in, standing too deep or moving slowly to the ball).

Perceptual skills

The limited technical skills of young players means that they often have little experience of taking singles and as a consequence find it difficult to recognise opportunities to score runs. Task simplification by requiring the batter to throw the ball can be used to enhance this awareness and provides a fun yet realistic way of helping players to learn to decide when and when not to run. In essence, the coach removes the problem of lack of batting technique by modifying the game (see Table 9.1 and Figure 9.5). The aim of the game is for batters to develop judgements about "placing" and "pacing" the ball to facilitate running singles. Allowing

Table 9.1 The singles game organisation

- 6 v 6 (2 batters as per cricket).
- Set up a field that is 25 m × 30 m.
- Stumps should be placed so that the "batting" stumps are 2 m from the rear boundary.
- Fielders can stand anywhere in the field (but MUST NOT stand within 5 m of the "batter").
- The feeder (one of the batting team) throws the ball (tennis or incrediball) to the batter, who must catch it and then throw the ball underarm into a space. The batters MUST run at least ONE run, but may run more if they choose. Batters can run overthrows (even if the ball goes over the boundary).
- Batters are out if they are caught, run-out, or throw the ball over the boundary.

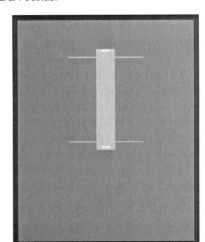

Figure 9.5 The singles game. The aim of the game is for batters to develop judgements about "placing" and "pacing" the ball to facilitate running singles. Allowing the batter to throw the ball means that they can quickly build up their awareness of where to throw the ball and how hard to throw it.

the batter to throw the ball means that they can quickly build up their awareness of where to throw the ball and how hard to throw it. Of course, the game allows fielding and captaincy skills to be developed at the same time and the principle of co-adaptation (see Renshaw *et al.*, 2009) will apply.

An extension to this practice is to introduce hitting using tennis rackets, and then bats against co-operative feeds (the batting team provide the bowler), before eventually playing competitive games as in the games shown in the previous section.

Mental skills

The mental approach of many batters is interlinked to their technical and perceptual skills and typically the consequence of the "block and bash" methodology adopted by young players means that they only look to score when they see an inaccurate delivery. As such, coaches need to find strategies to change this mindset by encouraging players to adopt a more positive approach to scoring runs. A useful approach is for coaches to develop awareness of the individual players by use of statistical performance analysis. For example, many singles are missed due to the non-striking batter not backing-up as the ball is bowled (not moving down the pitch after the ball has been bowled). In order to make players aware of the importance of backing-up, coaches could record the number of times that the non-striker fails to go past the 5 foot marker (a mark on the side of the pitch used by umpires to identify areas where bowlers must not run on the pitch). Similarly, rather than simply assessing performance on the number of runs scored, coaches could publish data showing the percentage of balls scored from and the runs per balls faced. These figures can be used with players to set goals on an individual and team level. Of course, a simple statistic that coaches could use is the percentage of singles scored in the innings. A good percentage for a young team to aim for would be 30–40%.

Application of this new-found "intention to score" can be developed using practice situations where "Yes" is the only accepted call (this does not imply that a run must be scored on every delivery) and any other call results in a batter's dismissal. This creates a sense of urgency for batters to score and raises expectations for both striker and non-striker to be prepared to run on every delivery. This method can be applied to regular net practice where batters work in pairs, centre wicket practice, or in conjunction with the games identified above to add a further dimension/level of difficulty.

Summary

For young players, learning to take singles is a crucial part of their development. The key to good running between the wickets is the development of good technical, perceptual and mental skills. Hitting the ball into the spaces between fielders requires batters to make controlled contact to direct balls and vary the pace of their shots. Additionally, it requires adopting a mindset where batters are actively looking to score at every opportunity. To develop these skills coaches must first of all identify the key rate limiters of performance and then design realistic practice tasks that allow players to develop functional solutions. Initially, players who have adopted a "block and bash" strategy will demonstrate mixed levels of performance and coaches should think carefully about when to introduce the intervention programme. However, regular adherence to the type of activities we have highlighted in the previous section will produce players with the skills and strategies that can only improve them as cricketers for the rest of their junior and senior careers.

Case Study: Applying constraint-led principles to improve cricket performance

Identify the problem

Young players who cannot score singles.

Setting

Junior cricket team.

Constraints

Technical, tactical and mental skills.

The Barnsborough School U-13 cricket team were unbeaten, but were about to come up against the only other unbeaten team, Victoria Road School. Greg

---

Buchan, the Barnsborough coach, had his side well-drilled. He had coached his batters to be able to hit the short, leg side ball for four and his bowlers to bowl straight and outside the off-stump – there would be no free gifts for the Victoria Road batsmen. Barnsborough had based their success on the well-known approach in junior cricket – make sure you hit any ball the opposition bowl short on the leg side for four and don't bowl any there when you bowl.

Right from the start, Greg could see his team were going to struggle to score runs today. Victoria Road bowled very accurately and the batters were not able to find a way of scoring. Victoria Road bowled very few leg side balls and when they did, they had a fielder perfectly placed to stop the boundary. At the end of their 40 overs, Barnsborough had only managed 6 for 79.

Greg was a little worried, but he knew that his bowlers were just as accurate as the Victoria Road bowlers and he got his captain to copy their tactic of placing fielders to stop the bad balls being hit for four. When Victoria Road began their innings, Greg immediately noticed a difference in their approach And although they had only scored one boundary, the score was 0 for 30. Barnsborough took a couple of wickets but the new batters played with the same level of intent and by the 25th over Victoria Road had secured a well-deserved 7 wicket victory. Greg realised that the tried and trusted methods he had used up until that point were not going to work against the better teams and it was time for him and the team to explore new strategies.

Greg pulled the group together and congratulated them on their run of success but then moved on to say that Victoria Road had given them a lesson today – "their batters were looking to score off the good balls and hit the ball into the gaps between our fielders and 40% of their runs were in singles." Greg added "their batters were really good at using the 'nurdle to leg'". The team laughed and said "what's a nurdle to leg, Greg?" Greg described how it was a term used to describe a deflection into the leg side field. Greg finished by asking the players to go away and think about what they needed to do to improve, so that when they play Victoria Road in the last match of the season they could turn around this defeat.

On the Tuesday, Greg sensed a mood of pessimism in his players and heard them saying that they were never going to be good enough to beat Victoria Road. Rather than shout at the group and tell them to pick up their defeatist attitude he decided to get the players to become aware of their own strengths and weaknesses. Greg put the team into groups of three and asked them to answer the following questions: (1) What are we good at when batting and bowling?; (2) What were Victoria Road good at?; and (3) What did Victoria Road do that we didn't? Over the next 30 minutes, each member of the team was pleasantly surprised by the good things their teammates said about them, but they also realised that Victoria Road had a different attitude to batting and were looking to score off every ball by taking singles, hitting accurate balls into spaces. Greg tells the group he believes they have the talent to become the top team once more and that he will design a new training program for the rest of the season so that "we can turn the defeat around" and become the best team in the competition. James adds with a smile "… and I want to learn to play the nurdle to leg, Greg."

Over the next few weeks the players worked really hard on fun, exciting and challenging training activities designed by Greg (see Chapter 9, pp. 117–27). On the last day of the season, Barnsborough were ready for their re-match with the crack Victoria Road team. Victoria Road won the toss and decided to bat. The batters were quickly into their stride and looking to pick up singles off the accurate Barnsborough bowling. However, this time the Barnsborough fielders were much more alert to the tactics of the batters and after an attempted quick single resulted in a near miss run-out the Victoria Road batters were aware of how well Barnsborough were fielding and were a little more cautious. However, Victoria Park were still good at finding the gaps and ended up with a score of 120 off 40 overs. In reply, Barnsborough started well, working the ball into gaps and scoring at three runs an over. The Victoria Road bowlers and fielders were not accustomed to being put under so much pressure and a few wild throws resulted in welcome extra runs from overthrows. The bowlers began to panic and tried to bowl too fast resulting in more boundary scoring opportunities. However, Victoria Road fought hard and Barnsborough needed one run to win off the last ball of the game. James was facing as the ball was bowled on a good length. He stepped forward, adjusted the line of his shoulders to present the face of the bat, and placed the ball into the gap between square leg and midwicket and scampered through for the winning run. The team were jubilant and huddled around Greg for a quick debrief. "Hey Greg," said James, "we won it with a nurdle to leg!" All the team fell about laughing, while Greg allowed himself a contented smile and noted that his team had scored 42% of their runs in singles compared with the 35% of the Victoria Road team.

References

Beek, P. J., Jacobs, D. M., Daffertshoffer, A. & Huys, R. (2003). Expert Performance in Sport: Views from the Joint Perspectives of Ecological Psychology and Dynamical Systems Theory. In J. L. Starkes & K. A. Ericsson (eds), *Expert Performance in Sports: Advances in Research on Sport Expertise*, Champaign: Illinois, Human Kinetics, pp. 321–344.

Davids, K., Button, C., & Bennett, S. J. (2008). *Dynamics of Skill Acquisition: A constraints-led approach*. Champaign: Human Kinetics.

English Cricket Board (n.d.). *Cricket Coaches Manual*. Birmingham: English Cricket Board Coaches Association.

Gibson, J. J. (1986). *The Ecological Approach to Visual Perception*. Hillsdale, NJ: Lawrence Earlbaum Associates.

Pinder, R. A., Renshaw, I. & Davids, K. (2009). Information–movement Coupling in Developing Cricketers under Changing Ecological Practice Constraints. *Human Movement Science*, 28, 468–479.

Renshaw, I., Oldham, A. R. H., Davids, K. & Golds, T. (2007). Changing Ecological Constraints of Practice Alters Co-ordination of Dynamic Interceptive Actions. *European Journal of Sport Science*, 7, 157–167.

Renshaw, I., Davids, K., Chow, J. W. & Shuttleworth, R. (2009). Insights from Ecological Psychology and Dynamical Systems Theory can Underpin a Philosophy of Coaching. *International Journal of Sport Psychology*, 40, 580–602.

10 Manipulating tasks constraints to improve tactical knowledge and collective decision-making in rugby union

Pedro Passos, Duarte Araújo, Keith Davids and Rick Shuttleworth

Introduction

In team sports such as rugby union, a myriad of decisions and actions occur within the boundaries that compose the performance perceptual-motor workspace. The way that these performance boundaries constrain decision-making and action has recently interested researchers and has involved developing an understanding of the concept of constraints. Considering team sports as complex dynamical systems signifies that they are composed of multiple, independent agents (i.e. individual players) whose interactions are highly integrated. This level of complexity is characterized by the multiple ways that players in a rugby field can interact. It affords the emergence of rich patterns of behaviour, such as rucks, mauls, and collective tactical actions that emerge due to players' adjustments to dynamically varying competition environments. During performance, the decisions and actions of each player are constrained by multiple causes (e.g. technical and tactical skills, emotional states, plans, thoughts, etc.) that generate multiple effects (e.g. to run or pass, to move forward to tackle or maintain position and drive the opponent to the line), a prime feature in a complex systems-approach to team games performance (Bar-Yam, 2004).

To establish a bridge between the complexity sciences and learning design in team sports like rugby union, the aim of practice sessions is to prepare players to pick up and explore the information available in the multiple constraints (i.e. the causes) that influence performance. Therefore, learning design in training sessions should be soundly based on the interactions amongst players (i.e. teammates and opponents) that will occur in rugby matches. To improve individual and collective decision-making in rugby union, Passos and colleagues proposed in previous work a *performer-environment* interaction-based approach rather than a traditional *performer*-based approach (Passos et al., 2008b).

Suggestions for a dynamical systems approach to training

Previous research (e.g. Passos et al., 2008a; 2009) has suggested that learning in rugby union must begin by developing tasks that allow players to become attuned to principles of play. These principles are ubiquitous task constraints that bound performance environments and emerge from players' behaviour to influence collective decisions and actions. This collective behaviour is responsible for the emergence of sub-units (e.g. four players forming a diamond-shape structure) that function as a complex dynamical system. In this type of subsystem, the interacting elements (i.e. the players) are capable of rich and varied patterns of behaviour, which clearly differ from the behaviour of each component acting separately (Gréhaigne *et al.*, 1997).

According to the New Zealand Rugby Football Union (2002),

> The Principles of Play are the Golden Rules upon which rugby is based – they are generalizations that cover most situations. (…) provide simple guidelines by which your team should base its play and also provides a checklist for coaches to analyse their team's performance.
>
> (NZRFU, 2002, p. 8)

The NZRFU goes on to state the principles of attack as: (1) to gain possession of the ball; (2) to move forward; (3) to support the ball carrier; (4) to maintain continuity; and (5) to exert pressure to score points. The principles of the defence are: (1) to move forward and reduce time and space for attackers; (2) to support your teammates, communicating your role within a defensive pattern, and cover the widest field area; and (3) to regain possession to counter attack (NZRFU, 2002; Greenwood, 2003).

The main question here is: How do players decide and act to successfully perform according to these principles of play? These principles can be characterized with time and space task constraints that link a set of players and lead them to decide collectively as sub-units, functioning as imperatives that recur cyclically in every attack situation (Greenwood, 2003). This means that to succeed, players must be attuned to (i.e. be aware of) the decisions and actions of their own teammates and opponents (see Chapter 1 for more information regarding the process of attunement). Despite the importance of learning and practising technical skills, players need to know "when" and "where" to perform those technical skills as well as knowing how to perform them. Technical skills are a precious tool for solving tactical problems posed by opponents, and it makes sense to practice them as demanded by the game. Additionally, technical skills practice suggests an analytical approach to training, that breaks a system (i.e. a team or sub-units) into its most simple constituent elements (i.e. the players) (Gréhaigne *et al.*, 1997). The need to evolve technical skills emerges when those skills are not sensitive to external perturbations induced by the performance context. For this reason a player needs the ability to adapt to a continually changing environment (e.g. problems posed by different opponents, performance conditions and competitive situations). Therefore, the aim is to develop technical skills that will equip players with more effective tools to actively explore dynamic performance environments, such as a rugby union match.

To train decision-making we suggest the adoption of a *non-linear pedagogical* methodology, based on principles of dynamical systems theory (see Chow *et al.*, 2007). This approach seeks to improve collective decision-making skills of players under practice task constraints that provide an appropriate balance between variability and stability. A non-linear pedagogical methodology promotes training programmes infused with an exploration process, confronting players with variability in practice tasks designed for them to seek unique performance solutions. The term *non-linear* refers to the emergence of a collective property of any open system (e.g. an attacker–defender dyadic system in rugby union), not uniquely possessed by any of the individual system components (i.e. the players), that leads to the spontaneous appearance of co-ordinated patterns of behaviour (Kauffman, 1995). In non-linear pedagogy practice tasks are designed to simulate many different performance situations that are likely to be faced by performers. In these simulations, tasks and environmental constraints used to design practice tasks should allow players to actively explore the same perceptual variables that they will encounter in performance. During practice, players learn by exploring the information present and, as a result, adapt their actions to achieve specific task goals such as running past defenders with the ball or defending space.

Despite the stability imposed by their goals and roles, players should be provided with opportunities to exploit the "order for free" available in the organization of team games, such as rugby union (i.e. the variations of possibilities for action that exist in the performance context that can be actively explored by the players). The most relevant information that a dynamical system needs in order to self-organize (i.e. to evolve over time without the direct external influence of a coach's prescriptive instructions) is available in the performance context; this is what is signified by the term "order for free". The "order" that a dyadic system needs to reach a stable state (e.g. a dribbling action to pass a defender or a successful tackle), exists in the performance context ready to be explored and harnessed by learners. This "order for free" exploration occurs through action and can move a dyadic system into critical periods (i.e. brief windows during which a system's organization is mainly open to alterations from external and internal influences (Anderson, 2002). Within these critical periods a team game can enter a state of criticality, (i.e. a state to which a system evolves so that it is poised for a transition (Bak, 1996). It is necessary for every dynamical complex system to evolve to this state. This approach to practice will allow performers to enhance their tactical understanding (e.g. from principles of play) for competitive matches.

Manipulating constraints to teach principles of play in rugby union

In this section we present an example of practice design that is based on the constraints-led perspective that aims to develop players' decisions and actions. For example, an essential principle of attacking play suggests that "… the quintessential pressure of every attack is speed in going forward into space". (Greenwood, 2003, p. 22), which implies that practice trials must be performed at competitive pace. Performing in these simulated settings provides an advantage because players are allowed to explore similar task constraints to those they will face in a real game. In previous research on 1 versus 1 game sub-phases (see Passos *et al.*, 2008a) we concluded that for an attacker to be successful in destabilizing a dyad with a defender, he/she must enter the region of self-organizing criticality (SOC) (i.e. approximately 4 m of interpersonal distance for youth level players) with increasing velocity compared to a defender's decreasing velocity. To achieve this aim an attacker must actively create a time and space window (i.e. a region of SOC) in order to decide when and where to increase speed and go forward to pass the defender and score a try. This requires a fine tuning of the way that learners couple their actions to available perceptual information, which can only be possible if the practice session includes the same task constraints that are faced in performance (e.g. makes use of an active defence and relevant field dimensions).

In summary, the findings from Passos *et al.* (2008a) suggested that to succeed in destabilizing a dyad with a defender, attacking players must enter SOC regions with increasing speed. Being successful in this task involves using principles of play, which coaches find an outcome that is difficult to achieve through instructions, since players manage their own speeds with regards to opponents. In order to create conditions in which players actively explore how to enter SOC regions with increasing velocity towards an opponent, coaches need to manipulate task constraints.

To develop players' performance according to the principles of play (that are present in every tactical situation), it is necessary to manipulate five types of practice task constraints: (1) change or add new rules of the game in order to facilitate the achievement of a specific team goal; (2) provide instructions based on information that is available in the playing field to drive players' attentional focus; (3) modify the performance field dimensions such as depth or width; (4) increase or decrease the number of players involved in every practice trial; and (5) set initial conditions, such as the interpersonal distance between attacker and defenders (a short interpersonal distance will favour the defence, a larger one will favour attackers).

For example, if the aim is to develop players' ability to perform according to the second principle of attack (i.e. to move forward and acquire territorial advantage), the first and the second type of task constraints manipulation above can be used (i.e. change or add rules and/or verbal instruction to drive players' attentional focus). To achieve this aim small side practice tasks can be created (i.e. with a reduced number of players, perhaps 3 versus 3; this number should be varied accordingly with the age and experience of the players involved). As a first task constraint manipulation a new rule can be added to the game – the running line trajectory of the player with the ball can only be forward (i.e. towards the goal line). This constraint does not mean that players must run in a straight line, since there can be variability in running forward towards a goal line. This variability is emergent due to the relative positioning and proximity of opponents. However, in the practice task, every time a player adopts a running line with a sideways or backward trajectory (i.e. not towards the goal line), a foul can be called and ball possession goes to the opponents. As an example of the second type of task constraint manipulation we can provide an instructional constraint to the ball

Grey circles – defenders
White circles with numbers – attackers
Black arrow – ball trajectory
Black dashed trajectories – players' trajectories
Grey dashed line – score imaginary line

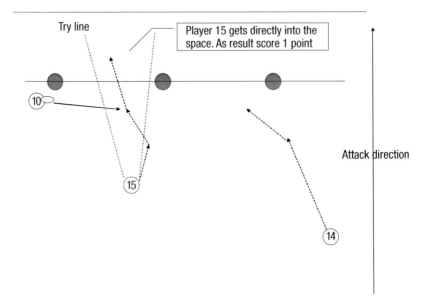

Figure 10.1 Get into space to score.

carrier to explore a running line trajectory on the defender's loose side shoulder, after receiving a pass from a teammate.

For support players who aim to get into space (i.e. pass across a defensive line between two defenders) as a task constraint manipulation we can add a new rule. Every time a ball is received in the space between two defenders that allows the ball carrier to get into the space directly (i.e. without being tackled), his/her team will score a point. The ball is placed on the floor and the game restarts from that point (Figure 10.1).

Other tasks constraints can be manipulated, such as field dimensions, number of players involved in attacker and defender functions, and initial interpersonal distance between attackers and defenders, in order to increase or decrease the level of task difficulty for attackers or defenders. The same kind of task constraints manipulation is also valid for the third principle of the game (i.e. support the ball carrier). Similar to the previous situation a new rule can be established: every time a player performs a pass to a teammate, he/she immediately must support the ball carrier. Failure to do so is considered a foul, and the opponents gain ball possession.

Manipulating constraints to develop tactical skills: an example using a four-player sub-unit

A rugby union match evolves through the behaviour of localized sub-units (or *mini-teams* as Greenwood (2003, p. 30), calls them). These sub-units are composed of three or four players that have a tendency to co-ordinate decisions and actions as a complex dynamical system leading to rich and varied patterns of collective behaviour. A key question is: how to plan a training session that aims to co-ordinate the collective decisions and actions of four players? Supported by empirical data from an ongoing research programme (see Passos *et al.*, 2008c), an example is provided for an attacking situation with a sub-unit of four players forming a diamond-shape structure. In this research programme Passos *et al.* (2008c) used a task design of four attackers playing against a first defensive line of two defenders plus a second defensive line also with two defenders, on a performance field 10 m wide and 22 m deep. Players' performance was recorded with a video camera and the images

White circles – players
Oval black shape – ball
Black arrows – players running line direction
Black dashed arrows – players' relative position and interpersonal distance

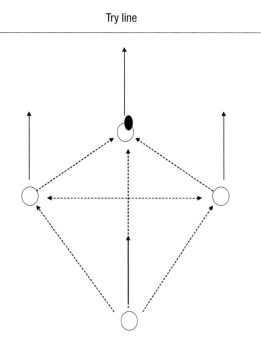

Figure 10.2 Diamond-shape structure.

were digitized to extract each player's position co-ordinates. It was hypothesized that there would be an optimal value of interpersonal distance amongst players within a sub-unit that allowed them to succeed. The data revealed a tendency for decreasing interpersonal distances amongst players within the attacker sub-unit as interpersonal distance to the defensive line decreased. However, this grouping tendency in the attacker sub-unit, when close to the defence line, was an emergent pattern that depended on the attacker–defender relationship.

In training, the first step is to set roles for each position in the sub-unit. The ball carrier is always the player in front; the players on the left side and right side are support players as well as the axial player, who usually may function as the "extra man". When practising these functions away from a match situation (i.e. no opposition), the intra-sub-unit co-ordination needed to create a diamond shape is quite easy to acquire. The four players involved must keep a specific interpersonal distance from each other. The side supporters also have to acquire a certain depth angle relative to the ball carrier, and the axial support player must also remain a certain interpersonal distance apart from the ball carrier and maintain a depth angle to both side support players (Figure 10.2).

The main issue is that within performance, when faced by opponents, this diamond-shape structure displays a tendency to desegregate. With decreasing interpersonal distance and due to players' decisions and actions to keep the initial structure, one of two outcomes may occur: (1) the ball carrier may pass the ball to one of the support players, with this player acquiring the role as ball carrier (i.e. the player in front). In this event the former ball carrier must support the current ball carrier, and the two left-sided players must occupy the space available in order to guarantee that the diamond-shape structure reorganizes to face the next defensive line as soon as possible; or (2) the defenders can put the ball carrier on the ground and spontaneous formation of a ruck emerges. In this event, the diamond structure disaggregates, and another structure emerges with a different functional organization. The most desirable situation for the attack sub-unit is to maintain the diamond shape, so that this pattern ensures tactical fluency and penetration of opposition territory.

The following task design illustrates task constraint manipulations to train collective decisions and actions for a four-player attacker sub-unit forming a diamond-shape structure. The task constraint manipulation is based on: (1) field dimensions; (2) number of players in opposition; (3) providing feedback to reinforce the main goal (i.e. keeping the diamond shape running towards the tryline); and (4) initial interpersonal distance between attacker and defenders.

A performance field of 10 m width and 22 m depth was established with four players in the attack forming a diamond-shape structure. In the initial stages of this practice, and in order to allow more space to be explored by the attackers, only two defenders were involved. The initial interpersonal distance between attacker and defenders was 10 m. The attackers must pass through this defensive line and score a try. In order to increase task difficulty, aiming to take this practice situation closer to a competitive performance situation, we can add a second defensive line 12 m behind the first one. The goal is for the attackers to pass through the

White circles – attack players
Grey circles – defence players
Oval white shape – ball
Black arrows – players running line direction
Grey dashed lines – players' relative position and interpersonal distance

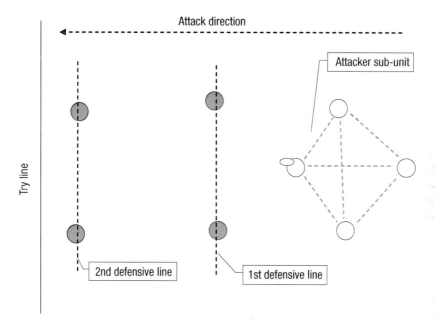

Figure 10.3 Task design 4 vs 2+2.

first defensive line and then reorganize as a diamond-shape sub-unit to face the second defensive line. When the rate of success is sufficiently high we can add more players to defensive lines, first in the first line and after that in the second defensive line (Figure 10.3).

Manipulating constraints to learn and develop technical skills: an example of passing and kicking

Handford (2006) has previously criticized the "one size fits all" methodology that traditionally characterizes the learning design for practice of technical skills in a broad way for all performers in team games. The main point of criticism focuses on the supposition that there is a common "optimal movement pattern" that acts as a model for a movement skill towards which each performer must progress. Put another way, he criticized traditional assumptions about the existence of a "text-book" tackle, hooker's throw, scrummaging technique, place kick, all of which are considered as discrete skills and taught to all learners in the same way, using a

Table 10.1 Task constraints manipulation for technical skills development

Ball carrier initial conditions	Stopped	i) with ball
		ii) receiving a pass from a teammate
	In movement	
Target (i.e. receiving player) initial conditions	Stopped	Distance, width and depth to the target
	In movement	
Opposition (i.e. defenders)	With	i) passive defence
		ii) active defence
		iii) initial distance from the defence
		iv) number of defenders
	Without	
Field dimensions	Width and depth	

"one-size-fits all" approach. This learning design is based on the postulation that the human brain acts like a computer. It implies that decisions and actions are based on mental representations that evolve from practice. However, to respond to performance dynamics with regard to problems of co-ordinated patterns of movement, coaches are encouraged to search for movement solutions that do not reside wholly inside an individual but that emerge from the confluence of a specific performer, task and environmental constraints (Handford, 2006).

The mutual and reciprocal interactions between individual, task and environmental constraints highlight that variability is an inherent feature of motor output between and within individuals in all categories of tasks (Newell *et al.*, 2006). Table 10.1 displays an example of several ideas about task constraints manipulation to enhance pass and kicking accuracy.

The design of practice tasks to augment passing (as well as kicking) accuracy can be focused on the following manipulations: (1) setting player initial conditions, such as if he/she is stationary or running, if he/she is running with the ball in the hands or has received the ball from a teammate before performing a pass; (2) performing a pass to a stationary target (e.g. a teammate, the coach), to a moving target (i.e. the support player), or to a predictable space where the target player will move. Moreover a technical skill such as a pass is not an end by itself but a constraint to achieve a tactical advantage, in other words, an accurate pass will put the receiver in position to advance into opposition territory. For these situations one also needs to define the distance, width and depth to the target; and (3) practising with and without opposition. For both situations one also needs to determine if a passive (i.e. with no physical contact) or an active defence is used (i.e. with physical contact). Additionally, one also needs to set the opponents' initial start distance from an individual learner. This is also a valid constraint for practice of kicking.

Considering the ecological dynamics in the learner-environment relationship it is possible to combine several types of task constraints manipulation with a common aim. This aim is to design a practice task that develops players' functional variability, helping each player to search the perceptual-motor landscape and find an optimal performance solution. As Handford (2006, p. 73) stated "variability clearly plays a key role in attaining consistent outcomes".

In summary, training programmes planned to improve collective decision-making and actions in complex dynamical systems should aim to attune players' perception-action couplings. The tasks proposed in these practice sessions must ensure that players become aware of the most significant sources of information that allow them to explore relevant action and perceptual variables, during the critical periods (i.e. time and space brief windows) that might lead to system structural re-organization. In other words, those players who learn to become more aware of the most relevant information for action are those who can more accurately explore time and space windows to gain a competitive advantage (Passos *et al.*, 2008a; 2009).

References

Anderson, D. I. (2002). Do Critical Periods Determine When to Initiate Sport Skill Learning? In F. L. Smoll and R. E. Smith (eds), *Children and Youth in Sports: A Biopsychosocial Perspective*, 2nd edn. Indianapolis: Brown & Benchmark, pp. 105–148.

Bak, P. (1996). *How Nature Works. The Science of Self-organized Criticality*. New York: Copernicus.

Bar-Yam, Y. (2004). *Making Things Work. Solving Complex Problems in a Complex World*. Cambridge, MA: NECSI. Knowledge Press.

Chow, J., Davids, K., Button, C., Shuttleworth, R., Renshaw, I. and Araújo, D. (2007). The Role of Non-linear Pedagogy in Physical Education. *Review of Educational Research*, 77(3), 251–278.

Greenwood, J. (2003). *Total Rugby. Fifteen-man Rugby for Coach and Player*, 5th edn. London: A & C Black.

Gréhaigne, J. F., Bouthier, D. and David, B. (1997). Dynamic-system Analysis of Opponent Relationships in Collective Actions in Soccer. *Journal of Sport Sciences*, 15(2), 137–149.

Handford, C. (2006). Serving up Variability and Stability. In K. Davids, S. Bennett and K. M. Newell (eds), *Movement System Variability*. Champaign, IL: Human Kinetics, pp. 73–84.

Kauffman, S. (1995). *At Home in the Universe: The Search for the Laws of Self-organization and Complexity*. New York: Oxford University Press.

Newell, K. M., Deutsch, K. M., Sosnoff, J. J. & Mayer-Kress, G. (2006). Motor Output Variability as Noise: A Default and Erroneous Proposition? In K. Davids, S. Bennett & K. Newell (eds), *Variability in the Movement System: A Multi-Disciplinary Perspective*, Champaign, IL: Human Kinetics, pp. 3–22.

New Zealand Rugby Football Union (2002). *Rugby Skills and Drills Manual*. Wellington: NZRU.

Passos, P., Araújo, D., Davids, K., Gouveia, L., Milho, J. and Serpa, S. (2009). Interpersonal Coordination Patterns, Decision-making and Information Governing Dynamics in Rugby Union. In D. Araújo, H. Ripoll & M. Raab (eds), *Perspectives on Cognition and Action in Sport*. New York: Nova Science Publishers, pp. 27–42.

Passos, P., Araújo, D., Davids, K., Gouveia, L., Milho, J. & Serpa, S. (2008a). Information

Governing Dynamics of Attacker–defender Interactions in Youth Level Rugby Union. *Journal of Sports Sciences*, 26(13), 1421–1429.

Passos, P., Araújo, D., Davids, K. and Shuttleworth, R. (2008b). Manipulating Constraints to Train Decision-making in Rugby Union. *International Journal of Sport Sciences and Coaching*, 3(1), 125–140.

Passos, P., Borges, J., Milho, J., Leandro, H., Sousa, J., Araújo, D. and Davids, K. (2008c). *Collective Decision-making – New Challenges to Match Analysis*. Communication at the 13th Annual Congress of the European College of Sport Science. 9–12 July, Estoril, Portugal.

11 The ecological dynamics of decision-making in sailing

Duarte Araújo, Luís Rocha and Keith Davids

Introduction

Competitive sailing is characterized by continuous interdependencies of decisions and actions. All actions imply a permanent monitoring of the environmental conditions, such as intensity and direction of the wind, sea characteristics, and the behaviour of the opponent sailors. These constraints on sailors' behaviour are in constant change implying continuous adjustments in sailors' actions and decisions. Among the different parts of a regatta, tactics and strategy at the start are particularly relevant. Among coaches there is an adage that says that "the start is 50% of a regatta" (Houghton, 1984; Saltonstall, 1983/1986). Olympic sailing regattas are performed with boats of the same class, by one, two or three sailors, depending on the boat class. Normally before the start, sailors visit the racing venue and analyse wind and sea characteristics, in order to fine-tune their boats accordingly. Then, five minutes before the start, sailors initiate starting procedures in order to be in a favourable position at the starting line (at the "second zero"). This position is selected during the start period according to wind shifts tendencies and the actions of other boats (Figure 11.1). Only after the start signal can the boats cross the imaginary starting line between the race committee signal boat "A" and the pin end boat. The start takes place against the wind (upwind), and the boats start racing in the direction of mark 1.

Based on the evaluation of the sea and wind characteristics (e.g. if the wind is stronger at a particular place on the course), sailors re-adjust their strategy for the regatta. This strategy may change during the regatta, according to wind changes and adversary actions. More to the point, strategic decisions constrain and are constrained by on-line decisions during the regatta.

Decision-making in sailing

Decision-making and cognitive processes have been widely studied in sport sciences with the "expert-novice paradigm" (Williams *et al.*, 1999; Williams & Ward, 2007). Surprisingly, only about 8% of the studies reviewed by Starkes *et al.* (2001) addressed dynamic sports, other than ball games (e.g. combat sports, fencing). This is important since the task constraints of dynamic non-ball sports are unique, and

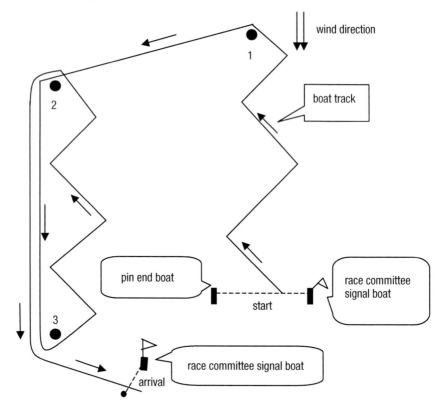

Figure 11.1 Regatta course and possible boat track in a regatta.

it is uncertain whether similar principles to ball sports underlie decision-making, given that "thrust and counter-thrust" strategies characterize ball games due to their "invasive" nature (see McGarry *et al.*, 2002). In sailing, task constraints are characterized by the combination of weather and adversary influences on the ever-changing boat displacement and location (e.g. Saltonstall, 1983/1996; Saury & Durand, 1998; Wisdorff, 1997). All competitors share the entire area of the regatta, with no specific location for each boat to defend. We argue that an ecological approach is needed, considering the whole decision-making process as an integral part of goal-directed behaviour influenced by ecological constraints at the scale of the environment-athlete relationship.

In sailing, prior to the regatta start, the sailor can explore the racing venue to detect information for performance, in order to adjust his or her strategy. These information sources mainly concern the wind and how it influences the regatta course. The sailor tries to perceive the relationship between the wind and the starting line, and the relationship between wind direction and regatta marks. These sources of information help in setting goals for action during the start (Figure 11.2).

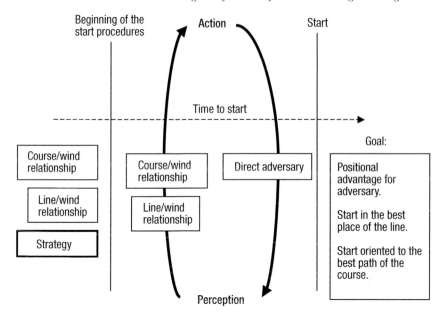

Figure 11.2 Ecological dynamics of decision-making at the regatta start.

During regattas, sailors actively explore the performance context, to detect better information about wind changes, when to avoid or confront adversaries, aiming for the better side for start in the starting line, in a perception-action cycle. The exploration of these sources of information adjusts the sailors' strategical and tactical actions, and decisions are embedded in actions towards performance goals. These ideas are congruent with Gibson's (1979) proposition that control lies in the agent-environment system, and behaviour can be understood to be self-organized, as opposed to organization being imposed from without.

From the performer's viewpoint, the task is to exploit physical (e.g. waves and tide) and informational constraints (e.g. an opponent's speed approach) to stabilize intended behaviours. Emergent performance solutions may rely more or less on physical or informational regularities, depending on the nature of the task, and within given constraints there are typically a limited number of stable solutions that can achieve a desired outcome. In sport, a player's expertise is only revealed in the consequences of movement and perception embedded in actions, as observable properties of the environment-actor system. Decision-making, therefore, is a complex, temporally extended process expressed by actions at the ecological scale (Turvey & Shaw, 1995). To make decisions is to direct a course of personal interactions with the environment towards a goal; decisions then emerge from this cyclical process of searching for information to act and generate behaviour that will detect more information (Figure 11.2).

This interaction is evident at the start of match racing in sailing, where the sailors should select a place to start based on the moves of adversaries. According to regatta rules, five minutes before the start, sailors need to initiate starting procedures in order to be in the optimal position (relative to the wind) at the starting line. This position is selected during the start period according to wind shift tendencies and the actions of other boats. Indeed we have observed transition phases in starting line location (order parameter) by manipulating the wind-line angle (control parameter) in previous research. We have observed this phenomenon when participants have started races with and without adversaries (Araújo *et al.*, 2003, 2006). We found that the boats' positions tended to be at the extremities of the start line with the higher angle values (> ±10°). In fact, when the wind favoured one of the extremities of the starting line, the nearer to that extremity the boat was positioned, the more direct was the required trajectory to the first mark of a regatta. However, in a zone where the wind was neutral (between about –10° and +10°) we observed higher variability in start location, because there was no advantage from boat positioning for a required trajectory. The start position near the committee boat tends to be underestimated because of the starboard priority. Following similar procedures, we investigated if the same phase transition occurred with the presence of opponents. We found that phase transitions occurred in the same region (between about –10° and +10°) whether opponents were present or not.

Expertise effects on dynamic decision-making in sailing

The purpose of a regatta can be described as attempting to master the use of the wind in order to arrive at the finish line as quickly as possible. This goal must be obtained through performance manoeuvres that aim to control the direction and the speed of the boat. In one study (Araújo *et al.*, 2005), we analysed how concurrent verbalized information and performed actions evolved during a computer-simulated regatta and how they corresponded to the performance of participants. Dynamic tasks in sailing were provided through interactive computer simulations, used to reveal the utilization of information, and the active exploration of ecological constraints by participants. Nowadays, advances in technology make it relatively straightforward to represent the circumstances toward which findings may be generalized. There are computer simulations of a system with the specific conditions in terms of their representativeness of complex judgement tasks in human ecology (Brehmer, 1996). These computer simulations are not designed to be high-fidelity simulations. Instead, they incorporate key task features so that it is possible to recognize what is being simulated, without enormous detail. This is important because it means that no special knowledge is needed by participants about the characteristics of various types of sailing equipment, for example, and they can perform in simulations with very little training. This does not mean that perception and action are decoupled. Instead the representativeness of the situation implies that participants can achieve their goals by acting to create information to guide action (Kirlik, 2006).

We found that when active exploration of the task was possible, even non-sailors with little knowledge of this complex task could achieve task goals. A strong relationship was predicted and found between expertise in sailing and performance on a dynamic decision-making sailing task. Also, we found that each of the three groups (expert, skilled, and international sailors) used the available information differently, creating distinct patterns of utilization and of exploration of perceptual variables, although expertise effects were found to reveal greater attunement to the most relevant information for goal achievement.

Next, we explore further the results of this study, using the three phases for the development of decision-making proposed by Araújo and colleagues (Araújo *et al.*, 2009). In an ecological approach, learning to make successful decisions entails the education of intention, attunement, calibration (Fajen *et al.*, 2009; Jacobs & Michaels, 2007) and mastering perceptual-motor degrees of freedom (Newell, 1985; Savelsbergh and Van der Kamp, 2000; Vereijken *et al.*, 1992). In line with this view, Araújo *et al.* (2009) presented three possible phases of the development of decision-making: (1) exploration; (2) discovery and stabilization; and (3) exploitation.

1 Exploration: manipulating degrees of freedom

In specific performance situations, certain perceptions and actions are more functional than others and, with experience, individuals improve in choosing the most functional perceptions and actions. Different intentions are presumed to organize action systems differently. Given particular intentions, some variables can be said to be informational while others are not. In perceiving, an observer explores the available stimulation in an environment of complex, structured energy fields. These fields of ambient structured energy are an environmental resource to be explored by goal-directed, active observers. Psychological processes begin with the obtaining of stimulation by the organism, not with the imposition of stimulation by an environment. Thus the distinction between stimulus and response should be replaced by a distinction between modes of activity, such as exploratory and performatory (Reed, 1997).

When the performer creates an intention to achieve a specific task goal there is a need to co-ordinate the redundant degrees of freedom of his/her movement system. Performers can establish basic relationships with the environment to acquire minimum control over degrees of freedom, both intrinsic and transactional, to realize the task (Davids *et al.*, 2008). Control may be obtained by "freezing" movement solutions that may facilitate goal achievement (Vereijken *et al.*, 1992; Savelsbergh & van der Kamp, 2000), or by increasing movement variability in the performance environment to find a functional task solution (Araújo *et al.*, 2005). This was observed in a group of non-sailors, who increased their exploratory actions in order to identify relevant information for action. At this stage, movements may be coupled to specific sources of functional information, but they may not specify properties of the environment that the performer intended to perceive, i.e. they may be non-specifying variables. When performers increase variability of movements this is due to difficulty in discriminating which properties of the environment constitute information and which do not. Exploration of a performance situation can reveal what environmental properties are informative relative to specific intentions (Araújo *et al.*, 2005). The organization of activities involved in scanning the environment for information is determined by the information a performer is seeking, and by the information that is available in that environment (Reed, 1997).

The appearance of control over abundant degrees of freedom characterizes this first stage through the exploration of the relationship between movement and information. The degrees of freedom that need to be constrained are more than those needed to control the performer-environment system to achieve the task goal. This is expressed in the fact that the non-sailors could achieve the goal of finishing the simulated regatta, but not with the same results as the sailors (Araújo *et al.*, 2005). The faster the performer was in the simulated sailing regatta, the higher was his expertise level in sailing. The non-sailors needed more time but they could still achieve the task goal, since they could act in order to perceive the affordances that enabled better actions. Non-sailors explored the simulated regatta environment and regulated changes in their activity patterns on the basis of variation in environmental information, not as a function of internal states (Araújo *et al.*, 2005). Therefore we can presume that this is the minimal condition for the development of expert decision-making.

2 Discovering solutions and stabilizing them

In the next phase, the performer uses these tentative solutions (information-action couplings) in order to regulate action when performing the task. A way to stabilize a functional movement solution is to "de-freeze" in some cases (Vereijken *et al.*, 1992) the previous constriction of movement system degrees of freedom. In the non-sailors, this second stage was characterized by a reduction of exploration (Araújo *et al.*, 2005). This means that some relevant degrees of freedom for achieving the task goal are identified, and also that the conditions when an informational variable might be useful are also identified and acted upon.

During this stage, the same intention might lead to the detection of different informational variables. The process of attending to more useful variables is referred to as the education of attention, or perceptual attunement (Gibson, 1966, 1979). Thus, even if an intention does not change, with experience, perceivers can learn to attend to more useful variables. Perceptual attunement is the process of learning which sources of information to attend to in which situations and when to attend to these variables. With practice, performers converge from sources of information that may be only partly useful in one particular situation (i.e. non-specifying) to sources of information that are more useful (i.e. specifying), under a variety of performance circumstances. For example, in our study the intermediate sailors used more manoeuvres and adversary information, than the other groups of sailors with higher levels of expertise (Araújo *et al.*, 2005). The skilled sailors used more adversary information during the regatta than the expert sailors. With experience, the non-expert groups can learn how to use more specifying information, as exemplified by the expert group who used wind information more than any other group. The stabilization of discovered solutions, as well as the exploration of the limits of these solutions, and consequent search for new information-action couplings, are the dominant characteristics of this phase.

3 Exploiting degrees of freedom

The exploitation of motor and perceptual degrees of freedom allows adaptation to situational demands and effective goal achievement. In this phase performatory activity can go beyond the use of particular information sources towards the creation of change in the environment. An important point at this stage is the manifestation of attunement to higher-order spatial and temporal variables, and more sensitivity to the consequences of one's actions. In sailing we can see that skilled sailors, instead of focusing directly on manoeuvres or on an opponent, focus on the spatial organization of the regatta field (Araújo *et al.*, 2005). Attunement to this information contrasts with the less-skilled sailors' focus of attention. Moreover, expert sailors are attuned to even higher order information, such as how the wind constrains their sailing progress as well as that of their adversaries. Although more flexibility in actions may occur, this variability is constrained and convergent to goal achievement.

A relevant process at this stage is that of calibration, or the scaling of the action system to information, as specifying information can appropriately constrain a perception or an action. Body dimensions and action capabilities are not fixed, but often change across short and long timescales. For example, in sailing, the size of a boat changes perception of the capacity to pass through spaces between the boats of adversaries. Action capabilities change across short timescales as a result of factors such as fatigue and injury, and across longer timescales as a result of development and training. When body dimensions and action capabilities change, actions that were once possible may become impossible (or vice-versa see, Fajen *et al.*, 2009). In perception and action, calibration and recalibration are necessary to establish and update the mapping between the units in which the relevant properties of the world are perceived, and the units in which the action is realized. Calibration in practice makes it possible for performers to perceive the world in intrinsic units even after changes in body dimensions and action capabilities. Successful calibration results in judgements that are appropriately scaled to the property to be perceived, independent of which informational variable is used for perception. For a properly calibrated performer, body-scaled and action-scaled affordances can be directly and reliably perceived by simply picking up the relevant sources of information (Fajen *et al.*, 2009). Although recalibration occurs quite rapidly, it is likely that continued experience leads to further improvements in calibration.

Importantly, the development of decision-making for action is not a normative or homogeneous process, and idiosyncratic manifestations are expected to occur (Newell *et al.*, 2003). It is worth mentioning also that processes like education of intention, attunement, and calibration can occur in all three phases of skill development.

Training the regatta start

There are several constraints, such as boat position in relation to the starting line, direction of the wind, distance to the adversary, or time to start, that channel decisional behaviour in the start procedures (Araújo & Rocha, 2000). Therefore, it is important that sailors learn to act according to contextual demands rather than merely acting on memorized behaviours – and ignoring relevant informational variables can be detrimental for performance (Araújo et al., 2005). In previous studies we realized that sailors with low and medium levels of expertise erroneously perceived the place to start a regatta (Araújo et al., 2003). We observed that sailors may not perceive changes at the most favourable side of the starting line, particularly during the final 15 seconds. This may have been due to weaknesses in their position during these moments that may not have let them detect the relevant wind-starting line angle (see Oudejans et al., 2000). Another possibility that may have consequences for training is that these sailors had some difficulties in starting near the pin end boat, even when this was the most favourable place to start.

The coach may develop the decision-making ability of the sailors relative to these tactical issues by manipulating constraints such as: (1) the angle of the starting line with the wind direction; (2) the regatta course, by changing the starboard mark to the left or to the right of wind direction; (3) the presence or the absence of adversaries (and the number of them) in certain parts of a training regatta; (4) the signals made by the coach during performance; (5) the number and place of marks in the regatta; and (6), the time to the start. Obviously interaction between these constraints during training is to be encouraged. For example, with a shorter starting line, the influence of adversaries is higher than with a longer line. Next we examine some concrete examples of task constraints manipulation for the development of decision-making at the start of a regatta.

It is important that the coach knows what the key task constraints are to manipulate. This interaction of relevant constraints allows for the development

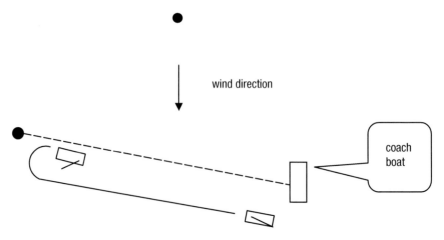

Figure 11.3 Exercise to develop the perception of the most favourable side for starting.

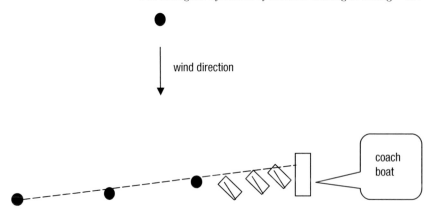

Figure 11.4 Exercise to develop the capability to identify the area of the starting line where the sailor starts. Figure with the starting line is favored on starboard end.

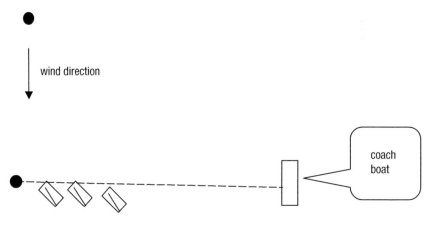

Figure 11.5 Exercise with non-square course when the success of the task is very dependent on a port end start.

of decision-making performance, according to a sailor's personal constraints. Importantly, the aim of training the start in sailing, is not only the start per se, but to ensure the boat is placed in an advantageous position relative to adversaries.

Conclusions

Decision-making performance emerges from the interaction of multiple constraints (personal cognitions, morphology, opponents, space constraints, wind, etc.). As we have discussed, decision-making should be analyzed at the ecological scale of analysis. A performer-environment system exhibits an initial state of order, which is broken during a transition to a new state, signifying that decision-making is an emergent phenomenon. This interplay of constraints eliminates the need to posit any inordinate role for a single controlling factor (e.g. the mind). From this perspective, decision-making is an emergent process that can be developed through the active exploration of situational constraints. In general, sailors (and non-sailors) achieved their task goals, when allowed to act to obtain reliable information. Rather than solely using the knowledge base stored in memory, decision-making seems to be predicated on exploratory and performatory activities in the performance context. The acquisition of expert decision-making entails a transition from using non-specifying information sources (e.g. wind and manoeuvre information used with the same probability) to a greater attunement to relevant informational variables (e.g. wind). For the coach, different expertize levels entail different information-action couplings, where different processes should predominantly occur (education of intention, attunement, calibration). The transition between different levels of decision-making performance may be achieved with the manipulation of performer, environment and task constraints in a sailing representative task or context. The coach acts as a facilitator for the development of decision-making performance, more than a prescriber of the "best" decisions.

Case Study: Sailing

Case Study a

Diagnostic

The sailor does not accurately perceive the most favourable side of the line to start.

Possible causes

Not enough exploratory actions are directed to detect wind changes at the starting line.

Task organization

The coach places a course upwind/downwind. The starting line is placed between a mark and the coach's boat (Figure 11.3). During every repetition, the coach can change the starting line in relation to wind direction. This can be done during the start procedures. The first mark is placed only 50 m from the starting line (highlighting the need for accurate perception of the most favourable side to start).

Task goal and sub-goals

The goal is to start at the most favourable side of the starting line, and then to move upwind and downwind. During the start procedures, the sailor moves from the stern of the coach's boat towards the starting mark, where the sailor should tack and return to the coach's boat. Once there, the sailor should discuss which side he/she perceived as the most favourable one for starting and why.

Cues for solving the problems created by the task

When a boat is sailing from one end of the starting line to the other, the sailor can find the most favoured side, by tacking and sailing back to the side she started from. For this, she has to pull in her sheet once she is sailing closer upwind. However, if she has to slack the sheet, this means that the most favourable side is not the one towards which she is directing her boat.

Case Study b

Diagnostic

The sailor cannot accurately identify his/her position on the start line at the start signal.

Possible causes

Difficulty in detecting the three areas of the starting line.

Task organization

The coach sets a course upwind/downwind with a starting line divided into three equal areas with marks. The windward mark is set about 50 m from the starting line (see Figure 11.4).

Task goal and sub-goals

Identical to Case Study a.

Cues for solving the problems created by the task

The sailor can choose to start between the marks that he/she has established as the most favourable.

Case Study c

Diagnostic

Difficulty in starting on port side and difficulty in detecting relevant aspects of the course.

Possible causes

The sailor may have an inaccurate perception that the leeward boat is losing to the windward boat. A beat angle that is too parallel to the start line creates difficulties in passing the pin end boat, avoiding tacking.

142   D. Araújo et al.

> ### Task organization
>
> Identical to Case Study b but the starting line shall be perpendicular to the wind. The windward mark shall be set much closer to the port side (see Figure 11.5).
>
> ### Task goal and sub-goals
>
> Identical to Case Study a.
>
> ### Cues for solving the problems created by the task
>
> The start should take place in the area of the starting line where the sailor can control (perceive) the fleet and arrive at the windward mark in front of opponents.

References

Araújo, D. & Rocha, L. (2000). The Trainability of Decision-making in Sport: The Example of the Portuguese Olympic Sailing Team. In B. Carlsson, U. Johnson, & F. Wetterstrand (ed), *Proceedings of the Sport Psychology Conference in the New Millenium*, Halmstad, Sweden: CIV, SSHS, pp. 94–98.

Araújo, D., Davids, K., Rocha, L., Serpa, S. & Fernandes, O. (2003). Decision-making in Sport as Phase Transitions. *International Journal of Computer Science in Sport*, 2(2), 87–88.

Araújo, D., Davids, K. & Serpa, S. (2005). An Ecological Approach to Expertise Effects in Decision-making in a Simulated Sailing Regatta. *Psychology of Sport and Exercise*, 6(6), 671–692.

Araújo, D., Davids, K. & Hristovski, R. (2006). The Ecological Dynamics of Decision-making in Sport. *Psychology of Sport and Exercise*, 7, 653–676.

Araújo, D., Davids, K. & Passos, P. (2007). Ecological Validity, Representative Design and Correspondence between Experimental Task Constraints and Behavioral Settings. *Ecological Psychology*, 19, 69–78.

Araújo, D., Davids, K., Chow, J. & Passos, P. (2009). The Development of Decision-making Skill in Sport: An Ecological Dynamics Perspective. In D. Araújo, H. Ripoll, & M. Raab (eds), *Perspectives on Cognition and Action in Sport*. New York: NOVA, pp. 157–169.

Brehmer, B. (1996). Man as a Stabiliser of Systems: From Static Snapshots of Judgment Processes to Dynamic Decision-making. *Thinking and Reasoning*, 2, 225–238.

Davids, K., Button, C. & Bennett, S. (2008). *Dynamics of Skill Acquisition. A Constraints-led Approach*. Champaign: Illinois. Human Kinetics.

Fajen, B., Riley, M. & Turvey, M. (2009). Information, Affordances and the Control of Action in Sport. *International Journal of Sport Psychology*, 40, 79–107.

Gibson, J. (1966). *The Senses Considered as Perceptual Systems*. Boston: Houghton Mifflin.

Gibson, J. (1979). *The Ecological Approach to Visual Perception*. Boston: Houghton Mifflin.

Houghton, D. (1984). *Wind Strategy*. London: Fernhurst Books.

Jacobs, D. & Michaels, C. (2007). Direct Learning. *Ecological Psychology*, 19, 321–349.

Kirlik, A. (2006). Abstracting Situated Action: Implications for Cognitive Modeling and Interface Design. In A. Kirlik (ed.), *Adaptive Perspectives in Human–technology Interaction*, New York: Oxford University Press, pp. 212–224.

McGarry, T., Anderson, D., Wallace, S., Hughes, M. & Franks, I. (2002). Sport Competition as a Dynamical Self-organizing System. *Journal of Sports Sciences*, 20, 771–781.

Newell, K. (1985). Coordination, Control, and Skill. In D. Goodman, R. Wilberg & I. Franks (eds), *Differing Perspectives in Motor Learning, Memory and Control*. Amsterdam: North-Holland, pp. 295–317.

Newell, K., Liu, Y.-T. & Mayer-Kress, G. (2003). A Dynamical Systems Interpretation of Epigenetic Landscapes for Infant Motor Development. *Infant Behavior & Development*, 26, 449–472.

Oudejans, R. Verheijen, R., Baker, F., Gerrits, J., Steinbrückner, M. & Beek, P. (2000). Errors in Judging 'Off-sides' in Football: Optical Trickery can Undermine the Assistant Referee's View of this Ruling. *Nature*, 404(6773), p. 33.

Reed, E. S. (1997). The Cognitive Revolution from an Ecological View. In D. M. Johnson, & C.E. Erneling (ed), *The Future of the Cognitive Revolution*, New York: Oxford University Press, pp. 261–273.

Saltonstall, J. (ed.) (1983/1996). *The RYA Race Training Manual*, 3rd edn. Hong Kong: Wing King Tong.

Saury, J. & Durand, M. (1998). Practical Knowledge in Expert Coaches: On-site Study of Coaching in Sailing. *Research Quarterly for Exercise and Sport*, 69, 254–266.

Savelsbergh, G. & Van der Kamp, J. (2000). Information in Learning to Co-ordinate and Control Movement: Is there a Need for Specificity of Practice? *International Journal of Sport Psychology*, 31, 467–484.

Starkes, J., Helsen, W. & Jack, R. (2001). Expert Performance in Sport and Dance. In R. Singer, H. Hausenblas & C. Janelle (eds), *Handbook of Sport Psychology*, 2nd edn. Chichester: John Wiley, pp. 174–201.

Turvey, M. T. & Shaw, R. E. (1995). Toward an Ecological Physics and a Physical Psychology. In R. L. Solso & D. W. Massaro (eds), *The Science of the Mind: 2001 and Beyond*. New York: Oxford University Press, pp. 144–169.

Vereijken, B., van Emmerik, R. E., Whiting, H. T. & Newell, K. (1992). Free(z)ing Degrees of Freedom in Skill Acquisition. *Journal of Motor Behavior*, 24, 133–142.

Williams, A. M., Davids, K. & Williams, J. G. (1999). *Visual Perception and Action in Sport*. London: E & FN Spon.

Williams, A. M. & Ward, P. (2007). Anticipation and Decision-making: Exploring New Horizons. In R. E. G. Tenenbaum (ed.), *Handbook of Sport Psychology*, 3rd edn. Hoboken, NJ: Wiley, pp. 203–223.

Wisdorff, D. (1997). Tactique, Stratégie et Micrométéorologie [Tactics, Strategy and Micrometeorology]. In J. Saury & J. F. Talon (eds), *L'entrainement de Haut Niveau en Voile [High Level Training in Sailing]*. Paris: Ed. Federation Française de Voile, pp. 19–28.

12 Using constraints to enhance decision-making in team sports

Adam D. Gorman

Introduction

Individuals from a range of domains, including medical practitioners, military personnel, and sportspeople, typically require the ability to execute a diverse range of motor tasks with extreme precision. However, superior performance is also characterised by an enhanced ability to determine the appropriateness of the skill for the demands of the environment (Chamberlain & Coelho, 1993). For example, a perfectly executed kick in a game of Australian Rules Football (AFL) is pointless if the better decision was to handball (pass the ball by hitting it with the hand). In short, superior performance is a combination of both skill execution *and* decision-making. The purpose of this chapter is to provide a basic understanding of the theoretical underpinnings and research findings that explain the factors that contribute to good decision-making in team sports. The intention is to highlight the benefits and applications of a constraints-led approach to enhance decision-making in the applied setting.

The importance of maintaining representative task constraints

An important consideration in the development of skilled performance is the interaction between the environment and the performer. When a task is practiced in an environment that is not an accurate representation of the typical perform-ance setting, or when the environment contains insufficient levels of variability, expert performance can deteriorate to the level of novices (Allard *et al.*, 1980; Araújo *et al.*, 2005) and learners will tend to rely on non-specifying information if that information allows reasonably accurate performance (Beek *et al.*, 2003; Jacobs *et al.*, 2001). Furthermore, the ability of the learner to converge upon more useful specifying information proceeds at a slower rate than if the learner had been exposed to a more representative and variable environment (Beek *et al.*, 2003).

A study by Egan *et al.* (2007) further highlights the need to maintain reliable perceptual variables in the training environment. Experienced and less experi-enced soccer players were required to quickly and accurately kick a stationary or moving soccer ball towards a vertical target. The results showed that the experi-enced participants scored more highly during the moving ball condition compared to the stationary ball condition, whereas the less experienced participants scored more highly in the stationary condition. In the stationary condition, the kick itself was self-paced (internally timed) and therefore initiated at a time determined solely by the player. In contrast, when kicking the moving ball, the task became more complex because the player had to regulate the co-ordination of the kick with the moving ball. Given that players kick considerably more moving balls compared to stationary balls in games, the authors concluded that the experienced participants were more accurate in this condition because they had developed a more functional movement solution through vast amounts of task-specific practice. In contrast, the lesser skilled participants performed better in the stationary condition because the players could only co-ordinate their kick in a very stable and intrinsically timed environment.

Although the study by Egan *et al.* (2007) was primarily concerned with skill execution, the results provide an important message for practitioners attempting to develop decision-making in team sports. The experienced soccer players had learned to better co-ordinate their kick by using information from an extrinsically timed stimulus (the moving ball) because this was a core requirement for successful performance in the sport. In other invasion games such as AFL, players are required to co-ordinate the execution of a kick or handball in both intrinsically and extrinsically timed conditions by searching for the appropriate perceptual information in the environment. Therefore, an overemphasis on training drills that primarily involve the execution of intrinsically timed skills may not only fail to accurately replicate the demands of the game, but it can also act to inhibit the development of functional movement solutions required in dynamic game environments.

The previous discussion highlights the importance of creating representative tasks and reliable perceptual variables in the practice setting to allow learners to become attuned to the information that is most relevant for executing movement solutions (Araújo *et al.*, 2005; Beek *et al.*, 2003). By maintaining the essential links between the information that is perceived (perception) and the movement solution that is executed (action), the perception-action coupling can be accurately mapped and the learner can become attuned to the important specifying variables that underpin successful decision-making in games.

The benefits of open training drills to maintain representative task constraints

In many team games, the traditional approach to enhancing performance is to compartmentalise training by addressing the physiological components separately from the skill components. The common belief is that fitness can be developed as a separate entity, typically with non-sport-specific drills so that training volumes can easily be quantified. It is often thought that this form of fitness work can make it difficult for "lazy" players to "hide" during the training session (Farrow *et al.*, 2008). When it comes to skill-based training drills, the tendency is to position markers on the field in a predetermined pattern to indicate where players should move as they complete the drill. Defenders are often excluded from drills so that players are better able to execute the skills of the game, without the distraction created by an opponent. Coaches can sometimes be wary of using more open training drills because they believe that the increased complexity can reduce the volume of skill repetitions and this may detrimentally affect skill development (Farrow et al., 2008).

Whilst this approach may have intuitive appeal, it is clear from the earlier discussion that a major limitation of this form of training is the substantial reduction in the critical information sources contained within the typical performance setting. Player movements are intrinsically timed, highly prescribed, and provide limited opportunities to explore the full range of temporal and spatial variables present in the performance environment. Similarly, while the removal of defenders would undoubtedly simplify the playing environment and allow skills to be executed with reduced error, the execution of those skills would often occur with little reference to appropriate specifying variables. Instead, players learn to map solutions to non-specifying variables, thus reducing the likelihood of the skills transferring to the normal competitive setting. The lack of variability in "closed" training drills reduces the opportunity for players to learn how to adapt movement solutions to changing environmental demands. It is likely that players simply develop a core repertoire of solutions that are successful in closed, intrinsically timed situations, but lack the necessary adaptability and functionality for more dynamic, complex, and extrinsically timed environments.

A recent study by Farrow et al. (2008) explored this area further by comparing the physiological and skill demands of open versus closed drills in AFL. Participants were required to complete two different training sessions involving a series of three closed drills and three open drills. In effect, Farrow et al. (2008) manipulated a key task constraint, namely, the absence or inclusion of defenders, in order to examine the changes that occurred as a result. The closed drills required players to execute intrinsically timed skills in a highly repetitious environment with no decision-making requirements. In contrast, open drills were more game-like in nature and required the skills to be executed in more unpredictable environments with decision-making and extrinsically timed variables being key ingredients. The open drills were designed to closely replicate the aims of the closed drills but with the addition of opponents.

Physiologically, the results showed that the open drills were more demanding in terms of the distance covered and the relative intensity. There were more moderate velocity efforts in the open drills but the number of high velocity and high acceleration efforts were similar between the open and closed drills. These results are similar to those obtained from research examining other team sports where the physiological demands of conditioning drills were compared to those experienced during game-based training activities (Gabbett, 2003; Hoff et al., 2002; Sassi et al., 2004). The general consensus suggests that open, game-based training drills can provide an equivalent physiological stimulus to that typically encountered in interval training and conditioning drills (Farrow et al., 2008; Gabbet, 2006). In fact, open drills have been shown to elicit similar heart rate and blood lactate concentrations to those typically experienced during actual competition (Gabbett, 2003).

Analysis of the skill demands showed that the closed drills contained a greater number of opportunities for skill execution, however, the open drills had more opportunities for game-based decision-making. One of the interesting findings was that participants perceived the open drills to be significantly more mentally taxing than the closed drill equivalents, presumably due to the increased demands on decision-making caused by the addition of defenders, and importantly, this may have also led to greater task engagement. It is also likely that the addition of defenders allowed players to contextualise their disposals (kicks and hand-balls) and to choose an appropriate decision based upon realistic perceptual variables. This was demonstrated by the fact that the players opted to kick more than handball in the open drills, which was often the better solution because the addition of two defenders meant that handballing was less functional than kicking (Farrow *et al.*, 2008). In effect, the changes to the drill encouraged the players to adapt by attuning their movement solutions to the differing demands of the playing environment. Overall, the study provides a practical example of the holistic benefits of game-based training and the importance of representative task design. While closed drills may provide a simplified environment that allows players to execute skills with increased precision and reduced error, open drills provide players with an opportunity to better calibrate the execution of the skill with relevant and reliable perceptual variables, such as the locations of defenders relative to teammates.

A constraints-led approach for developing decision-making in AFL

An ideal method of encouraging exploratory behaviour during practice, and simultaneously assisting the learner to differentiate between specifying and non-specifying variables, is to use a constraints-led approach. By manipulating specific task, environmental, or organismic constraints, the practitioner can shape and guide the co-ordination patterns that emerge as the learner attempts to perform particular movement solutions to satisfy task goals (Handford *et al.*, 1997). In the example above, Farrow *et al.* (2008) manipulated a key task constraint by includ-ing or removing defenders. The presence or absence of opponents had a marked influence on the playing environment and this differentially affected the solutions that emerged from the drills. The greater variability that existed in the open drills allowed players to actively search the perceptual-motor workspace for functional movement solutions, and importantly, encouraged players to adapt those solutions to changes in the environment. A similar approach can also be used to elicit other outcome goals.

If, for instance, an AFL coach wants to develop the ability of players to quickly recognise open teammates or scoring opportunities, an "up-and-down" drill can be used to promote broad visual scanning and the ability to identify reliable per-ceptual variables that underpin good decision-making. In the "up-and-down" drill, players are required to play a modified game of AFL, in an area of about 50 m², but the locations and movements of particular players are manipulated by the coach. During play, the coach can call out the name of any player on the field, and that player must immediately drop down to the ground and lay on his/her stomach for two seconds before resuming play. If the coach calls the name of a defender, for example, this results in an attacking player being undefended and provides opportunities for exploitation by the attacking team. At the same time, the defending team must adapt and restructure to cover the gap, preventing the attackers from utilising their brief numerical superiority. Importantly, the instability in the defence is only present for a few seconds while the defender is lying on the ground, meaning that the attackers need to very quickly determine the extent of the instability in the defence and decide whether to directly exploit the missing defender or simply wait and use another option. One of the other advantages of this situation is that the excluded defensive player (who was previously lying on the ground) must quickly assess the current state of play and co-ordinate him/herself with other teammates to minimise the extent of the instability. The rapid changes in the playing environment also promote the need for communication amongst teammates. This can be facilitated by calling short "time-outs", where each team must discuss different strategies that can be used to exploit the dynamic nature of the game. Rather than passively receiving information from the coach, this process can be augmented by using questioning techniques that encourage the players to actively seek solutions to the tactical problems created (Chow et al., 2007).

The "up-and-down" drill is one example of the many ways in which a coach can manipulate key constraints to create a training environment where players are provided with opportunities to explore and solve new movement solutions. Importantly, players are encouraged to map their solutions to relevant perceptual information, thus ensuring that decisions are appropriate for the demands of the game. Attunement to the specifying information within the environment is likely to lead to better skill execution and decision-making. One of the key considerations for coaches is to ensure that the drills are designed to provide an appropriate level of challenge for the players. Overly complex drills may create so much mayhem and chaos (i.e. variability) that players struggle to find any effective solutions. Conversely, closed and intrinsically timed drills are likely to diminish the important perceptual information, reducing the ability of the players to develop a broad repertoire of functional movement solutions that transfer to the normal competitive setting. The Case Study below, highlights the benefits of using a constraints-led approach for developing decision-making in team sports.

Case Study: The case of Merloo South Junior AFL Club

John Price was the coach of a very successful Under 14 AFL club in the small country town of Merloo South. For years he had worked tirelessly to instil the importance of repetition, consistency, and perfection in his team. John's philosophy was simple: If players are to learn how to perform the skills of the game to a high standard they must repeatedly practice those skills until they are executing them perfectly.

He had a repertoire of drills that were ideal for developing these attributes and in all his years of experience as a coach, he had never had any reason to change the drills that had served him and his team so well. He preferred to use drills where players could execute their skills without making errors and he liked to use large volumes of skill repetitions so that the correct technique was "drilled" into players. He also felt that this was important to ensure that the skills would hold up under the pressure of competition. Given that the team was restricted to only two training sessions per week, John thought that it was necessary to avoid using complicated drills because the time could be better spent by completing additional skill repetitions.

John's training sessions invariably started with a few short warm-up laps followed by some stretching. He then progressed into a series of "breakdown" drills where he placed markers on the ground to dictate the pattern of ball movement. He carefully placed the markers in positions that would replicate the style of play and attacking structures that he wanted the players to use during a game. To finish the session, John always used one of his favourite drills which he liked to call "circlework". Players were given three or four footballs and told to kick or handball the balls up and down the full length of the ground, following the same playing style that he had just taught them in the earlier breakdown drills. There were no other specific rules, and no defenders, and John felt that the drill provided the players with an opportunity to practice their skills in a more game-like environment.

After a recent training session, Sam Jones, a parent of one of the players, told John that he thought the team were looking pretty good at training, but he was surprised that they had only won two out of their first ten games of the season. Sam said that he had watched a number of games and taken some stats on the number of kicks, handballs, marks, and tackles. When he compared those stats to previous seasons, he found that the numbers were much the same. However, when he looked more closely into the decision-making statistics, Sam noticed that the quality of the decisions were considerably lower than the stats he had collected from previous seasons. Moreover, when Sam compared Merloo South to the other teams, he found a huge discrepancy in the level of decision-making. The teams were evenly matched in terms of the number of possessions, but Merloo South were considerably lower than every other team in the competition when it came to the quality of their decisions. John decided to investigate this further.

During the week, he visited a few of the surrounding teams and watched several of their training sessions. He noticed that the other teams were using game-based training drills where the players competed against each other in small-sided games with slightly modified rules. Most drills included some form of defensive pressure and whilst this increased the amount of skill errors, John liked the intensity of the drills and the amount of pressure that was created by the defenders.

John thought that this approach would be a great addition to his favoured circlework drill. The following Tuesday, he implemented his new ideas and suddenly found that the players not only enjoyed the new challenge, but they started to attempt different types of kicks and handballs that he had rarely seen them do in the past. The drill also highlighted that the quality of their decision-making was quite poor and he wondered why he hadn't noticed this before. John decided to persist with his new training strategy over the remaining weeks of the season and he designed some entirely new drills and discarded a number of his older drills. Importantly, he always included the relevant perceptual variables to ensure that the players learned when and where it was appropriate to execute certain types of skills. When he called players together during a drill, he questioned them to encourage them to think about new solutions and tactics. Whilst some training sessions were better than others, he started to notice a gradual improvement in the standard of decision-making. The players were no longer running aimlessly around the field, kicking to players who were heavily defended, or rushing forward in attack when they should have been slowing the play. At times, the number of errors would increase and some players started to lose confidence in their ability. John simply explained to the players that the purpose of the drills was to provide opportunities for them to perform in a game-like environment and whenever that happens, more mistakes are likely to occur. But, the important thing was to learn from those mistakes and to search for other solutions that are more successful. John never fully dispensed with some of his favourite closed drills because he found that he could use them to inflate the player's confidence. However, he found that he was using them less and less, particularly once he noticed that the decision-making of his team was improving more than he ever thought was possible.

References

Allard, F., Graham, S. & Paarsalu, M. E. (1980). Perception in Sport: Basketball. *Journal of Sport Psychology*, 2, 14–21.

Araújo, D., Davids, K. & Serpa, S. (2005). An Ecological Approach to Expertise Effects in Decision-making in a Simulated Sailing Regatta. *Psychology of Sport and Exercise*, 6, 671–692.

Beek, P. J., Jacobs, D. M., Daffertshofer, A. & Huys, R. (2003). Expert Performance in Sport: Views from the Joint Perspectives of Ecological Psychology and Dynamical Systems Theory. In J. L. Starkes & K. A. Ericsson (eds), *Expert Performance in Sports: Advances in Research on Sport Expertise*. Champaign, Illinois: Human Kinetics, pp. 321–344.

Chamberlain, C. J. & Coelho, A. J. (1993). The Perceptual Side of Action: Decision-making in Sport. In J. L. Starkes & F. Allard (eds), *Cognitive Issues in Motor Expertise*. Amsterdam: North-Holland, pp. 135–157.

Chow, J. Y., Davids, K., Button, C., Shuttleworth, R., Renshaw, I. & Araújo, D. (2007). The Role of Non-linear Pedagogy in Physical Education. *Review of Educational Research*, 77, 251–278.

Egan, C. D., Savelsbergh, G. J. P. & Verheul, M. H. G. (2007). Effects of Experience on the Co-ordination of Internally and Externally-timed Soccer Kicks. *Journal of Motor Behavior*, 39, 423–432.

Farrow, D., Pyne, D. & Gabbett, T. (2008). Skill and Physiological Demands of Open and

Closed Drills in Australian Football. *International Journal of Sports Science & Coaching*, 3, 485–495.

Gabbett, T. (2003). Do Skill-based Conditioning Games Simulate the Physiological Demands of Competition? *Rugby League Coaching Manual*, 32, 27–31.

Gabbett, T. (2006). Skill-based Conditioning Games as an Alternative to Traditional Conditioning for Rugby League Players. *Journal of Strength and Conditioning Research*, 20, 309–315.

Handford, C., Davids, K., Bennett, S. & Button, C. (1997). Skill Acquisition in Sport: Some Applications of an Emerging Practice Ecology. *Journal of Sports Sciences*, 15, 621–640.

Hoff, J., Wisløff, U., Engen, L. C., Kemi, O. J. & Helgerud, J. (2002). Soccer-specific Aerobic Endurance Training. *British Journal of Sports Medicine*, 36, 218–221.

Jacobs, D. M., Runeson, S. & Michaels, C. F. (2001). Learning to Visually Perceive the Relative Mass of Colliding Balls in Globally and Locally Constrained Task Ecologies. *Journal of Experimental Psychology: Human Perception and Performance*, 27, 1019–1038.

Sassi, R., Reilly, T. & Impellizzeri, F. (2004). A Comparison of Small-sided Games and Interval Training in Elite Professional Soccer Players. *Journal of Sports Sciences*, 22, 562.

13 Skill development in canoeing and kayaking

An individualised approach

Eric Brymer

Introduction

Leaders of outdoor experiences are often required to facilitate development of motor skills. However, as Thomas (2007) reported most outdoor leadership training courses do not include topics on motor learning. Physical activities such as canoeing and kayaking, skiing and climbing require the development of specific perceptual-motor skills for successful performance. Even the humble backpacker changes walking gait and requires new skill patterns (Orloff & Rapp, 2004). At a practical level understanding how learners acquire functional movement patterns is essential for considering issues such as: (1) selecting ergonomically designed equipment for each learner; (2) organising and structuring learning environments and teaching tasks; (3) planning and management of exercise and practice programmes; (4) prevention of injury and associated health and safety considerations; and (5), understanding the nature of individual differences at various levels of performance (Davids *et al.*, 2008).

Beyond pure skills development, outdoor education is also promoted as a medium for the development of broader issues such as group support (Brymer & Gray, 2006). Thus, understanding skill development needs to allow for the broader picture. This chapter overviews the constraints-led perspective to motor learning in canoeing and kayaking and examines how this approach is particularly suited to outdoor leaders. To a large degree the constraints-led approach to skill development seems to encompass the holistic and environmentally focused perspective that outdoor leaders already follow (Hayllar, 2005). In this way the constraints-led approach might effectively frame good leadership practice. Throughout this chapter the term "leader" will be used to describe anyone introducing, instructing, teaching or coaching canoeing or kayaking in a sport, recreation, education or tourism context.

Arguably the most important session for the development of canoeing or kayaking is the introductory session carried out by the educational or recreational canoe or kayak leader (from this point forward I will use the term "paddlesport"). Neither activity is provided through school sport but through the educational camp, scouts/ guides or local club and this initial session has the potential to imbue a desire to continue or not. Thomas (2007) concluded in his analysis of two different motor learning models typically used in canoeing that effective canoe coaching depends on understanding theoretical principles. So how can the constraints-model of skill acquisition help paddlesport coaches understand ineffective learning design and facilitate effective learning? The following sections explore how understanding of the constraints-led approach to learning new skills might influence the management and delivery of an introductory session into canoeing, particularly the first few hours from first meeting the group to introducing them to the intricacies of steering their new craft. First I will outline a traditional approach to undertaking the introductory canoe or kayak session and highlight potential constraints on learning. Next, I will outline a constraints-led approach to an introductory canoe/kayak session. As the aim of this chapter is to examine learning I will be starting with the premise that environmental, technical and personal risk issues have already been effectively managed.

The traditional introductory session

In the traditional introduction session the leader would start by organising equipment. This entails fitting the learner with a personal flotation device from a standard style and range (e.g. extra small to extra large), a standard paddle (small, medium or large) and boat from a fleet of identical boats. Typically, this approach does not take into account the vast range of unique individual physical characteristics. The standard style of flotation device does not consider individual physical differences such as height, weight, girth size, chest size, limb length. The traditional approach does not accurately match each learner with equipment. Whilst it is common practice for educational and recreational centres to have general purpose small, medium and large (or even extra large) flotation devices, leaders should also think about how well these devices fit individual learners. A poorly fitting flotation device will adversely affect a learner's ability to acquire useful motor skills (Brymer *et al.*, 2000). For effective facilitation of skill acquisition the leader needs to ensure that the learner's flotation device is comfortable, unrestrictive to the body's movement, contains the appropriate buoyancy for the learner's body weight and also suits the type of craft to be used.

It is also not enough just to have small, medium and large paddles. Paddle size needs to be scaled to the individual user's arm length, boat flotation, sitting/kneeling position, eventual paddle style and even upper body: lower body ratio. A leader may also have to consider blade shape and feather, blade size, shaft and grip diameter or type, and paddle weight to take into account individual factors such as strength and hand size (Brymer *et al.*, 2000). This individualisation process might even require experimentation with different paddles when on the water.

Equally the type of craft should also fit the individual learners. A leader will need to consider matching an individual to a craft based on the relationship between individual differences and boat weight, boat length, gunwale depth (for canoes), primary and secondary stability and buoyancy. It is not enough to have a one size fits all. The typical notion of having a fleet of identical boats might actually work against the development of effective learning. Activities such as skiing have been taking an individualised approach to skill learning and performance for years and ski resorts are well organised with a vast range of skis and adjustable bindings based on individual skill level, height and strength (Schmottlach & McManama, 2006).

As well as ensuring a good fit between person and equipment the leader will need to consider the task constraints. A boat that does not meet the task requirements will negatively affect learning, for example, a kayak designed for fast-moving rivers when the task relates to flat-water racing. Typically the next stage involves preparing the learner's body and mind for the session to come. In the traditional approach the leader would gather the group together for off-water "warm-up" activities designed to prepare the body for exercise and focus the mind for undertaking an activity considered risky. Leaders are encouraged to guide learners through a series of "fun" group activities such as "Simon Says" (a game of follow the leader as he/she runs around) or "Pass the Ball" (a game where participants run around in a circle whilst passing a ball) or more serious activities such as running on the spot followed by focused stretching routines (Hampton, 2002). The argument for undertaking a thorough warm-up before getting on the water is that learners will need to work hard in order to reach the desired goal of being out of breath. A beginner will not have the required level of skill to do this when on the water (Hampton, 2002). However, if a learner does not have the required level of skill to get out of breath when on the water it is also feasible that the same learner will not need to warm-up so vigorously before getting on the water. Another potential downfall of the recommended off-water warm-up is that activities invariably involve the lower body (e.g. running, jumping on the spot and so on). However, canoeing and kayaking are more heavily biased towards the upper body. To keep the warm-up representative of the task in hand it is perhaps more appropriate to undertake simple explorative exercises on the water.

In this traditional approach the leader is also encouraged to structure time introducing basic skills such as what to do in a capsize, boat handling, how to hold the paddle or even basic forward paddling before "risking" the real environment (Gilbertson et al., 2006). The downside of this approach is that the activities do not represent the desired on-water performance. Learners might even be initiated into ineffective habits away from the appropriate environment, which might negatively influence skill development.

The traditional approach to getting a beginner group on the water involves a highly regimented process. Generally, the paddlesport leader takes the group to a standard entry point on a standard stretch of water that was chosen for its general suitability or nearness to the centre. The paddlesport leader gives strict instructions that need to be obeyed for safety reasons. Learners are told how to get into the boat and instructed to head for a point on the water (most often another leader) where they would wait until the whole group was ready. Almost immediately the traditional paddlesport leader will launch into teaching a basic stroke such as the sweep stroke or forward paddle. Learners are allowed little room for exploration despite more experienced paddlesport coaches arguing against this tight management structure (Tipper, 2002).

The problem with this tightly managed approach is that learners are introduced in a standard way on a standard stretch of water that is used for all stages of learning. There is little connection between the learner's state of readiness and the environment. The tightly managed session is a way of counteracting any unwanted environmental effect and providing comfort to the instructor. As a result learners are not given opportunities to get used to the environment or the equipment and might even become nervous based on interpretations of the instructor's behaviour.

The important point is that a leader needs to ensure that the physical environment is appropriate to each person in the group so that the beginner can explore within specified boundaries and without having to struggle against current or wind. A leader will need to consider physical issues such as the intensity of the water, size of the water body, the wind influence, the bank condition and type (e.g. overhanging trees, deep mud), the weather (e.g. mist, rain, sun, snow) and time of year, tides and currents, time of day and available light. From a socio-cultural perspective the age of group members, readiness to participate, reason for attending (e.g. just to have fun, wanting to learn more) and even the leader's style will all serve to influence learning. The paddlesport leader needs to be aware of his/her own style and ability but focus the session on the learner's readiness and ability.

In the first instance the instruction is focused on overcoming the troublesome problem of getting the boat to travel from point A to point B in a reasonably direct way (Bailie, 1991). The typical issue that a beginner encounters is that canoes and kayaks turn, and one of the instructional methods proposed to counteract this issue is to teach the new learners a basic skill used to turn the boat, called the sweep stroke.

The basic skills approach to canoeing that emphasises acronyms such as EDICT (Explain, Demonstrate, Imitate, Coach or Critique and Test), DEDICT (EDICT with an initial Demonstration) and IDEAS (Introduction, Demonstration, Explanation, Activity, Summary) focuses on the teacher's processes, perhaps to the detriment of the learner. Whilst these acronyms are often presented as methodologies to help novice coaches (see Taylor, 2002), the lack of motor learning or skill acquisition in outdoor education courses frequently results in long-term acronym-focused teaching. The main premise highlighted by the three instructor-focused approaches is the strong belief that there is one best way of undertaking a manoeuvre. The instruction techniques are stroke-focused and are about helping learners adapt their body and mind to fit the ideal. All three approaches emphasise the use of demonstrations, verbal instruction, physically trying the manoeuvre under guidance and a final summary or testing stage. The demonstration aims to provide a model that the students can attempt to emulate when undertaking the activity. The verbal stage provides a detailed summary of a few essential points (usually about three) to provide focus for students to interpret the demonstration. The activity, imitation and coaching elements then typically involve repeating an activity over and over again whilst the coach "floats" about attempting to correct or coach technique, based on the original ideal model. Finally, some sort of test or game is set up to assess how well the learner has modelled the ideal movement pattern.

The traditional method of teaching canoe skills is to decompose the task into convenient components as a way of managing the information load on learners. An obvious example occurs when the complex kayak roll is taught through a manoeuvre called the "pawlata roll", which requires that the learner adopt a paddle grip that will not be used once the kayak roll is mastered (Collins, 2004; Thomas, 2007). In addition, the sweep stroke is traditionally taught by asking learners to spin the boat over and over again on one spot. Yet the intended aim of the sweep stroke is to turn the boat whilst on the move, either as a means to straighten the boat if it is going off-course or to turn the boat if the learner needs to avoid an object or change direction (Bailie, 1991). The stroke is perhaps only undertaken once or, if ineffective, twice, not over and over again on one spot.

The downside of this approach is that the task is *decomposed*, which affects the relevant information-movement coupling so that it becomes quite challenging for learners to perform the intended action in context (Handford, 2006). Instead the paddlesport leader should *simplify* the task, which strengthens the information-movement couplings. That is skill development should always take place in the natural performance environment, but on occasions the context can be simplified. Task simplification in paddlesport can occur as learners begin by experimenting with how the boat and environment interact, perhaps even before focusing on the use of the paddle. A coach who wishes to explore how to turn a boat might use this exploration time by asking learners to experiment with turning the boat to avoid an object or to change direction, or by asking students to paddle to point B whilst experimenting with different ways of keeping the boat straight.

Another disadvantage of the traditional instruction process is that it does not consider affordances for action. Affordances are simply opportunities for action that combine the objective nature of the environment with the subjective nature of the learner (Gibson, 1986). An example of affordances in paddlesport could include the fact that two learners turning a canoe on the same stretch of flat water would be working with the same environmental properties, but differences in limb length and body length would result in different perceptions and actions. At the same time an action that is simple to undertake in calm conditions, such as paddling in a crosswind might present different complexities as the wind picks up. Opportunities to attune to affordances are important because they strengthen the learner's connection to the environment and ability to be in step with, or attuned to, the nuances that are peculiar to the relationship between the environment, task and individual constraints. For long-term effective development, learners need to be placed in realistic learning environments where they can attune to information enabling them to make intelligent and informed decisions based on a good understanding of their own capabilities in any given environment.

In summary, the traditional method of managing the learning process for a beginner's session does not fully take into account individual, task or environmental constraints. Often the processes are not fully representative of the intended task. For this reason, even before the learners arrive, the paddlesport leader should search out an appropriate environment. The first stages of an effective basic paddlesport session will need to take into account individual differences with regards to psycho-emotional readiness, clothing, flotation device, paddle and canoe. A coach should take time to ensure that equipment fits the individual and that each individual is appropriately outfitted for the particular environment in order to ensure a valuable introduction to paddlesport. From this point off-water sessions should be minimised to the essentials and any activities that are undertaken should closely represent the future on-water task.

The paddlesport leader needs to manipulate a variety of appropriate constraints to help learners effectively search for successful movement solutions in a practice environment. The search process should allow for flexibility and adaptability so that learners can generate a movement solution that is unique to his or her personal, task and environmental constraints. Functional variability in movement facilitates a discovery type of approach in paddlesport settings by allowing learners to establish effective co-ordination patterns which satisfy task constraints.

As mentioned in the introduction Thomas (2007) concluded in his analysis of two different motor learning models that effective canoe coaching depends on understanding theoretical principles. So how can the constraints-model of skill acquisition help paddlesport coaches facilitate effective learning? To recap: skills acquisition depends on constraints in the task, individual and environment, as well as the effective coupling of perception and action through task representation and affordances for action.

The constraints-based approach in practice

Paddlesport leaders already accept that any planned session undergoes an effective risk management process long before the session takes place, based on understanding the relationship between risk and people, the environment and the task (or equipment). The constraints-based approach requires a similar process in order to ensure effective learning management. The paddlesport leader will need to prepare long before the session takes place in order to ensure that individuals are effectively prepared for the session with appropriate equipment and so on. The leader will also need to choose a physical environment that allows for flexibility whilst keeping the learner's needs in mind. Ideally the leader has a vast range of non-standardised paddles, boats and flotation devices to ensure that individual differences can be effectively taken into account. This range should be planned with the potential clientele in mind (e.g. young people, adults, male, female and so on). In a beginners session a leader should also have a range of clothing to fit all potential client sizes, task requirements and environmental conditions. A wetsuit when it is very warm is not ideal, as is wearing a T-shirt when it is very cold. These experiences can negatively influence the learner's experience.

Setting appropriate challenges for learners is in itself a demanding task for paddlesport leaders. A key skill is identifying the most important performance aspect that an individual or group needs to work on at any specific stage of development. In most beginner sessions, the paddlesport leader will only be able to determine this relationship once the session has started. From this perspective it makes sense to omit the land-based activities and get the group on the water as soon as practicable. As an appropriate environment has already been chosen it should be unlikely that learners will have to struggle against wind, current or tides and the paddlesport leader should set boundaries and allow students to initially explore within those boundaries. The leader should encourage the learner to explore the interaction between brain, body, boat, blade and the environment by providing activities that do not focus on movement in any direction but instead explore stability and balance (Brymer et al., 2000). For example, once all learners are on the water the leader could ask learners to explore what happens with the connection between boat, body and environment when the learner moves the body backward and forward. A leader might also ask learners to experiment with body positions when using the paddle by asking them to move forward whilst leaning back or setting a challenge to find the most effective body position for using the paddle.

Instead of bringing the group together to teach a stroke the leader would also be in a strong position to observe individuals and provide challenges appropriate to each individual. It is possible that whilst one person is struggling to keep the boat straight another is finding this easier. A leader can then provide challenges to the struggling learner through asking the learner to brainstorm or experiment with different ways of keeping the boat straight. Then the leader could contextualise the movement by setting questions and challenges around travelling from point A to point B whilst physically practising different ways of keeping the boat straight. In the meantime the person finding the task easier can be challenged in other ways. For example, a leader could ask them to explore ways of moving the craft with minimum bow (front of the boat) bobbing or whilst it is on edge or even finding the most effective way of turning a boat, or challenging them to manoeuvre their boat in a precise and accurate manner by coming alongside a specific point on the bank. The challenges cannot be standardised and should be designed to meet the needs of individual learners. This adds a particular responsibility to the leader's "tool box", as to do this effectively, the leader will need to be highly skilled and open or attuned to the learner's individual requirements.

The leader's role is to provide appropriate challenges whilst allowing the learner the space to explore responses to the challenge. This could be achieved by asking the group to undertake different forward, sideways and backwards movements by increasing the task complexity through setting experiential challenges to travel within set boundaries. On occasion it might be necessary to provide some coaching that necessitates the use of a demonstration. If this were the case, the demonstration should be seen as a visual guide as opposed to a model to emulate and further exploration should allow the learner space to determine his/her own unique response. From a constraints-led perspective demonstrations are useful to provide a rough "ballpark" understanding of what a particular movement pattern should achieve, and a guide to support a learner's exploration of a particular desired outcome, in this case turning the boat (Davids et al., 2008). This will ideally be done as a means towards helping a particular learner at a specific point in their development.

A constraints-led perspective suggests that movement variability is significant because it provides the flexibility required to consistently achieve a movement goal in any dynamic sporting environment (Williams *et al.*, 1999). In fact, even the most highly skilled individuals find it hard to replicate a movement pattern across trials (Davids *et al.*, 2008). Variability in movement patterns permits flexible and adaptive motor-system behaviour, encouraging the free exploration necessary in dynamic learning and performance contexts as found in canoeing and kayaking. During skilled performance it is important to consistently repeat a performance outcome, although the movement pattern used to achieve this outcome may not be replicated in an identical way every time. In human movement, this quality of repetition without replication (Bernstein, 1967) presents learners with an opportunity to conceive of novel variations to solve typical motor problems. This seemingly inconsistent relationship between stability and variability is actually beneficial because skilled performers need to be capable of both persistence and change (Davids *et al.*, 2008). The paddlesport leader needs to accept that movement variability may be an integral process in learning and acquiring effective movement patterns that are specific to a task goal. However, this does not mean that the constraints approach encourages paddlesport leaders to merely allow "free play" in some vain hope that learners will eventually complete a set task in whatever way they deem appropriate! The essence of the constraints-led perspective is to facilitate new movement solutions by designing learning environments that provide controlled boundaries of exploration in dynamic settings through the provision of relevant task constraints.

Thus, in the second part of the session, depending on the group and if the physical environment allows, the leader could undertake a short journey whilst providing small goal-centred challenges, such as allowing learners to explore moving backwards or sideways without turning the boat. It may be appropriate to develop more challenges designed to support the process of self-organisation in the learner. This can be done by moving to an area with slight current or wind and challenging the learner to undertake similar tasks.

By effectively manipulating task or environment constraints whilst being attuned to individual learners, the paddlesport leader can support the learner's formation of useful and co-ordinated movements. Many paddlesport educators and practitioners seem to have understood that learners have this self-organising capability, even though they may not have referred to the constraints approach. For example, Thomas's (2007) description of the FERAL (Frame the problem, Explore solutions, Report back with solutions, Adjust our thinking and motor plans, Learn by testing the new solutions) seems to effectively consider the environmental, task and individual constraints through a discovery approach. However, even within this approach the group is asked to undertake the exploration as one (even if they may come up with different solutions) and each individual is treated as if at the same state of readiness with a focus on boat manoeuvring. The essence in the constraints approach is to manage the session in such a way that the leader is able to utilise individual affordances for learning through effective task representation whilst empowering individuals through the manipulation of task and environmental constraints.

Summary

The constraints-led approach has become a widely accepted theoretical exploration of how effective motor skills are developed. This student-centred perspective provides an ideal perspective for the paddlesport leader to design effective learning settings. Furthermore, this open style of facilitation also allows students to learn other concepts such as teamwork, leadership and so on.

References

Bailie, M. (1991). *Canoeing and Kayaking: Technique, Tactics, Training.* Malborough: The Crowood Press.

Bernstein, N. A. (1967). *The Control and Regulation of Movements.* London: Pergamon Press.

Brymer, E. & Gray, T. (2006). Effective Leadership: Transformational or Transactional? *Australian Journal of Outdoor Education*, 10(2), 13–19.

Brymer, E., Hughes, T. & Collins, L. (2000). *The Art of Freestyle.* Bangor, North Wales: Pesda Press.

Collins, L. (2004). *Kayaking Rolling: The Black Art Demystified.* Bangor: Pesda Press.

Davids, K., Button, C. & Bennett, S. J. (2008). *Dynamics of Skill Acquisition: A Constraints-led Approach.* Champaign: Illinois. Human Kinetics.

Gibson, J. J. (1986). *The Ecological Approach to Visual Perception.* Hillsdale, NJ: Lawrence Erlbaum Associates.

Gilbertson, K., Bates, T., McLaughlin, T. & Ewert, A. (2006). *Outdoor Education: Methods and Strategies.* NIRSA Education & Publication Center.

Hampton, K. (2002). Safety and Leadership. In F. Ferrero (ed.), *Canoe and Kayak Handbook.* Bangor: Pesda Press.

Handford, C. H. (2006). Serving Up Variability and Stability. In K. Davids, C. Button & K. Newell (eds), *Movement System Variability.* Champaign: Illinois. Human Kinetics, pp. 73–83.

Hayllar, B. (2005). Leadership and Facilitation. In T. J. Dickson, T. Gray & B. Hayllar (eds), *Outdoor and Experiential Learning: Views from the Top.* Dunedin: Otago University Press.

Orloff, H. A. & Rapp, C. M. (2004). The Effects of Load Carriage on Spinal Curvature and Posture. *Spine*, 29(12), 1325–1329.

Schmottlach, N. & McManama, J. (2006). *Physical Education Activity Handbook*, 11th edn. San Fransisco: Pearson Education.

Taylor, B. (2002). Coaching. In F. Ferrero (ed), *Canoe and Kayak Handbook.* Bangor: Pesda Press, pp. 115–137.

Thomas, G. (2007). Skill Instruction in Outdoor Leadership: A Comparison of a Direct Instruction Model and a Discovery-learning Model. *Australian Journal of Outdoor Education*, 11(2), 10–18.

Tipper, L. (2002). Foundation Kayak Skills. In F. Ferrero (ed.), *Canoe and Kayak Handbook.* Bangor: Pesda Press, pp. 47–68.

Williams, A. M., Davids, K. & Williams, J. G. (1999). *Visual Perception and Action in Sport.* London: E & F. N. Spon.

14 A constraints-led approach to coaching association football

The role of perceptual information and the acquisition of co-ordination

Matt Dicks and Jia Yi Chow

Introduction

An ability to execute the right pass at the right time in association football requires the accurate perception of information coupled to the skilled co-ordination of movement. The fact that skilled perceptual anticipation is complementary to successful action has led sport scientists to seek to determine its precise role in a variety of sport tasks. In this chapter, we will briefly explore the literature on perceptual anticipation in association football before providing evidence that demonstrates that changes in ecological task constraints (i.e. information display and response requirements) can directly influence the visual anticipatory behaviour of goalkeepers. We then turn our attention to research examining the co-ordination of a football kicking action. We will share how task constraints provided in the learning environment help to shape the emergence of different but equally successful movement solutions among novice learners. Finally, we provide an example of how practitioners can exploit understanding from the combined body of empirical evidence for the design of coaching activities.

Perceptual skill in football

When in possession of a ball, a footballer continuously scans the pitch for information to guide action: should the player attempt to pass, run with the ball or shoot? If they pass, to whom, and when? With every ensuing movement, information in the surrounding environment (e.g. position of teammates and opponents) will alter, presenting new information and imposing a new set of constraints on action. Furthermore, individual and game constraints such as the player's level of physical fatigue and location on the pitch can affect the ensuing time available for perception and action. Therefore, an ability to accurately anticipate the intentions of other players provides the player with a mechanism to successfully cope with the temporal demands of performance in complex game environments. Indeed, many of the world's most gifted players are often said to be blessed with an ability to "read the game". Therefore, an interesting question is whether the perceptual skill of expert players is underpinned by the pickup of different information in comparison with their lesser-skilled peers. In the following section, we briefly discuss research that has measured football players' visual search strategies, which are thought to reveal the information sources used during visual anticipation and decision-making (Williams *et al.*, 1999).

Visual search strategies of association football players

Traditionally, the visual search strategies and decision-making abilities of football players have been measured using experimental designs that simulate the visual information of "open" game sub-phases (e.g. 3 vs 1 or 4 vs 3: Vaeyens *et al.*, 2007) and comparatively "closed" set-plays (e.g. the penalty kick: Savelsbergh *et al.*, 2002) using "life-size" video displays. For example, Vaeyens *et al.* (2007), recently examined the search strategies and decision-making behaviours of outfield players (international, national, regional and novice) in response to variations on the video simulation of training ground drills consisting of different numbers of attackers and defenders (2 vs 1, 3 vs 1, 3 vs 2, 4 vs 3 and 5 vs 3). Participants were required to make decisions as though they were one of the attacking players depicted in the film display. The trend of results suggested that decision time became slower and response accuracy decreased as the number of players within the training drill increased. Similarly, there was a greater visual search rate, comprising more fixations of shorter duration for the 3 vs 2, 4 vs 3 and 5 vs 3 scenarios in comparison with the 2 vs 1 and 3 vs 1 display conditions. The findings suggest that an important constraint on decision-making skill and search strategy in simulated open game situations is the number of players presented in the video display, a finding corroborated by other research examining the performance of outfield players (see Williams & Davids, 1998).

However, perhaps a more pertinent issue for understanding learning from a constraints-led perspective is the necessity to determine whether the video simulation task constraints as used in the example of Vaeyens *et al.* (2007) are representative of competitive game conditions (see Araújo *et al.*, 2007; Davids, Chapter 1). Indeed, technological advances have enabled recent experimental designs to measure participants, search strategies while facing an opponent(s) *in situ* as they would in sport performance conditions (for an example in ice hockey see Martell & Vickers, 2004). Much like the example of Renshaw *et al.* (2007) for cricket strokes against a bowler and bowling machine (see Davids, Chapter 1), performance may differ between video simulation and *in situ* constraints due to the *nature* of the information presented (Gibson, 1979) in the respective conditions. Importantly, skilled players may have learnt distinct information-movement couplings for *in situ* conditions that are not actualised when performance is measured in response to video simulation task constraints.

Recently, we have attempted to verify this pertinent issue through a series of experiments where we measured experienced goalkeepers visual search strategies and movement responses for video simulation and *in situ* task constraints of the penalty kick in football (see Dicks *et al.*, under review). The goalkeepers were required to predict the outcome of penalty kicks verbally or with a simplified body movement for video and *in situ* conditions. The *in situ* condition required goalkeepers to produce a whole-body movement (i.e. side step), with arms directed towards the anticipated goal location. As in previous research (e.g. Savelsbergh *et al.*, 2002), the video simulation condition required the goalkeepers to move a joystick as though to save the kick. Performance was also measured for an *in situ* interception condition in which the goalkeepers were required to move and attempt to save the penalty kicks. It was found that the experienced goalkeepers were more accurate at anticipating penalty kick direction as the task constraints became more representative of real-life conditions (i.e. *in situ* interception condition). Performance was more accurate for the *in situ* in comparison with the video simulation tasks while there was a trend of improved accuracy across the three different *in situ* conditions.

In each experiment, we recorded the goalkeepers' visual search strategies. The data presented in Figure 14.1 depicts the percentage viewing time of eye fixations on the penalty taker's body (e.g. head, torso, kicking leg and non-kicking leg), compared with fixations upon the ball during the run-up for the different task constraints.

The findings demonstrate that task constraints that more closely represent sport performance environments increase the requirement of the goalkeepers to spend more time fixating upon the ball than the penalty taker's body. A possible interpretation of this finding is that the video simulation conditions force players to rely on information presented by the penalty taker to anticipate kick direction as only minimal ball-flight information was available for these conditions. This

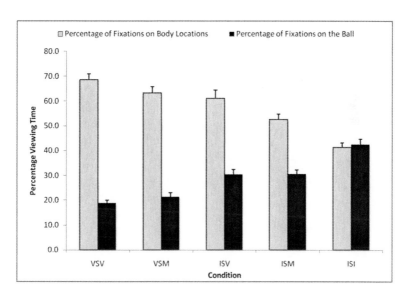

Figure 14.1 Cumulative percentage time spent viewing anatomical locations in comparison with the ball for all experimental conditions (adapted from Dicks *et al.*, under review). Note: VSV = video simulation verbal condition; VSM = video simulation movement; ISV = *in situ* verbal; ISM = *in situ* movement; ISI = *in situ* interception.

creates a non-representative simulation of the task constraints that are normally encountered *in situ*. Indeed, the findings further suggest that the two anticipatory *in situ* simulations fail to adequately represent the task requirements for the *in situ* interception condition. The results emphasise the importance of specificity in the design of training practices that emphasise the learning of representative and functional information-movement couplings that are most important to success in real game situations (Savelsbergh & van der Kamp, 2000). Failure in the design of training drills to fully capture the *nature* of information (Gibson, 1979) available to players during sport performance conditions may result in the acquisition of a diminished set of perceptual skills that are not compatible with the precise co-ordinated actions that are replete in expert football performance.

In the next section, we will demonstrate how skilled footballers are able to use different, functional co-ordination solutions to successfully overcome the same task goal in a football chipping task. Similarly, we will illustrate the variable co-ordination changes that take place among novice learners for a comparable chipping task over an extended period of practice.

Co-ordination in football

Passing ranks as one of the most important skills in football. Passes are made on the ground, around or over the opposition to teammates. While research has been conducted to investigate kicking and especially shooting (see Putnam, 1983; Lees & Nolan, 2002), less emphasis has been placed on examining passing and even less on passing the ball over opponents (e.g. chipping the ball). Building on the ideas of a constraints-led approach as discussed in the early chapters (see Davids, Chapter 1), it would be insightful to determine how task constraints can be manipulated to direct learners to explore different movement solutions, taking into account the performer constraints and the characteristics of the environmental boundaries in the performance and learning context. In the case of passing in football, it would be pertinent to examine whether different co-ordination solutions are acquired by respective performers.

Recently, our laboratory investigated the specific features of movement behaviours of different levels of skill performers in a kicking task that mimics the task demands for a football chip pass (Chow *et al.*, 2006; 2008). The focus of the investigations was to examine whether different co-ordination patterns were used by skilled footballers under the specific task constraints studied and to determine the pathway of co-ordination acquisition of novice participants as a function of practice. Specifically, we attempted to determine how co-ordination changes with practice in the absence of explicit instructions on kicking techniques. We aimed to examine whether there was a common movement solution utilised by novices or even skilled players for the kicking task.

For the football passing task, participants were required to kick a football over a height barrier to a receiver with their dominant foot. No explicit instructions were given saying how to strike the ball over the height barrier and participants were simply informed that the task goal was to kick the ball over the height barrier so

Expert 1

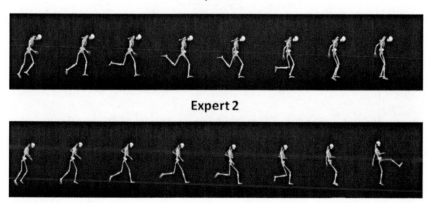

Expert 2

Figure 14.2 Representative skeletal illustrations of kicking actions for skilled players with different kicking movement patterns that are equally successful in meeting the task goal.

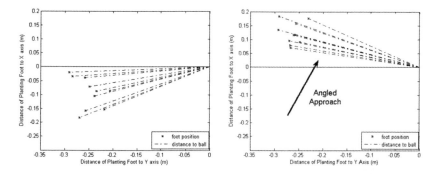

Figure 14.3 Planting foot position relative to stationary position of the ball for two different skilled players (adapted from Chow *et al.*, 2006).

that it would land at the feet of a receiving player or within the landing zone in front of the receiver, appropriately weighted to allow for easy control of the pass.

Prior to the learning study, skilled participants kicking patterns were analysed in order to determine whether there were any functional differences between the co-ordination patterns used by skilled players (Chow *et al.*, 2006). While most skilled players employed a kicking pattern with little follow-through and with a stabbing action, some participants used a scooping kicking pattern that was equally successful in meeting the task goal (see Figure 14.2).

The skilled players tended to adopt either a planted foot position to the side and back, or to the side and front of the ball (see Figure 14.3). While planting foot characteristics were different, all skilled players were just as successful in getting the ball over the height barrier and weighted the passes appropriately and accurately to the live receiver. The skilled players who adopted a forward

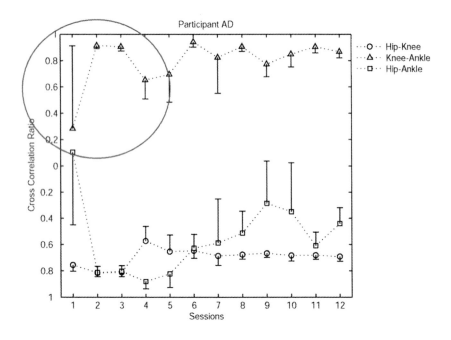

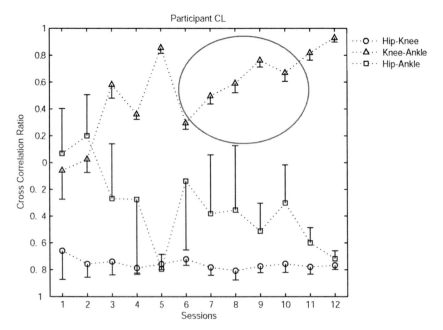

Figure 14.4 Cross-correlation ratios for joint relations of four novice players plotted as a function of practice sessions. Circles highlight the difference changes in to knee–ankle cross-correlation ratios with practice for the novice players (adapted from Chow *et al.*, 2008).

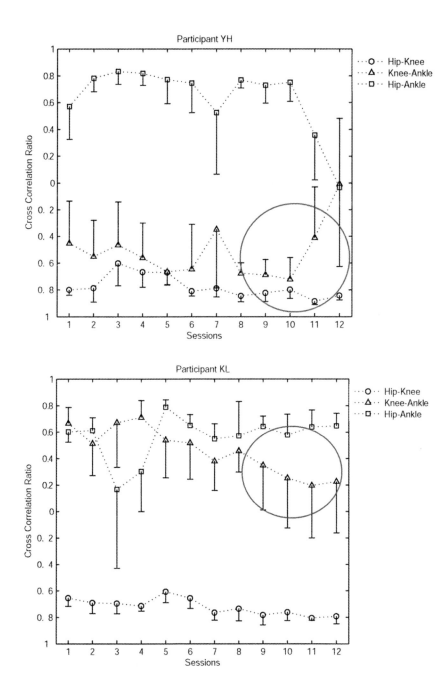

planting foot position also used an angled approach to the ball. Based on these observations, there seems to be an absence of an optimal kicking pattern for this task across all performers. Even though the task constraints were constant for all skilled participants, the performer constraints were different and the interaction mainly between the task and performer constraints allowed the establishment of different but functionally skilled movement behaviours.

Following this examination of skilled players, we sought to measure the change in co-ordination of kicking for novices as a function of practice under the same kicking task constraints (see Chow et al., 2008). Four male adult novices with little or no experience in football were recruited for the study. The novice participants had to undergo 12 sessions of practice over four weeks, with 40 trials per session. Similar to Chow et al. (2006), no explicit instructions on kicking technique were provided and the task goal was made known to the participants with a video clip.

Cross-correlation analysis was administered to determine how tightly coupled the joints (i.e. hip–knee, knee–ankle and hip–ankle) are with each other for all individual participants. High cross-correlation ratios suggests that the joints are tightly coupled and low cross-correlation ratios suggests that the joints are loosely coupled between the two joints. Figure 14.4 shows the cross correlations for the four novices as a function of practice sessions. From the figure, it was observed that there are no clear similarities in terms of the change in coupling between the joints among all four novices. For example, when knee–ankle cross-correlation ratios were compared (as highlighted by the circles), some participants started with loosely coupled joint relations before proceeding to tightly coupled joint relations, while some participants demonstrated otherwise.

While the route to success differed among the participants, all were equally successful by the end of the practice phase. This finding supports the concept that there are different functional learning pathways during the acquisition of successful kicking solutions under the same task constraints for different participants.

The programme of work shared in this section highlights how different constraints (especially task and performer in this instance) can result in the emergence of different goal-directed behaviours. Particularly, it was interesting to note that even for skilled players, there was no common optimal movement pattern and individual performer constraints can exist to channel the different players to search for their own functional movement solutions. Moreover, the data demonstrated how different individualised pathways of co-ordination can emerge for novices following the interaction of different constraints over an extended period of practice. The following Case Study will exemplify some practical implications for coaches to follow, aimed at the development of skilled perception and acquisition of functional co-ordination in association football.

Case Study: Development of skilled perception and functional co-ordination in football

Identify the problem

Developing a range of representative practice constraints for the acquisition of functional co-ordination and decision-making behaviours for learners in association football.

Setting

Junior football team.

Primary constraints

Performer (lack of experience), task (accurate perception of teammates to pass to and co-ordination pattern used to execute the pass).

At eight years of age, Simon loved football. He was always glued to the television watching matches with his father, before going into the back garden and recreating the game highlights by kicking a ball against the garage wall. James, Simon's father, recognised his son's appetite for the game and decided to take Simon along to play for a local junior team.

During his first game, Simon, like the other children, found it difficult to adapt to a game environment and playing in a team. Each child wanted possession of the ball, they chased around the pitch in a big group, getting in each other's way and even tackled their own teammates on occasions. Some of the parents did their best to encourage the children to "spread out", "find space" and "pass the ball" but this instruction had little positive effect. Simon, more than most, did his best to pass, but typically he kicked the ball as hard as he could to the first teammate he saw on the pitch, even if they were not looking at him or surrounded by other players. Osman, the team's coach, realised the children needed to significantly improve and learn a competent set of passing techniques that could be used correctly in game situations when teammates are in space and aware of the player's intention to pass.

At the start of the next training session, Osman split the children into groups of four and marked out a small square (10 m × 10 m). Osman gave a football to each group and asked the children to walk around the square and pass the football. "Try exploring different ways of passing the ball," he suggested. "Don't be afraid to make mistakes, try kicking the ball with different parts of your foot and see what works best for you," he said reassuringly. The children became comfortable performing within the initial task constraints so Osman decided to change the task slightly. He made the playing area bigger and instructed the children to begin jogging rather than walking. "You may need to try something different now. The area is bigger so you will need to kick the ball over longer distances and you will all be moving around at a faster pace." Osman continually encouraged the children to try new techniques without the fear of making mistakes, "Keep exploring different ways of passing. Do your best to make sure the pass is accurate and that it allows your teammate to receive the pass comfortably." At the end of training, the children were put into two teams and Osman said, "Try to remember what you've just learnt in practice. Look to pass the ball and don't be afraid of making mistakes." Osman emphasised, "I'm not going to tell you a right or wrong way of doing things, just do your best to express yourselves and enjoy playing".

With each training session over the season, Osman was consistent in his instruction to encourage the players to explore different techniques. He continually modified the task, changing the number of players in each group and altering the size and shape of the practice areas used as well as coaching instructions to encourage the children to focus on the outcome and task goal of the small-sided activities. In some conditions, he placed a series of different shaped targets within each area for the children to pass between, around, and over. He also began including a defender(s) into each area who would try to gain possession of the ball. The learning environment permitted the acquisition of functional movement solutions. Actions were coupled to information that supported the decision-making of appropriate passing options such as the force and trajectory required for a pass to reach a teammate without interception by an opponent.

Reciprocal to the development of different co-ordination solutions, the players learnt to pick up information that offered the opportunity to anticipate the intended kicking actions of their teammates. That is, the players began to couple their movements to the information that unfolded in a teammate's kicking action and thus they began to "read the game". For example, rather than responding to a pass direction once it had left the foot of a teammate, players were moving prospectively to place themselves at locations in the passing area in order to receive and control the pass. The instruction for players to continually move around the area meant that they were learning to act and create information about spaces on the pitch and player positions that would have been unavailable to them had they remained at the same pitch location. For instance, the players learnt to move to different locations within the passing area to produce passing options for a teammate if they were blocked by an opponent or an obstacle was placed in the task environment. The exposure to the variable kicking actions of teammates also meant that the players developed complementary perceptual skills that emphasized a variety of different information-movement couplings for variable kicking actions.

Where appropriate, Osman simplified task constraints to aid the children's learning if they found any aspects of the practice conditions difficult to cope with. Learning took time, but steadily the children began to improve in training and this transfer became evident in games as they started to show competence in constructing passing sequences. Towards the end of the season, James noticed that Simon was using both the inside and outside of his foot with considerable success. When next in possession, Simon flicked the ball over an opponent's head to create a shooting opportunity for his teammate. James looked across to Osman with pride in his son's ability and asked, "Did you teach him that?" Osman turned and smiled at James, "No, that's nothing to do with me. Simon's discovered that for himself!"

In summary, the above case study highlights the important role of a coach as a *facilitator* of learning. In this context, the coach may emphasise explorative learning by the players with encouragement of freedom of expression, whereby young players are encouraged to seek out different co-ordination solutions coupled to the representative simulation of perceptual information made available in the training context. Moreover, the coach can continually alter the task constraints to force players to adapt and learn alternative coordinative solutions to satisfy successful performance under differing conditions.

References

Araújo, D., Davids, K. & Passos, P. (2007). Ecological Validity, Representative Design, and Correspondence between Experimental Task Constraints and Behavioral Setting: Comment on Rogers, Kadar, and Costall (2005). *Ecological Psychology*, 19(1), 69–78.

Chow, J. Y., Davids, K., Button, C. & Koh, M. (2006). Organization of Motor System Degrees of Freedom during the Soccer Chip: An Analysis of Skilled Performance. *International Journal of Sport Psychology*, 37, 207–229.

Chow, J. Y., Davids, K., Button, C. & Koh, M. (2008). Co-ordination Changes in a Discrete Multi-articular Action as a Function of Practice. *Acta Psychologica*, 127, 163–176.

Davids, K. (in press). The Constraints-based Approach to Motor Learning: Implications for a Non-linear Pedagogy in Sport and Physical Education. In K. Davids, I. Renshaw & G. Savelsbergh (eds), *A Constraints-led Approach to Motor Learning: Designing Effective Practice*. London: Routledge, forthcoming.

Dicks, M., Button, C. & Davids, K. (in review). Ecological Constraints Shape the Visuomotor Behaviors of Association Football Goalkeepers in the Penalty Kick, *Attention, Perception & Psychophysics*, forthcoming.

Gibson, J. J. (1979). *The Ecological Approach to Visual Perception*. Boston, MA: Houghton Mifflin.

Lees, A. & Nolan, L. (2002). Three-dimensional Kinematic Analysis of Instep Kick under Speed and Accuracy. In W. Spinks, T. Reilly & A. Murphy (eds), *Science and Football IV*. London: Routledge, pp. 16–21.

Martell, S. G. & Vickers, J. N. (2004). Gaze Characteristics of Elite and Near-elite Athletes in Ice Hockey Defensive Tactics. *Human Movement Science*, 22(6), 689–712.

Putnam, C. A. (1983). Interaction between Segments during a Kicking Motion. In H. Matsui & K. Kobayashi (eds.), *Biomechanics 4B*. Champaign, Illinois: Human Kinetics, pp. 688–694.

Savelsbergh, G. J. P., Williams, A. M., van der Kamp, J. & Ward, P. (2002). Visual Search, Anticipation and Expertise in Soccer Goalkeepers. *Journal of Sports Sciences*, 20(3), 279–287.

Savelsbergh, G. J. P. & van der Kamp, J. (2000). Information in Learning to Control and Co-ordinate Movements: Is there a Need for Specificity of Practice? *International Journal of Sport Psychology*, 31, 467–484.

Vaeyens, R., Lenoir, M., Williams, A. M., Mazyn, L. & Philippaerts, R. M. (2007). The Effects of Task Constraints on Visual Search Behavior and Decision-making Skill in Youth Soccer. *Journal of Sport and Exercise Psychology*, 29, 147–169.

Williams, A. M. & Davids, K. (1998). Visual Search Strategy, Selective Attention, and Expertise in Soccer. *Research Quarterly for Exercise and Sport*, 69(2), 111–128.

Williams, A. M., Davids, K. & Williams, J. G. (1999). *Visual Perception and Action in Sport.* London: E. & F. N. Spon.

15 Identifying constraints on children with movement difficulties

Implications for pedagogues and clinicians

Keith Davids, Geert J. P. Savelsbergh and Motohide Miyahara

Introduction

A constraints-based framework for understanding processes of movement co-ordination and control is predicated on a range of theoretical ideas including the work of Bernstein (1967), Gibson (1979), Newell (1986) and Kugler, Kelso & Turvey (1982). Contrary to a normative perspective that focuses on the production of idealized movement patterns to be acquired by children during development and learning (see Alain & Brisson, 1996), this approach formulates the emergence of movement co-ordination as a function of the constraints imposed upon each individual. In this framework, cognitive, perceptual and movement difficulties and disorders are considered to be constraints on the perceptual-motor system, and children's movements are viewed as emergent functional adaptations to these constraints (Davids *et al.*, 2008; Rosengren *et al.*, 2003).

From this perspective, variability of movement behaviour is not viewed as noise or error to be eradicated during development, but rather, as essentially functional in facilitating the child to satisfy the unique constraints that impinge on his/her developing perceptual-motor and cognitive systems in everyday life (Davids *et al.*, 2008). Recently, it has been reported that functional neurobiological variability is predicated on system degeneracy, an inherent feature of neurobiological systems that facilitates the achievement of task performance goals in a variety of different ways (Glazier & Davids, 2009). Degeneracy refers to the capacity of structurally different components of complex movement systems to achieve different performance outcomes in varying contexts (Tononi *et al.*, 1999; Edelman & Gally, 2001). System degeneracy allows individuals with and without movement disorders to achieve their movement goals by harnessing movement variability during performance. Based on this idea, perceptual-motor disorders can be simply viewed as unique structural and functional system constraints, which individuals have to satisfy in interactions with their environments. The aim of this chapter is to elucidate how the interaction of structural and functional organismic and environmental constraints can be harnessed in a non-linear pedagogy by individuals with movement disorders.

Functional coupling of perception and movement: the role of constraints

Gibson's (1979) theory of direct perception emphasized the role of perceptual information as a major constraint on the co-ordination of action with environmental events, surfaces and objects. In direct perception information about objects, places and events in the environment are unambiguously specified, for example, by the change or persistence of optical patterns in the environment. Task practice and experience result in the acquisition of specific information-movement couplings that guide actions such as negotiating a cluttered environment or reaching for an object. During development, children have to learn to pick up and select the appropriate information that tailors an action in a specific task and individuals with movement difficulties may or may not have structural and functional variations to perceptual systems. Any structural alterations to perceptual systems, as a result of disease, disorder or injury, may require individuals to adapt their behaviours and to rely on different sources of information (Davids *et al.*, 2008). The functional variability exhibited by degenerate movement systems is an important way that individuals can adapt their actions to maintain performance consistency. An important role for researchers and practitioners is to search for the sources of information used by individuals in guiding their actions, and to understand how a disability may provide an organismic constraint in the coupling of information to actions. Subsequently, pedagogic programmes should be based on the design of learning environments that align the coupling of perceptual and motor systems, such as when a visual impairment requires better attunement of a learner to available acoustic or haptic information.

Bernstein (1967) formulated one of the central issues in the study of the development of motor co-ordination: the "degrees of freedom" problem, arguing that the complex interactions between the different components of the movement apparatus (i.e. muscles, tendons, joints etc.) make separate control of all these components impossible. Bernstein's ideas led to the recognition that, whether a child faces movement difficulties or not makes no difference to the problem of co-ordinating available degrees of freedom in adapting to environmental constraints. Children with and without movement difficulties face the same challenge of satisfying the unique constraints acting on them during development.

Constraints have been defined as boundaries or features, which interact to limit the form of biological systems searching for optimal states of organization (Newell, 1986). Given the potential for interaction between the degrees of freedom in degenerate movement systems, hypothetically, there are a number of functional organizational states that can be adopted in goal-directed movement behaviour. Constraints help to alleviate the co-ordination problem in dynamical movement systems by structuring the available state space and reducing the number of configurations available. With regards to movement difficulties, organismic constraints relate to the unique properties and characteristics of each individual. These constraints can be structural, such as a lesion impairing the visual system or a traumatic injury to the lower limb, or functional, such as a deficit in attentional processes. Task constraints relate to the specific activities undertaken by individuals in their environments, such as a visually-impaired child locomoting with a stick or interpreting a sign in braille. Finally, environmental constraints refer to physical (e.g. gravity) or social (e.g. societal expectations) factors that might shape the way individuals behave.

It is important to note that constraints should not be regarded as intrinsically negative, but as unique to each of us as individuals, and continually interacting to shape the emergence of perceptual-motor behaviour. In attempting to satisfy the constraints on them, individuals can harness variability in movements to produce functional and specific behaviours (Rosengren *et al.*, 2003). With respect to the theme of this chapter, the motor patterns observed in children with movement difficulties due to cerebral palsy, ataxia or tardive dyskinesia should not be viewed as dysfunctional, but as an emergent and functionally adaptive response to the interaction between unique organismic constraints with task and environmental constraints.

These ideas have significant implications for pedagogical practice involving children with perceptual-motor impairments. They have resulted in the development of a non-linear pedagogy (Chow *et al.*, 2007). Non-linear pedagogy is an approach to pedagogical and rehabilitation practice that is based on a model of the individual as a complex, non-linear dynamical system (Chow *et al.*, 2007). In non-linear dynamics it has been shown how complex neurobiological systems continuously adapt and change their organizational states by harnessing intrinsic processes of spontaneous self-organization (Kelso *et al.*, 1995; Newel *et al.*, 2008; Thelen & Smith, 1994). The property of system degeneracy supports the exploitation of inherent self-organization processes by non-linear neurobiological systems in satisfying organismic constraints, such as different types of perceptual-motor disorders, to interact with the environment. The aim of non-linear pedagogy is not to ensure that each individual complies with an "idealized motor pattern" for achieving functional behaviours. Instead, opportunities should be provided for specific individuals to functionally adapt their movements as they use inherent system degeneracy to seek individualized movement solutions to satisfy the unique constraints on them. In this respect, Kugler & Turvey (1987) argued that descriptions of goal-directed movement behaviour should focus on the functions of an action, not on the specific anatomical units involved because "... an act is functionally specific, its variability is in reference to preserving the function it fulfils rather than preserving any particular aggregation of body parts that it happens to involve" (p. 407). Such inherent system variability is functional in providing developing movement systems with the capacity to adapt movement solutions to a variety of different cognitive and perceptual-motor constraints.

During development, changes brought on by the interaction between environmental and organismic constraints lead to inter- and intra-individual variability. This type of movement system variability is central to the process of facilitating transitions from one developmental state to another. Next we elucidate findings from studies of children with movement difficulties that demonstrate that they have the capacity for functional adaptation to constraints, although the nature of the specific co-ordination solutions that emerge will differ from movement solutions observed in other children.

Emergent behaviour under constraints in children with movement difficulties

In order to perform mundane tasks like crossing a road safely, one needs to perceive the time-to-arrival of approaching traffic. An important informational constraint on this action is the temporal information directly specified in the optic array provided by a retinal image of an approaching car, as long as the velocity of the approaching object and the observer is constant. If one attempts to cross a road safely, the perceived approaching time of the oncoming traffic has to be longer than the time it takes to reach the far curb. Accordingly, the temporal information of approaching traffic has to be related to the pedestrian's own walking speed. Presumably, action-scaled information that relates temporal information of oncoming vehicles to the pedestrian's own walking speed is used to determine when a road affords crossing. Children with cerebral palsy (CP) regularly experience challenges in tasks such as getting themselves across the road in environments typically designed for able-bodied individuals. However, assistive devices, such as splints, crutches, and wheelchairs not only enable them to transfer themselves physically, by modifying their functional organismic constraints, but also safely, by adjusting their perception for the modified action.

Te Velde *et al.* (2004) studied whether children with CP could negotiate traffic as safely as their peers without CP. Problems in motor control have often been related to perceptual deficits (see Wilmut & Wann, 2008), which may complicate the perception of temporal and spatial properties of the environment, and can act as an additional impediment for safely crossing roads by CP children. The aim of the study by Te Velde *et al.* (2004) was to examine whether children with CP had the capacity to perceive safe traffic gaps in the context of actual road crossing. To perceive safe gaps, they needed to be able to perceive information that specifies time-to-arrival of approaching traffic, and, of course, the time-to-arrival of traffic had to be specified in terms of their own constrained walking abilities.

In the study by Te Velde *et al.* (2004) the basic capacity of children with CP to make safe decisions about crossing a single-lane road was assessed and compared to the performance of children without CP. Te Velde *et al.* (2004) used a simulated road on which a slowly approaching bike was moving at different speeds. Children were required to judge whether or not to cross the road, while standing still and while walking on the curbside. They were asked to cross the road if they thought the situation was safe. The basic capacity of children with CP to perceive and act according to temporal information in relation to their own abilities, required for safe participation in traffic, was examined in a natural, but safe manner.

Results showed that when road crossing was assessed in relation to the children's own walking abilities, in general, children with CP performed as safely as children without CP. This finding is in line with data from Savelsbergh *et al.* (1998) who found that children with CP were able to make similar decisions when scaled to their own abilities as other children when a task was actually performed. After making a distinction between children with left and right hemispheric lesions (LHL and RHL), Te Velde *et al.* (2004) found that children with RHL almost exclusively had difficulties in safely crossing the road. This subgroup made more unsafe decisions than children with LHL or non-disabled peers. Furthermore, children with RHL sometimes crossed the road when there was not sufficient time to cross safely, while they also remained on the curbside when gaps were safe to cross. This inconsistent behaviour was not observed in the other subgroup or in the non-CP group. Moreover, crossing time was not related to time-to-arrival of the oncoming bike. Children with RHL did not compensate for risky or unsafe decisions by walking faster. A possible explanation for this finding might be that these children were not able to perceive time-to-arrival of the bike accurately and therefore did not adjust crossing time (i.e. they did not see that they were crossing unsafely). Children with LHL, on the other hand, were able to make safe decisions like other children. In addition, LHL children adjusted their crossing time to time-to-arrival information from the approaching bike. Similar to children with RHL, the non-CP children did not adjust crossing time to time-to-arrival of the bike, but perhaps such adjustments were not necessary.

Concerning safety of decisions, Te Velde *et al.*'s (2004) findings suggested that children with LHL seemed able to make safe decisions for low-speed traffic approaching from one direction, and moreover, they tuned their crossing time to time-to-arrival of an oncoming object. Therefore, these children seemed to have the basic perceptual-motor capacity to visually adjust time for road crossing safely. On the other hand, the children with RHL made significantly more unsafe decisions than non-CP children and children with LHL. Because the children with RHL already experienced problems on this relatively simple task, their fundamental capacity to perceive whether a road was safe to cross might have been impaired. Accordingly, when crossing a real two-lane road they might experience even greater difficulties.

This study showed how damage to specific parts of the central nervous system (CNS) should be interpreted as unique structural constraints on movement behaviours of children. Caretakers, therapists and pedagogues should, besides training motor abilities and modifying instruments, pay attention to perception for action in children with movement difficulties. Sometimes, it is possible that structural organismic constraints, due to inordinate levels of CNS damage, can provide powerful limitations (i.e. RHL) on perception and action. But the data from this study clearly showed that, provided that CNS damage is not of inordinate magnitude to prevent CP children from performing a perceptual-motor task, successful learning design could involve opportunities to practice functionally specific behaviours in highly safe "real world" situations by relating perception and action. Training then should involve perceiving spatial and temporal properties of the environment in relation to the children's unique capacities to prevent them from ending up in unsafe situations.

Upper arm movements in children with spastic hemiparetic cerebral palsy

Children with mild to moderate spastic hemiparetic cerebral palsy (SHCP) can perform functional movements with their impaired and non-impaired arms (e.g. Van der Weel & Van der Meer, 1991; Van der Weel *et al.*, 1996). Since most children with SHCP are not able to fully stretch the impaired arm, and/or have problems with flexing/extending the knee or foot on the impaired side of their body, they are constrained to find solutions within their own action capabilities. There has been a limited number of studies on the intra-limb and inter-limb co-ordination of these functional reaching movements in children with SHCP. Research has shown that task context can be of great importance in improving movement performance in individuals with movement disorders or disabilities (Volman *et al.*, 2002; Wu *et al.*, 2000). In children with CP, it has been shown that functional and relevant task constraints are more effective for movement planning, increasing the range of motion and performing smoother movements (Steenbergen *et al.*, 2004; Volman *et al.*, 2002; Wu *et al.*, 2000). For instance, Van der Weel and Van der Meer (1991) showed that the range of motion of the impaired arm increased when children with SHCP were confronted with specific task constraints (e.g. to bang a drum with their hand), compared to a condition where they were given non-specific instructions (such as to "move as far as you can with your arm"). As well as the relevance of the task context, the nature of the timing constraints (i.e. whether the task is internally or externally paced) has been shown to influence the motor response of individuals with movement disorders or disabilities (e.g. Van Thiel *et al.*, 2000).

Recently, Ricken *et al.* (2005) examined how children with SHCP adapted the hemiparesis to their action systems. They studied how the kinematics of reaching, and the co-ordination and recruitment of degrees of freedom, were adapted when using the impaired arm compared to the non-impaired arm in children with SHCP. They also determined how the reach response of the impaired and non-impaired arms was influenced by a task that required interception of a stationary object (internally paced) or an approaching object (externally paced). Participants reached and grasped a ball with either their impaired or non-impaired arm. The ball was either stationary on a table (stationary ball condition) or rolled down an open tube (moving ball condition).

In line with predictions of the constraints-based framework, results clearly illustrated that children with SHCP were able to successfully achieve similar movement outcomes as controls, but with different movement patterns. SHCP participants showed longer deceleration time and movement times, and greater trunk contribution following decreased elbow and shoulder excursion when reaching with the impaired arm compared to the non-impaired arm. The co-ordination of joint angle pairs showed little linearity for the impaired arm, indicating more segmented movements of shoulder and elbow. Additionally, it was found that the co-ordination patterns between elbow, shoulder and trunk displayed less similarity when reaching with the impaired arm compared to the non-impaired arm in both stationary and moving ball conditions. Regardless of the timing constraints, children with SHCP were able to make successful interceptions when using the impaired arm, indicating that they co-ordinated and controlled their motor system degrees of freedom in a functional manner (see Table 15.1).

Children with SHCP used a different movement strategy to satisfy constraints of reaching with the impaired arm compared to the non-impaired arm, neatly illustrating how system degeneracy supported functional variability. This movement outcome was achieved by a prolonged movement time and deceleration time, and an increased trunk contribution, which might be related to the decreased elbow and shoulder excursion. The effect of the impairment was also evident in the continuous measures of joint co-ordination. Participants reached with a less linear and hence more segmented co-ordination of elbow excursion and shoulder flexion when using the impaired compared to non-impaired arm. In addition, the similarity of co-ordination was influenced by the arm used. Participants exhibited less similar co-ordination between elbow excursion and shoulder flexion, and

Table 15.1 Means of dependent variables (SD in parentheses) as a function of condition and arm. Data from Ricken *et al.* (2005). N.B.: TAPVX and TAPVY = time after peak wrist-velocity until the moment of contact) in the horizontal and vertical directions respectively; PVX and PVY = peak velocity in the horizontal and vertical directions respectively (all data in seconds).

Variable	Standing-stationary ball				Standing-moving ball			
	Impaired		Non-impaired		Impaired		Non-impaired	
Movement time (s)	1.18	(0.37)	0.96	(0.25)	1.03	(0.37)	0.81	(0.32)
TAPVX (s)	0.68	(0.33)	0.52	(0.21)	0.42	(0.19)	0.29	(0.14)
TAPVY (s)	0.88	(0.30)	0.68	(0.15)	0.65	(0.21)	0.56	(0.27)
PVX (m/s)	0.32	(0.23)	0.25	(0.21)	0.40	(0.16)	0.46	(0.20)
PVY (m/s)	0.49	(0.14)	0.53	(0.18)	0.45	(0.17)	0.53	(0.25)
Trunk rotation (°)	21.22	(9.95)	15.24	(7.82)	19.43	(11.72)	13.77	(5.81)
Trunk flexion (°)	18.92	(15.30)	15.76	(20.26)	14.74	(8.28)	10.25	(9.76)
Trunk lateral-flexion (°)	29.11	(25.38)	9.86	(9.81)	35.14	(29.25)	15.35	(11.42)
Elbow excursion (°)	69.71	(24.95)	79.31	(22.10)	59.57	(17.24)	73.01	(20.19)
Shoulder flexion (°)	26.78	(11.89)	31.84	(19.03)	25.83	(10.71)	29.63	(8.5)
Shoulder elevation (°)	11.24	(6.46)	8.32	(4.99)	18.12	(14.69)	9.77	(5.90)

elbow excursion and shoulder elevation in the stationary ball condition compared to a moving ball condition when reaching with the impaired rather than non-impaired arm. In other words, although participants maintained a similar type of co-ordination in the stationary and moving ball conditions when reaching with the non-impaired arm, they did not maintain the same co-ordination across the different task contexts when reaching with the impaired arm.

When the task context was externally paced and participants reached for a moving ball, there was less obvious modification to the discrete kinematic measures. Contrary to previous work with children without SHCP (see Ricken *et al.*, 2004), who deal with the impact demands of an approaching object by lengthening deceleration time and movement time, it was observed that children with SHCP exhibited a reduced deceleration time in the moving ball condition compared to the stationary ball condition. These findings demonstrated neatly how functional perception-action couplings can be achieved, depending on the task constraints.

Constraint-based approach in practice

DiRocco & Klein (2001) reported an outcome of a specific programme for children who had developmental delays in learning how to ride a two-wheel bicycle. Getchell & Gagen (2006) also demonstrated how to conduct a constraint-based task analysis for children with a wide variety of disabilities ranging from limb deficiency to cerebral palsy to attention deficit hyperactivity disorder. DiRocco & Klein (2001) reported that 75% of their studied sample succeeded in riding the bike after a week of daily two-hour interventions that considered the structure of the bike, gears, width of tires, the environment of practice, and motivational factors. Getchell & Gagen (2006) provided feasible examples of adapting tasks, equipment and environmental constraints to a variety of disabilities, in other words, structural and functional constraints of the individual. Although these papers have highlighted the potential usefulness of the constraint-based approach in designing therapeutic interventions, more work is needed to verify the advantages that this approach has over other popular intervention methods.

One example of how this evaluation work might be conducted was by Miyahara *et al.* (2008) who examined whether additional knowledge of the constraints-based approach over knowledge of the traditional information processing approach in student teachers would significantly impact on their capacity to enhance motor co-ordination of children with developmental co-ordination disorder (DCD). In that study, a total of 20 student teacher-child dyads were retrospectively selected from the 1996–2005 database of the Movement Development Clinic, a research and teaching laboratory at the School of Physical Education, University of Otago. Exclusion criteria of the children consisted of the presence of diagnosable neuromuscular disorders, mental retardation, pervasive developmental disorders, and missing data of the Movement Assessment Battery for Children (MABC; Henderson & Sugden, 1992) at intake or after the first eight-week intervention programmes. The diagnosis of DCD was made by a registered psychologist on the basis of DSM-IV TR (American Psychiatric Association, 2000).

Table 15.2 Demographic data and matching variables

	IP Only		IP+CB		
	n		n		
Boys	4		6		
Girls	6		4		
	M	SD	M	SD	p
Children's age	6.8	1.23	6.8	1.23	1.00
MABC % at intake	8.2	16.68	6.6	12.08	0.81

Undergraduate student teachers from 1997 to 2001 learned the traditional information-processing approach to motor learning and control and motor development while teaching children with DCD in the third or fourth year of a four-year bachelor degree curriculum. In addition to the traditional approach, the student teachers in 2003 and 2004 studied the constraints-based approach to motor control in the second year, and the constraints-based approach to motor development while teaching children with DCD in the third or fourth year of the same degree curriculum. Based on children's age and initial motor performance

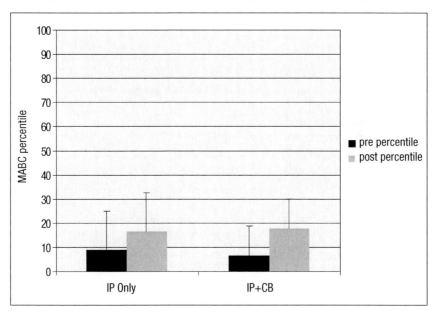

Figure 15.1 Percentiles on the Movement Assessment Battery for Children before and after intervention by student teachers. There are two categories of teachers: those with the knowledge of the information processing (IP) approach only and those who learned both the information processing (IP) approach and the constraints-based (CB) approach.

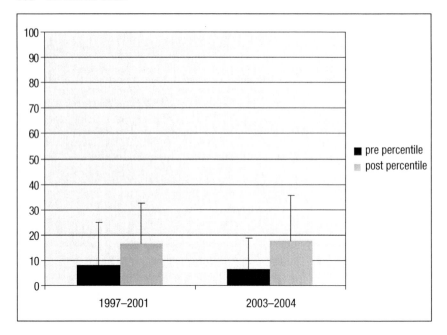

Figure 15.2 Proportion of student teachers with knowledge of both the traditional and the constraints-based approaches.

before intervention, 10 student teacher-child dyads out of 35 from 1996 till 2001 were matched with 10 student teacher-child dyads in 2003 and 2004. Table 15.2 shows demographic data and the means and standard deviations of matching variables.

Statistical analysis of the data yielded no significant interaction effects, and the main effect for intervention approached a statistically significant level, although the main effect for the group was not significant. Results indicated a lack of differential intervention outcome between those student teachers who only had knowledge of the traditional approach and those equipped with knowledge of both the traditional and the constraints-based approaches (See Figures 15.5 and 15.2). This finding is consistent with foregoing studies that failed to prove the effectiveness of a specific intervention technique over others (e.g. Miyahara, 1996; Miyahara & Wafer, 2004; Sims *et al.*, 1996) although all these intervention studies, including this study, demonstrated some substantial benefits of intervention. In that study, for example, the mean percentile of each of the two groups improved from below to above the cutoffs (2nd–15th percentile) for DCD.

It is possible that effective teachers, therapists and clinicians might have already been aware of the constraints on DCD children. The constraints-based approach allows professionals in the fields of disability and rehabilitation to be consciously aware of not only the service recipients' organismic constraints and task constraints, but also of the environmental constraints and the interaction between them by constraint-based task analysis (see Getchell & Gagen, 2006 for detail). Routine examinations of all three constraints are valuable, albeit not necessarily differentially effective, in planning and delivering services. To further expand awareness, it may be worth paying attention to Bronfenbrenner's (1989) ecological systems theory approach because this theory seems to be well utilized in special education, but not yet in rehabilitation settings.

Implications of research for a non-linear pedagogy

The research examples we have reviewed demonstrated that the movement patterns of children with movement difficulties should be viewed as functional adaptations to the unique and interacting constraints on each individual. The misconception of the existence of "common optimal movement patterns" is ubiquitous in the study of perceptual-motor disorders and has implications for clinicians interested in rehabilitation and movement disabilities. For example, in the area of disability studies, the implicit "medical model" or "disability as tragedy model" (see Barnes *et al.*, 2001), used by many clinicians has provided a unitary, internally determined perspective of health and movement behaviour in which variability, viewed as deviation from an "accepted" norm, is seen as dysfunctional and an index of abnormality. In this model, health and performance behaviours are identified as problems for the individual since they may deviate from what are perceived as population norms. As with early motor development literature, this approach suffers from a normative bias. Rather, an alternative view, in a non-linear pedagogical framework, is that variability in behaviour may be viewed as adaptation to unique organismic constraints such as genetic variations, perceptual-motor disorders, differences in CNS or motor system structure, or psychological characteristics. An implication of this view for clinicians is that behaviours exist on a spectrum characterizing the boundaries of naturally occurring variability.

The performance spectrum from "impaired" to "elite" movement performance needs to be understood in relation to the constraints on each individual (Latash & Anson, 1996). This is because the precise location that an individual movement system inhabits on the performance spectrum emerges from the multitude of constraints pressurizing it at specific points during the lifespan. Since the constraints on each individual are many and unique, it follows that movement solutions will differ within and between individuals in order to maintain functionality. As Latash & Anson (1996) noted, the "phenomena of variability of voluntary movements by themselves indicate that 'correct' peripheral motor patterns may form a rather wide spectrum" (p. 65). Latash & Anson (1996) proposed that adaptations to constraints should not necessarily be perceived as pathological since motor patterns may be optimal for the conditions affecting the individual's motor system at any given point in time. Typically, although motor patterns in individuals with cognitive, perceptual and motor deficits may be defined by some clinicians as "abnormal" in comparison to "common optimal motor patterns" idealized in the "medical model", they may be better viewed as functional and emergent under the confluence of constraints that each individual needs to satisfy.

Therefore, teaching of children with movement difficulties should not be directed towards the achievement and maintenance of an "ideal" movement pattern. The overarching aim of pedagogues should be to help individuals to satisfy the unique constraints on them and improving their functionality in the performance environment. This approach is likely to lead to the emergence of a range of movement patterns used to achieve similar performance outcome goals. Future studies are needed to understand how a non-linear pedagogy might benefit the practice of therapeutic and rehabilitation programmes and help in the evaluation of the efficacy of these programmes.

References

American Psychiatric Association. (2000). *Diagnostic and Statistical Manual of Mental Disorders*, 4th edn, Text Revision. Washington, DC: American Psychiatric Association.

Bernstein, N. A. (1967). *The Co-ordination and Regulation of Movements*. Oxford: Pergamon Press.

Brisson, T. A. & Alain, C. (1996). Should Common Optimal Movement Patterns be Identified as the Criterion to be Achieved? *Journal of Motor Behavior*, 28, 211–223.

Bronfenbrenner, U. (1989). Ecological Systems Theory. *Annals of Child Development*, 6, 187–249.

Chow, J.-Y., Davids, K., Button, C., Shuttleworth, R., Renshaw, I. & Araújo, D. (2007). The Role of Nonlinear Pedagogy in Physical Education. *Review of Educational Research*, 71, 251–278.

Davids, K., Button, C., & Bennett, S. J. (2008). *Dynamics of Skill Acquisition: A constraints-led approach*. Champaign: Human Kinetics.

DiRicco, P. & Klein, R. (2001). Dynamical Systems Approach to Bicycle Instruction. In M. Dinold, G. Gerber & T. Reinelt (eds) *"Towards a Society for All" – through Adapted Physical Activity. Proceedings of the 13th International Symposium for Adapted Physical Activity 2001*. Wien: Manz Verlag Schulbuch, pp. 462–465.

Edelman, G. M. & Gally, J. A. (2001). Degeneracy and Complexity in Biological Systems. *Proceedings of the National Academy of Science*, 98, 13763–13768.

Getchell, N. & Gagen, L. (2006). Adapting Activities for All Children: Considering Constraints can make Planning Simple and Effective. *Palaestra*, 22, 20–58.

Gibson, J. J. (1979). *The Ecological Approach to Visual Perception*. Boston: Houghton Mifflin.

Glazier, P. & Davids, K. (2009). Constraints on the Complete Optimization of Human Motion. *Sports Medicine*, 39, 15–28.

Henderson, S. E. & Sugden, D. A. (1992). *The Movement Assessment Battery for Children*. London: Psychological Corporation.

Kelso, J. A. S. (1995). *Dynamic Patterns: The self-organization of brain and behavior*. Cambridge, MA: MIT Press.

Kugler, P. N. & Turvey, M. T (1987). *Information, Natural Law, and the Self-assembly of Rhythmic Movement*. Hillsdale, NJ: Erlbaum.

Kugler, P. N., Kelso, J. A. S. & Turvey, M. T. (1982). On the Control and Co-ordination of Naturally Developing Systems. In J. A. S. Kelso & J. E. Clark (eds), *The Development of Movement Control and Co-ordination*. New York: John Wiley and Sons, pp. 5–78.

Miyahara, M. (1996). A Meta-analysis of Intervention Studies on Children with Developmental Co-ordination Disorder. *Corpus, Psyche et Societas*, 3, 11–18.

Miyahara, M. & Wafer, A. (2004). Clinical Intervention for Children with Developmental Co-ordination Disorder: A Multiple Case Study. *Adapted Physical Activity Quarterly, 21*(3), 281–300.

Miyahara, M., Yamaguchi, M. & Green, C. (2008). A Review of 326 Children with Developmental and Physical Disabilities, Consecutively Taught at the Movement Development Clinic: Prevalence and Intervention Outcomes of Children with DCD. *Journal of Developmental and Physical Disabilities, 20*(4), 353–363.

Morange, F. & Bloch, H. (1996). Lateralization of the Approach Movement and the Prehension Movement in Infants from 4 to 7 Months. *Early Development and Parenting, 5*, 81–92.

Newell, K. M. (1986). Constraints on the Development of Co-ordination. In M. Wade & H. T. A. Whiting (eds), *Motor Development in Children: Aspects of Co-ordination and Control*. Dordrecht: Martinus Nijhoff, pp. 341–360.

Newell, K. M., Liu, Y-T., & Mayer-Kress, G. (2008). Landscapes beyond the HKB Model. In A. Fuchs & V. K. Jirsa (Eds.), *Co-ordination: Neural, behavioral and social dynamics*. Berlin: Springer Verlag, pp. 27–44.

Ricken, A. X. C., Savelsbergh, G. J. P. & Bennett, S. (2004). Co-ordinating Degrees of Freedom During Interceptive Action in Children. *Experimental Brain Research, 156*, 415–421.

Ricken, A. X. C., Bennett, S. & Savelsbergh, G. J. P. (2005). Coordination of Reaching in Children with Spastic Hemiparetic Cerebral Palsy under Different Task Demands. *Motor Control, 9*, 357–371.

Savelsbergh, G. J. P., Davids, K., Van der Kamp, J. & Bennett, S. J. (eds) (2003). *Development of Movement Co-ordination in Children: Applications in the Fields of Ergonomics, Health Sciences and Sport*. London: Routledge.

Savelsbergh, G. J. P., Douwes-Dekker, L., Vermeer, A. & Hopkins, B. (1998). Locomoting Through Apertures of Different Width: a Study of Children with Cerebral Palsy. *Pediatric Rehabilitation, 2*, 5–15.

Savelsbergh, G. J. P., van der Kamp, J. & Rosengren, K. S. (2006) Functional Variability in Perceptual-motor Development. In K. Davids, S. J., Bennett, & K. M. Newell (eds), *Variability in the Movement System: A Multi-disciplinary Perspective*. Champaign, Illinois: Human Kinetics, pp. 185–198.

Skinner, B. F. (1974). *About Behaviorism*. New York: Knopf.

Sims, K., Henderson, S. E., Hulme, C. & Morton, J. (1996). The Remediation of Clumsiness. II: Is Kinaesthesis the Answer? *Developmental Medicine and Child Neurology, 38*(11), 988–997.

Steenbergen, B., Meulenbroek, R. G. J. & Rosenbaum, D. A. (2004) Constraints on Grip Selection in Hemiparetic Cerebral Palsy: Effects of Lesional Side, End-point Accuracy, and Context. *Cognitive Brain Research, 19*, 145–159.

Taub, E., Ramey, S. L., DeLuca, S. & Echols, K. (2004). Efficacy of Constraint-induced Movement Therapy for Children with Cerebral Palsy with Asymmetric Motor Impairment. *Pediatrics, 113*(2), 305–312.

Thelen, E. & Smith, L. B. (1994). *A Dynamic Systems Approach to the Development of Cognition and Action*. Cambridge, MA: Bradford.

Tononi, G., Sporns, O. & Edelman, G. M. (1999). Measures of Degeneracy and Redundancy in Biological Networks. *Proceedings of the National Academy of Science, 96*, 3257–3262.

Van der Meer, A. L. H., Van der Weel, F. R. & Lee, D. N. (1996). Gravitational Know-how in Neonates. *Scandinavian Journal of Psychology, 37*, 424–437.

Van der Weel, F. R. & Van der Meer, A. L. H. (1991) Effect of Task on Movement Control in Cerebral Palsy: Implications for Assessment and Therapy. *Developmental Medicine & Child Neurology, 33,* 419–426.

Van Hof, P., Van der Kamp, J. & Savelsbergh, G. J. P. (2002). The Relation of Unimanual and Bimanual Reaching to Crossing the Midline. *Child Development, 73,* 1353–1362.

Van Thiel, E., Meulenbroek, R. G. J., Hulstijn, W. & Steenbergen, B. (2000). Kinematics of Fast Hemiparetic Aiming Movements Towards Stationary and Moving Targets. *Experimental Brain Research, 132,* 230–242.

Velde, te, A. F., Savelsbergh, G. J. P., Barela, J. A. & Van der Kamp, J. (2003). Safety of Road Crossing in Children with Cerebral Palsy, *Acta Pediatrica, 92,* 1197–1204.

Volman, M. J. M., Wijnroks, A. & Vermeer, A. (2002). Effect of Task Context on Reaching Performance in Children with Spastic Hemiparesis. *Clinical Rehabilitation, 16,* 684–692.

Wilmut, K. & Wann, J. P. (2008). The Use of Predictive Information is Impaired in the Actions of Children and Young Adults with Developmental Coordination Disorder. *Experimental Brain Research, 191,* 403–418.

Wimmers, R. H., Savelsbergh, G. J. P., Kamp van der, J. & Hartelman, P. (1998). A Cusp Catastrophe Model as a Model for Transition in the Development of Prehension. *Developmental Psychobiology, 32,* 23–35.

Wu, C., Trombly, C., Lin, K. & Tickle-Degnen, L. (2000). A Kinematic Study of Contextual Effects on Reaching Performance in Person With and Without Stroke: Influences of Object Availability. *Archives of Physical Medicine and Rehabilitation, 81,* 95–101.

16 Augmenting golf practice through the manipulation of physical and informational constraints

Paul S. Glazier

Introduction

Over the years, the golf industry has flooded the market with a plethora of weird and wonderful practice tools and coaching aids. However, the vast majority of this equipment comes with nothing more than marketing hype promising a drastically improved game and few have been subjected to rigorous scientific analysis. Ubiquitous to many driving ranges and practice grounds around the world are the Explanar® Golf Training System and video feedback systems. In this chapter, I will evaluate the effectiveness of this teaching and training apparatus from a constraints-led, dynamical systems theoretical perspective.

The Explanar® Golf Training System

The Explanar® Golf Training System is a popular teaching and training aid endorsed by a number of reputable golf instructors, including, among others, Butch Harmon (ex-swing coach to World No. 1, Tiger Woods and current swing coach to World No. 2, Phil Michelson) and Peter Cowen. Indeed, Harmon regards the Explanar® Golf Training System as the "best training system I have seen in my 40 years as a teacher" (www.explanar.com). The apparatus, which consists of an adjustable circular hoop, a weighted roller, and a stance mat (see Figure 16.1), is designed to help golfers increase their distance and improve their accuracy and consistency by encouraging them to swing on their "optimal biomechanical swing plane" (www.explanar.com).

The swing plane concept was popularised by Ben Hogan in his famous text *The Modern Fundamentals of Golf* (Hogan, 1957) and is defined as an imaginary two-dimensional surface – extending from the centre of the golf ball through the sternum of the golfer – that the clubhead should travel on throughout the golf swing (see Figure 16.2). Users of the Explanar® Golf Training System are required to adjust the angle of inclination so that the outer edge of the circular hoop coincides with their "ideal" swing plane. Once they have taken up their correct stance inside the circular hoop, as guided by the stance mat, users are then required to swing the weighted roller whilst resting it on the outer edge of the circular hoop, enabling them to better "feel" their "correct" swing plane and to develop "muscle

Figure 16.1 The adjustable aluminium hoop, fin (Plane Fin™), roller (Power Roller™), and stance mat (Radial Stance Mat™) that comprises the Explanar® Golf Training System.

memory" (www.explanar.com).

In dynamical systems parlance, the circular hoop acts as a physical constraint, eliminating all other swing planes except the purportedly "optimal" swing plane. Theoretically, repetitive practice on the Explanar® Golf Training System promotes the development of deeper attractor regions in state space, leading to more robust movement solutions and greater stability of performance outcomes, particularly during perturbation (e.g. performing under pressure, inclement weather conditions, hilly terrain, etc.).

What the literature says about the Explanar® Golf Training System

Despite the plethora of testimonials endorsing the Explanar® Golf Training System, empirical support for this product is far less abundant. Indeed, only two scientific investigations examining the effectiveness of the Explanar® Golf Training System as a teaching and training aid have been published.

Building on previous work on the swing plane (Coleman & Rankin, 2005; Coleman & Anderson, 2007), Coleman & Ritchie (2008) compared swings performed using the roller on the Explanar® Golf Training System to normal swings using a golf club by a group (n = 8) of expert, single-figure handicap golfers.

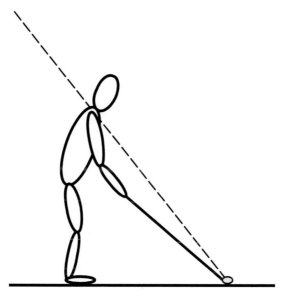

Figure 16.2 The swing plane concept was popularised by Hogan (1957) who suggested that it might best be visualised as a pane of glass inclined from the golf ball that rests on top of the shoulders. Over the years, the swing plane concept has been revised and now it is generally regarded to be an imaginary two-dimensional surface extending from the centre of the golf ball through the sternum of the golfer.

Image-based motion analysis was used to generate three-dimensional kinematic data (50 Hz) describing the motion of the club (6 iron) and roller from take-away to impact. Interpolating quintic splines were used to generate continuous time histories and better estimate the point of impact in both conditions. The digitised co-ordinates of the two markers affixed to the club and roller were entered into a multiple regression technique to calculate the swing plane in each condition (see Coleman & Anderson, 2007). The specific variables of interest were: angle of the swing plane to the horizontal, alignment of the swing plane to the target line, fit to plane (r^2) and fit to plane (RMS residuals). Average values for these variables during the backswing, downswing, and whole swing (i.e. the backswing and downswing combined) for the two conditions (normal vs Explanar® Golf Training System) were calculated and compared using inferential group mean difference statistics.

The results of this study revealed that no statistically significant differences existed between the swing performed on the Explanar® Golf Training System and normal swings with a golf club in the angle of the swing plane to the horizontal for any of the phases. However, there were statistically significant differences in the alignment of the swing plane to target line for all the phases, with the swing plane for the normal swing aligned more to the right of target than the swing plane for the Explanar® Golf Training System. The authors suggested that this finding might indicate that the Explanar® Golf Training System produces a different geometry of swing to a normal swing performed with a golf club. Conversely, it could be argued that these results may simply be an artefact of an incorrectly configured experimental setup. Although the authors argued to the contrary, citing favourable results from error assessments that they had conducted as part of their investigation, it is possible that these results had several determinants. They could be related to the alignment of the Explanar® Golf Training System, or to how the golfers aligned themselves in relation to the intended target, or a combination of the two.

In terms of the fit to plane variables, there were no statistically significant differences for any of the phases for the r^2, although the group data presented appeared to suggest that the single swing plane model fitted better to the normal swing with the golf club than to those performed on the Explanar® Golf Training System. Statistically significant differences were found in the RMS residuals, but only in the backswing phase, where they were lower in the normal swing condition than the Explanar® Golf Training System. However, as the authors note, it is only the motion of the club immediately prior to impact that determines the flight of the ball and analysis of consecutive club positions in the downswing revealed that golfers tended to be on a steeper plane approaching impact when swinging the golf club than when using the Explanar® Golf Training System. An issue not considered by the authors that could compromise the results of this study was the low sampling rate of their original data capture and the subsequent use of interpolation to effectively increase the number of (virtual) club positions. Clearly, further research utilising motion capture equipment of sufficiently high sampling rate (>200 Hz) is necessary to confirm these findings.

The only other published study to examine the Explanar® Golf Training System was by Bertram *et al.* (2008), who investigated the effects of kinesthetic practice on golf swing performance. In this study, 20 golfers were randomly assigned to either a self-guided or a kinesthetic group. The self-guided group was instructed to hit golf shots for 20 minutes without any kind of feedback except data on swing characteristics (club-head speed, club-face angle and tempo) produced by a launch monitor. The kinesthetic practice group were given 20 minutes practice on the Explanar® Golf Training System with verbal instruction. After a five minute warm-up period, a pre-test that involved golfers performing 12 shots on a launch monitor was conducted to determine baseline swing characteristics. Immediately following the 20 minute training sessions, each participant was asked to hit 12 shots on the launch monitor with a 5 iron (post-test 1). Following a 10 minute rest period, participants were requested to hit a further 12 shots on the launch monitor (post-test 2). A final testing session (post-test 3) was conducted one week later when all participants were asked to hit a further 12 shots on the launch monitor so that the long-term training benefits of being exposed to kinesthetic feedback via the Explanar® Golf Training System could be examined.

Statistical analyses of the launch monitor data indicated that there was a significant increase in the club-head speed in the kinesthetic practice group from the pre-test to the final post-test (no data provided). In contrast, there were no immediate changes in club-head speed for the self-guided group and, in fact, there was a slight decrease by the final post-test (no data provided). In terms of tempo, the kinesthetic group slowed significantly from the pre-test to the final post-test and the tempo variability (indicated by the standard deviation) also reduced. The self-guided practice group, on the other hand, had no statistically significant change of tempo from the pre-test to the final post-test and, indeed, it became increasingly more variable. There were no statistically significant differences in club-face angle at impact, although the general trend was that club-face angle variability increased slightly in the self-guided practice group across tests, whereas the club-face angle variability for the kinesthetic group decreased. The results of this study have since been used as empirical verification for the Explanar® Golf Training System and have featured prominently on the Explanar® website (see www.explanar.com).

A significant shortcoming of this study was that it was product-driven rather than process-driven. By focusing on outcome variables, the underlying movement dynamics were largely ignored.[1] Of course, one may argue, with some merit, that the method by which the outcome is achieved may be of little consequence providing the task goal is accomplished (see Wiren, 1990). However, the purpose of the Explanar® Golf Training System is to help facilitate changes in technique and encourage the adoption of the "optimal biomechanical swing plane", but as movement patterns were not analysed, the effectiveness of this apparatus in achieving this purpose could not be evaluated.

Is the Explanar® Golf Training System an effective coaching and practice tool?

The studies reviewed above are not only inconclusive in their assessment of the Explanar® Golf Training System but they also appear to be somewhat flawed in their methodologies. Consequently, they cannot be used to provide a definitive verdict either way about the suitability and effectiveness of the Explanar® Golf Training System as a coaching and practice tool.

From a constraints-led dynamical systems theoretical standpoint, the Explanar® Golf Training System might be useful during the initial stages of learning when the novice golfer is attempting to assemble a "ballpark" movement solution, as it acts as a physical constraint, thereby restricting or preventing superfluous movements of the golf club during the swing and encouraging the development of stable attractor regions. Furthermore, it may also help to reduce attentional demands in the early stages of learning. However, at more advanced stages of learning, the Explanar® Golf Training System should be used less frequently so that the golfer can explore and probe the boundaries of the "perceptuo-motor workspace" without restraint (see Newell *et al.*, 1989; Newell *et al.*, 1991; Newell & McDonald, 1992; Button *et al.*, 2008). It is important that more skilled golfers are allowed to "search and discover" their own unique movement solutions that better compliment their intrinsic dynamics[2] rather than having them forced upon them by overly restrictive physical constraints. Ultimately a naturally evolving technique is likely to have greater robustness when performing under pressure than an artificially enforced swing (see Masters, 1992).

These theoretical insights are consonant with a recent critique of the swing plane concept by Jenkins (2007), who suggested that there was not one single, or optimal, swing plane on which all golfers should swing the golf club. In fact, a quick survey of the golf-coaching literature seems to suggest that there is some degree of confusion about the definition of the swing plane with some renowned golf coaches arguing, for example, that it is simply an extension of the shaft at address (see Haney, 1986). Moreover, other coaching texts have advocated a "plane shift" during the golf swing, with the backswing following a more upright plane and the downswing following a shallower plane (see Leadbetter, 1990). Additionally, it is unclear whether the club-head, the shaft or the golfer's arms and hands should follow the plane. Considering the amount of conjecture surrounding what constitutes the swing plane, one could argue, as Cheetham (2007) did, that the swing plane concept is of little practical use so, therefore, by implication, neither is the Explanar® Golf Training System.

Video feedback technology

Possibly the most important contribution of technology to sports coaching over the past 30 years has been the advent and integration of video capture and playback facilities. High-definition digital video camcorders of ever-increasing sampling rates and sophistication are now readily available, as are purpose-built software applications such as cSwing®, V1 Pro Swing Analysis® and GASP Golf Swing Analysis®, which enable golf coaches to conduct frame-by-frame and semi-quantitative analysis of the golf swing almost in real-time *in situ* on the practice ground. However, is there any need for such fine-grained analyses of the golf swing? Is there any scientific evidence proving that video analysis leads to improvements in technique and performance?

In this section, I review the literature specifically related to the use of video feedback technology in the teaching and coaching of the golf swing. Owing to the plethora of theoretical and empirical studies that have considered video feedback in sport generally and the extensive reviews that have already been published on this topic (e.g. Liebermann *et al.*, 2002; Liebermann & Franks, 2008), I will only refer to this part of the literature where necessary.

What the literature says about video feedback in golf teaching and coaching

Comparatively few studies have examined the role and influence of video feedback in golf. Guadagnoli *et al.* (2001) set out to establish what type of feedback – verbal, video or a combination of the two – was most influential in teaching the golf swing. Forty-five apparently novice golfers participated in an initial pre-test that involved striking 15 golf balls with a 7 iron at a target 200 m away. "Accuracy distance" (AD) for each shot was calculated by subtracting the "error distance"

(ED) from "target distance" (TD) (see Figure 16.3 for definitions). Immediately after pre-test, a 20 minute instructional video about the grip, stance and swing mechanics was shown to each participant before they were randomly assigned to one of three experimental groups – verbal, video and verbal + video. The day following pre-testing, each participant hit 10 golf balls into a practice net with a 7 iron, which was followed by either verbal feedback from a qualified PGA teaching professional (verbal group), video feedback from high-speed video recordings (video group), or a combination of the two (verbal + video). This sequence was repeated four times so that 40 balls were hit in a single practice session and four practice sessions were conducted, separated by one day between each session where no practice was permitted. Once their four practice and feedback sessions had be completed, participants completed a post-test, which was identical to the pre-test.

No statistically significant differences in AD between the verbal, video and verbal + video groups for the pre-test were reported. However, the video and verbal + video groups performed significantly better than the verbal group during post-test, although there was no statistically significant difference between the video and verbal + video groups. There was also a statistically significant increase in AD between pre-test and post-test. However, the graphical representation of these results suggests that much of this difference was primarily attributable to large improvements for the video and verbal + video groups, with the verbal group only showing a very modest improvement. The results of this study suggest that video and verbal + video produces greater learning effects in novice golfers than verbal feedback, although the authors could not provide a convincing explanation as to why there was no significant difference between the video and verbal + video groups.

In a follow-up study, Guadagnoli *et al.* (2002) examined the efficacy of video instruction (i.e. practicing with the aid of a teacher or coach and video feedback) relative to that of verbal instruction (i.e. practicing with the aid of a teacher or coach) and self-guided instruction (i.e. practicing without the aid of a teacher or coach). Thirty experienced golfers (handicap range 7 to 16 strokes) volunteered to participate in this study and were randomly assigned to one of three experimental groups – video, verbal and self-guided. The research design used was the same as their previous study outlined above except that an additional post-test was introduced two weeks after the initial post-test. In addition, no instructional video was shown to the participants after the pre-test, presumably because they were already fairly accomplished golfers, and each of the four practice sessions lasted for 90 minutes in duration. In addition to calculating AD, variability of TD and ED were also calculated to determine consistency of performance.

No statistically significant differences in AD between the video, verbal and self-guided groups for the pre-test and the first post-test were reported. However, there was a statistically significant difference between the three groups on the second post-test, with the video group performing better than the verbal group, which, in turn, performed better than the self-guided group. Similar results were reported for variability of TD and ED. The authors concluded that these results indicate

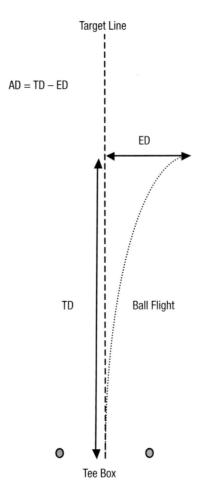

Target Line

AD = TD – ED

ED

TD

Ball Flight

Tee Box

Figure 16.3 Pre- and post-testing involved the calculation of "accuracy distance" (AD) by subtracting "error distance" (ED) from "target distance" (TD). ED was defined as the perpendicular distance from the initial ball-to-target line from where the ball landed and TD was defined as the distance where this perpendicular line bisected the initial ball-to-target line (adapted from Guadagnoli *et al.*, 2001).

that video instruction is an effective method of augmenting learning, although improvements in performance may take some time to develop.

In a more recent study, Bertram *et al.* (2007) combined and extended the previous two studies of Guadagnoli and colleagues. Of the 48 male and female golfers that were recruited for this study, half were considered novices (handicap ≥ 25) and the other half experts (handicap ≤10). An initial pre-test was conducted where each participant was required to hit 12 shots with a standard 6 iron into a practice net. Each stroke was captured on video and a launch monitor was used to calculate club-head speed at impact (CHS), club-face angle at impact (CFA) and tempo (T). Following the pre-test, each participant was randomly assigned to one of three experimental groups – verbal, verbal + video and self-guided. Participants in the verbal group were given 20 minutes of tuition from a qualified PGA teaching professional. During this period, each golfer was permitted to hit a maximum of 30 shots with the 6 iron used in the pre-test. Tuition provided by the teaching professional focused specifically on improving the quality and squaredness of the club-face at impact. Data obtained from the launch monitor was also available and used to supplement the coaching points being conveyed by the teaching professional. Participants in the verbal + video group followed the same procedure as the verbal group except that after their 5th, 10th, 15th, 20th and 25th shots, a video replay was shown of their preceding five shots. A set format was used for playing back video replays, which included replaying each shot: (1) three times at normal speed; (2) three times in slow motion with interactive commentary from the teaching professional; and (3) three times again at normal speed. Finally, participants in the self-guided group were permitted to hit 30 shots during their 20 minute practice session. No form of instruction was provided, although participants were allowed to view launch monitor data after each stroke. Approximately 20 minutes after their practice session, each participant was required to participate in a post-test, which was identical to the pre-test.

The results of this study showed that novice golfers in the verbal group significantly improved their club-head speed from pre-test to post-test, whereas neither the verbal + visual or the self-guided group showed any significant changes. In contrast, only expert golfers in the self-guided group showed any significant improvements in club-head speed from pre-test to post-test. No significant changes in club-head speed variability were observed across skill level or feedback conditions. In terms of club-face angle, verbal feedback significantly improved the squaredness and consistency of the club-face angle at impact for novice golfers. However, verbal + visual feedback had the opposite effect for novice golfers, causing a significant reduction in the squaredness and consistency of the club-face angle at impact. No significant changes were reported across feedback conditions for club-face angle and club-face angle variability for expert golfers. Finally, no significant differences in tempo were observed in any of the feedback groups for novice golfers, whereas expert golfers in verbal + video feedback group showed a significant slowing of tempo between pre-test and post-test. In terms of shot-to-shot tempo variability, there was a significant increase in consistency between pre-test and post-test for novice golfers in the verbal group. However, verbal + video feedback significantly reduced the consistency of tempo in novice golfers, although the opposite was true for expert golfers.

Despite the inherent limitations and lack of clarity of this study, it appears that novice golfers benefit more from verbal feedback than expert golfers. Conversely, expert golfers appear to benefit more from verbal + video feedback than novice golfers, which seemed to help slow, and make more consistent, their tempos. Self-guided instruction, according to this study, does not appear to lead to any substantial improvements in performance, which seems to be at odds with the literature on discovery learning (see Vereijken & Whiting, 1990).

A word of caution on the use of video feedback

Although not as unequivocal as some golf coaches may envisage, the preceding review of the work of Guadagnoli and colleagues provides some evidence that video feedback may be useful in the coaching process and could lead to improvements in performance. However, from a constraints-led dynamical systems theoretical perspective, caution should be applied when using video feedback technology. The main issue appears to be the implicit or explicit use of criterion models or templates of the "perfect" golf swing as a basis for detecting faults and directing remedial action (see also Sherman *et al.*, 2001). Many instructional texts advocate a standard grip, stance, backswing, downswing and follow-through that are generally considered to characterise the "ideal" golf swing. Indeed, support for this "one-size-fits-all" approach has even been forthcoming in the scientific literature. For example, Mann & Griffin (1998) produced a computer-generated model of the best features of the golf swings of over 100 US PGA, LPGA and Senior PGA tour players, which has since been promoted as *the* template or criterion golf swing that *all* golfers should aspire to achieve. However, owing to the unique confluence of constraints acting to shape and guide the co-ordination patterns of individual golfers, it could be argued, from a dynamical systems theoretical standpoint, that the "perfect" golf swing does not exist (Glazier & Davids, 2005). Accordingly, rather than using video feedback technology to compare the golf swings of specific individuals to those of leading tournament professionals in a bid to replicate their perceived picture-perfect form, it should primarily be used to improve the application, and increase awareness, of general mechanical principles as they relate to the golf swing (Button, 2008).

Conclusion

In this chapter, I have reviewed two of the most used (and sometimes abused) teaching and training aids in golf. Both the Explanar® Golf Training System and video feedback technology might be useful in helping golfers improve their games but it is important that they are used sparingly and in the correct manner to maximise motor learning and performance benefits. Over-reliance on the Explanar® Golf Training System or video feedback technology, or any other coaching and practice tool for that matter, may adversely affect motor learning and performance because they may prevent golfers from fully exploring their "perceptuo-motor workspace". Theoretical insights presented in this chapter suggest that "manufacturing" or "cloning" golf swings by using artificial mechanical devices or attempting to mimic the technique of a champion performer, respectively, may not be the most efficient or effective ways to learn how to play golf. Indeed, the development of a golf swing that is not consonant with the unique intrinsic dynamics of the individual golfer could be prone to breaking down in certain performance contexts (e.g. when performing under pressure in competition, during inclement weather conditions etc.) owing to lack of robustness.

Notes

1 This problem is not new. Indeed, a previous investigation by Yost *et al.* (1976) of the "Golfer's Groove" – a similar, but now defunct, training aid – had comparable issues focusing solely on outcome scores that may not have been valid (see Skrinar & Hoffman, 1978).
2 The term intrinsic dynamics is used here to refer to the spontaneous co-ordination tendencies or preferred modes of co-ordination that exist in the movement system at the start of the learning process (Corbetta & Vereijken, 1999).

References

Bertram, C. P., Grosser, L. & Guadagnoli, M. A. (2008). Getting the "Feel" for It: The Effects of Kinesthetic Practice on Golf Swing Performance. In D. Crews & R. Lutz (eds), *Science and Golf V*, Mesa, AZ: Energy in Motion, pp. 279–285.

Bertram, C. P., Marteniuk, R. G. & Guadagnoli, M. A. (2007). On the Use and Misuse of Video Analysis. In S. P. Jenkins (ed.), *Annual Review of Golf Coaching*, Brentwood, UK: Multi-Science Publishing pp. 37–46.

Button, C. (2008). Enhancing Skill Acquisition in Golf – Some Key Principles. *ISBS Coaches' Infoservice*. Available online at: http://www.coachesinfo.com (accessed 21 June 2009).

Button, C., Chow, J.-Y. & Rein, R. (2008). Exploring the Perceptuo-motor Workspace: New Approaches to Skill Acquisition and Training. In Y. Hong & R. Bartlett (eds) *Handbook of Biomechanics and Human Movement Science*, London: Routledge, pp. 538–553.

Cheetham, P. (2007). Golf Coaching and Swing Plane Theories: A Commentary. In S. P. Jenkins (ed.), *Annual Review of Golf Coaching*, Brentwood, UK: Multi-Science Publishing, pp. 23–24.

Coleman, S. G. S. & Ritchie, S. (2008). Mathematical Comparison of Swing Planes with and without the Explanar® Trainer. In D. Crews & R. Lutz (eds), *Science and Golf V*, Mesa, AZ: Energy in Motion, pp. 263–269.

Coleman, S. G. S. & Anderson, D. (2007). An Examination of the Planar Nature of Golf Club Motion in the Swings of Experienced Players. *Journal of Sports Sciences*, 25, 739–748.

Coleman, S. G. S. & Rankin, A. J. (2005). A Three-dimensional Examination of the Planar Nature of the Golf Swing. *Journal of Sports Sciences*, 23, 227–234.

Corbetta, D. & Vereijken, B. (1999). Understanding Development and Learning of Motor Co-ordination in Sport: The Contribution of Dynamic Systems Theory. *International Journal of Sport Psychology*, 30, 507–530.

Glazier, P. S. & Davids, K. (2005). Is There such a Thing as a "Perfect" Golf Swing? *ISBS Coaches' Infoservice*. Available online at: http://www.coachesinfo.com (accessed 21 June 2009).

Guadagnoli, M. A., McDaniels, A., Bullard, J., Tandy, R. D. & Holcomb, W. R. (2001). The Influence of Video and Verbal Information on Learning the Golf Swing. In P. R. Thomas (ed.), *Optimising Performance in Golf*, Brisbane: Australian Academic Press, pp. 94–103.

Guadagnoli, M., Holcomb, W. & Davis, M. (2002). The Efficacy of Video Feedback for Learning the Golf Swing. *Journal of Sports Sciences*, 20, 615–622.

Hall, M., Colclough, S., MacBeth, J. & Currie, S. (2008). The Effectiveness of Two

Commercial Golf Swing Training Aids in Teaching Beginning Golf. In D. Crews & R. Lutz (eds), *Science and Golf V*, Mesa, AZ: Energy in Motion, pp. 286–292.

Haney, H. (1986). The Robot Swing. *Golf Monthly*, 3, 45–50.

Hogan, B. (1957). *The Modern Fundamentals of Golf*. London: Kaye & Ward.

Jenkins, S. P. (2007). Golf Coaching and Swing Plane Theories. In S. P. Jenkins (ed.), *Annual Review of Golf Coaching*, Brentwood, UK: Multi-Science Publishing, pp. 1–19.

Leadbetter, D. (1990). *The Golf Swing*. London: Collins Willow.

Liebermann, D. G. & Franks, I. M. (2008). Video Feedback and Information Technologies. In M. Hughes & I. M. Franks (eds), *Essentials of Performance Analysis: An Introduction*, London: Routledge, pp. 40–50.

Liebermann, D. G., Katz, L., Hughes, M. D., Bartlett, R. M., McClements, J. & Franks, I. M. (2002). Advances in the Application of Information Technology to Sport Performance. *Journal of Sports Sciences*, 20, 755–769.

Mann, R. & Griffin, F. (1998). *Swing Like a Pro: The Breakthrough Scientific Method of Perfecting Your Swing*. New York: Broadway Books.

Masters, R. S. W. (1992). Knowledge, Knerves and Know-how: The Role of Explicit Versus Implicit Knowledge in the Breakdown of a Complex Motor Skill under Pressure. *British Journal of Psychology*, 83, 343–358.

Newell, K. M. & McDonald, P. V. (1992). Practice: A Search for Task Solutions. In R. W. Christina & H. M. Eckert (eds), *Enhancing Performance in Sport: New Concepts and Developments*, Champaign, Illinois: Human Kinetics, pp. 51–59.

Newell, K. M., Kugler, P. N., van Emmerik, R. E. A. & McDonald, P. V. (1989). Search Strategies and the Acquisition of Co-ordination. In S. A. Wallace (ed.), *Perspective on the Coordination of Movement*, Amsterdam: North-Holland, pp. 85–122.

Newell, K. M., McDonald, P. V. & Kugler, P. N. (1991). The Perceptual-motor Workspace and the Acquisition of Skill. In J. Requin & G. E. Stelmach (eds), *Tutorials in Motor Neuroscience*, Dordrecht: Kluwer, pp. 95–108.

Sherman, C. A., Sparrow, W. A., Jolley, D. & Eldering, J. (2001). Coaches' Perceptions of Golf Swing Kinematics. *International Journal of Sport Psychology*, 31, 257–270.

Skrinar, G. & Hoffman, S. (1978). Mechanical Guidance of the Golf Swing: The Golfer's Groove as an Instructional Adjunct. *Research Quarterly*, 49, 335–341.

Vereijken, B. & Whiting, H. T. A. (1990). In Defence of Discovery Learning. *Canadian Journal of Sports Sciences*, 15, 99–106.

Wiren, G. (1990). Laws, Principles and Preferences: A Teaching Model. In A. J. Cochran (ed.), *Science and Golf I: Proceedings of the First World Scientific Congress of Golf*, London: E & F. N. Spon, pp. 3–13.

Wiren, G. (2007). Golf Coaching and Swing Plane Theories: A Commentary. In S. P. Jenkins (ed.), *Annual Review of Golf Coaching*, Brentwood, UK: Multi-Science Publishing, pp. 21–22.

Yost, M., Strauss, R. & David, R. (1976). The Effectiveness of the Golfer's Groove in Improving Golfers Scores. *Research Quarterly*, 47, 569–573.

17 Skill acquisition in dynamic ball sports

Monitoring and controlling action-effects

Nicola J. Hodges and Paul R. Ford

Introduction

One of the central issues for theories of motor control is to account for how humans constrain the many degrees of freedom of the motor system (i.e. independent dimensions of the body that are free to vary, such as joints and muscles) to produce relatively complex actions. Initiating actions by anticipation of their sensorial effects (or action-effects) has been forwarded as a simple and economic way to automatically constrain the limbs into organized voluntary action (Kunde *et al.*, 2004). Dynamic ball-sports skills have naturally available external action-effects, such as ball-flight information in kicking. These actions also take place in environments that are rich in information, such as in a soccer match where the movements of opponents and other teammates serves to constrain the choice of action. The external effects of an athlete's own actions, the external performance environment, and variables within that environment act as task constraints upon performance. We review a number of studies where we and others have examined how external action-effect information (e.g. ball trajectory) and external action-percept information (e.g. visual monitoring of other players) constrain action. Although the majority of this research has been conducted in relatively controlled, laboratory-based tasks, in order to allow isolation of critical performance features, we attempt to contextualize the findings of this research for sport. We discuss the implications of this research for coaches and practitioners, particularly those involved in invasion, net, target and field sports.

A number of theoretical approaches have underpinned our program of research and have influenced how researchers view action planning and execution. The important approach is that of the common-coding hypothesis of Prinz (1997). This theory is based on the ideomotor hypothesis of James (1981) and it is related to the "theory of event coding" (Hommel, 2004). The major assumption of the common-coding (and related), hypothesis (es) is that perceptual and action codes are represented according to a shared neural code for action and perception. In this way, the association between an action and its sensorial effect(s) is bi-directional. Anticipation of an action's effect (i.e. its perceivable consequences) facilitates the initiation and execution of the action itself. The predictions of this theory have been confirmed in a number of laboratory-based, relatively simple tasks. For example, incidental auditory tones have been paired with finger responses and then after a period of practice the consequential tone acts to elicit the associated finger response (see Kunde, 2001; Kunde et al., 2002; Kunde et al., 2004). Some of these researchers have gone on to show that the associations between an action and its sensorial effects become stronger as a performer accumulates more hours in practice and becomes more skilled (see Drost et al., 2005; Koch et al., 2004). Koch et al. (2004) state that "practice at a skill makes the performer more sensitive to the produced action-effects, so that they can imagine and anticipate these effects more vividly as well" (p. 371).

External control of action

Some of the implications of the above research for skill acquisition in sport have been shown in a series of studies conducted by Gabriele Wulf and colleagues (for a review, see Wulf, 2007). In various tasks and sports skills, including throwing, hitting, balancing and jumping, Wulf has shown that people acquire skills more effectively when they have their attention focused on the effects of their action, rather than their own movements. For example, Wulf & Su (2007) had novice golf players practice a 9 iron shot to a target. Participants in three groups were first given basic instructions regarding stance, posture and grip. Two of the groups were given further instruction that directed them toward the motion of the club (external) or the motion of their arms (internal). In a retention test one day later, the external group was more accurate than the control and internal groups, who did not differ from each other. This finding replicated previous research showing the advantages of an external-focus of attention for skill acquisition over an internal focus or no instruction. In a second experiment, Wulf & Su (2007) also demonstrated the same performance advantage as a result of an external, or action-effects related, focus of attention for expert golfers.

One explanation for the advantage of an external-focus of attention is that it helps to promote a more automatic mode of movement control, whereas an internal focus causes individuals to intervene in processes that are believed to operate more effectively outside of conscious control. This has been termed the constrained-action hypothesis (McNevin et al., 2003). This hypothesis carries the implicit assumption that irrespective of the stage of learning, an automatic, or more proceduralized mode of control is beneficial to performance.

Skill dependencies

Skill-based differences in performance as a function of attention-directing cues or instructions have been shown by a number of authors (see Beilock et al., 2002). This research contradicts some of the findings (Wulf & Su, 2007) and conclusions of Wulf and colleagues, showing that experience moderates or even reverses the effects seen among novice learners. Novice performers have been shown to benefit from instructions that direct them to attend to the step-by-step control of the skill, or at least have performed better under these conditions than ones where their attention is directed externally. These researchers have argued that an external action-effects focus, defines more expert performance, as a result of the performer having proceduralized knowledge, which enables performance to run relatively automatically under reduced levels of conscious control. For example, Beilock *et al.* (2002) had novice and skilled soccer players dribble a ball through a slalom course. Participants performed the task with their dominant foot and again with their non-dominant foot under two conditions. Under skill-focused conditions they were prompted to focus on the side of the foot that last made contact with the ball. Under dual-task conditions they were prompted to monitor auditory words. Skilled players were faster than novices. Novices performed best under skill-focus (a more internally directed condition) compared to dual-task conditions (i.e. external monitoring). Experts with their dominant foot performed best under dual-task conditions, but with their non-dominant foot they behaved more like novices. Ford *et al.* (2005) also showed that the skill-dependent nature of the instructions mattered more than the attentional focus encouraged by the instructions (also Castenada & Gray, 2007).

One major limitation in studies where skill-based differences as a function of attentional-focus have been examined is that the majority of these research designs have been performance- rather than learning-oriented. Therefore, these designs only allow conclusions about the short-term effects of attention cues and instructions. In comparison, the majority of research by Wulf and colleagues has assessed learning as a result of specific instructions administered over many practice trials and following a short retention interval. In these learning studies, it may be the case that performers are allowed to adapt to the task constraints (i.e. the instructions) over multiple trials and progress to a new level of performance. What we think is of primary interest is not where attention is directed so much as what source of information most effectively constrains the action to bring about optimal performance and learning. Do, or can, performers, at all levels of skill, use action-effects' related information to plan, execute and modify their actions?

Action-effects

In our research, we wanted to know whether realistic action effects (e.g. trajectory of a ball) can help to beneficially constrain and foster learning among novice performers, or whether practice experience and skill are necessary to effectively use this information to plan, initiate and execute actions. In a first study we examined whether ball flight information acts as a beneficial constraint on novice action that brings about the acquisition of a soccer chip shot (Hodges *et al.*, 2006). Two groups who received either traditional movement form demonstrations or demonstrations of the desired ball flight were compared (both recorded from a well-practiced task expert). In both cases, the demonstration was coupled with response-produced feedback about either the person's action or their actual ball flight. Ball flights and outcome information were occluded during the shot through visual occlusion goggles, but both groups were shown where the ball landed in practice. Video cameras were positioned to record either a side-on view of ball flight (from toe release), or the action (up to ball-toe release), and these videos were projected onto a full size screen positioned to the side of the kicker and shown in between select trials. The ball flight demonstration was shown to be a beneficial learning strategy for novices in comparison to demonstrations and feedback about movement form. This effect was most pronounced during retention testing and there were no differences between the groups in terms of movement form.

In subsequent studies we have attempted to determine the importance of action-effects information for performance through the manipulation (i.e. removal and perturbation) of this sensorial information. Novice, intermediate, and skilled soccer players (as determined through playing level and years of experience) performed a modified soccer chip task with the intention of getting the ball over a height barrier to a near or far ground-level target (Ford *et al.*, 2006). This action was similar to that required during match-play, such as when making short and accurate passes or shots while overcoming a defender or goalkeeper. As illustrated in Figure 17.1, the removal of vision of the ball trajectory resulted in increased radial error (RE), in a skill-level-dependent manner. Contrary to our original expectations, the skilled players were not affected by the removal of ball vision. In contrast, intermediate and novice players performed less accurately when ball-flight information was removed. We concluded that skilled players may have developed the ability to maintain performance when vision was not available by imaging the action-effects and/or by relying on other sources of sensory information to perform the action, such as proprioceptive feedback.

Because of the lack of evidence showing that skilled performers were more

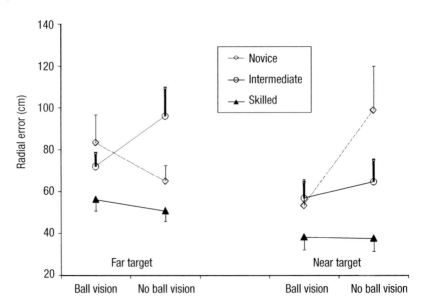

Figure 17.1 Mean (and Standard Error) radial error (cm) across the two vision conditions (ball vision and no ball vision) as a function of group and target (adapted from Ford *et al.*, 2006).

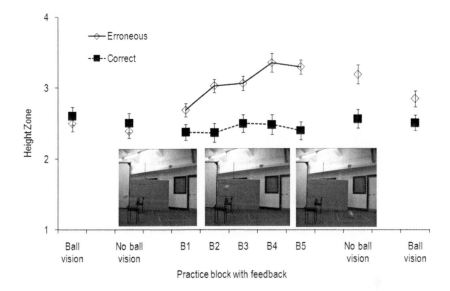

Figure 17.2 Mean apex of ball trajectory (and Standard Error) in terms of height zone for the two ball feedback groups (erroneous and correct) during the 2 pre-test blocks (with and without vision of the ball), 5 experimental feedback blocks (B1–B5), and 2 post-test blocks (with and without ball vision). An illustration of the ball trajectory information provided as feedback to participants via a large video screen is shown at the bottom of the figure. (adapted from Ford *et al.*, 2007).

attuned to external action-effects, a second study was conducted to determine whether skilled soccer players use ball trajectory information to plan and modify their movements when it is available (Ford *et al.*, 2007). Skilled players only kicked a ball to a target area using a lofted pass or chip shot in order that they would additionally clear a height barrier. Vision was occluded after the kick, preventing knowledge of ball flight information and outcome success. On approximately one third of all trials video feedback was provided pertaining to the flight of the ball and landing accuracy. Participants were assigned to one of two groups: correct or erroneous ball flight video feedback. For both groups, the ball was always shown landing in the actual achieved target zone (i.e. it was correct). However, for the erroneous group, the apex of the ball was always shown to be lower than actually achieved on that trial. As a result of the erroneous ball-flight feedback, participants adjusted their actions across trials, causing a significant bias toward higher ball trajectories and more target failures compared to the correct group. Figure 17.2 shows the mean apex of ball trajectory in terms of height zone for the erroneous and correct feedback groups across trial blocks. These two studies show that skilled performers use ball trajectory information to execute actions when it is available (even if it is incorrect). However, they are not reliant on this information and can perform as accurately when it is not available.

In a final study, when participants were asked to plan their actions in terms of their anticipated movements (i.e. the actual actions) or in terms of their anticipated effects (i.e. ball flight), both novice and skilled performers showed benefits from this latter type of action-effects planning (Ford et al., 2009). When visual feedback of outcome was withheld, using visual occlusion goggles that occluded ball flight as soon as the ball was kicked, accuracy was greater in effects' focus compared to movement focus. However, when vision was allowed, there was no difference between these two conditions and in a second experiment these outcome differences were not replicated. The skilled performers reported that planning their actions in terms of their anticipated effects was more "natural" than planning in terms of movement form. In general, skilled athletes in soccer use this action-effects information to constrain their actions, but they are not dependent on its physical presence for accurate performance.

Action-percepts

An extensive literature base exists to demonstrate systematic differences in the visual search behaviours of skilled soccer players during gameplay compared to less-skilled performers. Skilled players tend to fixate more on what have been deemed "informative" areas of the visual display (such as key attacking players) and show a different search pattern to less skilled players (for reviews, see Hodges et al., 2007; Williams et al., 1999). Systematic differences between experts and novices have been shown in relation to key variables, such as fixation duration, number of fixations, and the proportion of time spent fixating different areas. When playing soccer this visual search involves players gathering information from the performance environment with respect to their own location, the location and movements of teammates, the opposing team, and the ball. We term this information *external action-percepts*. Action-percepts differ to action-effects in that percepts are not caused by the individual performer, yet nevertheless they constrain the performers' actions.

During gameplay, soccer players must conduct this visual search often whilst performing soccer-specific motor skills, such as dribbling the ball. Hence it makes sense that actions become coupled or constrained by what we term external action-percept information. As detailed above, there have been a number of studies showing that skilled soccer players are able to dual-task, effectively focusing on the external environment without disrupting performance of their primary task (i.e. dribbling). There has also been evidence that visually-based, external monitoring is a characteristic of expert performance when performing sport-specific motor skills. For example, Smith and Chamberlin (1992) showed that skilled soccer players were not affected when dribbling a soccer ball through a slalom course even though they were required to simultaneously identify projected geometric shapes. However, this task did harm the dribbling of novice players.

The ability of skilled soccer players to dual-task (e.g. dribble or kick when vision is directed externally) appears to be acquired through the need for players in a soccer match (and other team sports) to use vision to constantly gather information from the external performance environment to dictate action. When playing soccer, the performer's vision and attention is often directed away from their own movements and the ball. Hence, we propose that skilled soccer players who have spent many hours playing soccer use a combination of both these information sources (i.e. action-effects and action-percepts) to plan, initiate and execute their actions in gameplay, but can perform successfully when these information sources are diminished or one is not available. The ability to quickly plan, initiate and execute an action based on the external surroundings is of course a significant advantage in dynamic ball games. In less dynamic, time-constrained situations, such as hitting a ball onto the green in golf, anticipation of an action-effect is more likely to dominate or constrain the action.

Practical implications

Action-effects

External action-effects do not contain prescriptions for the learner in terms of a correct co-ordinated movement solution (which is what an internal-focus instruction typically does). They leave the learner with options for finding a movement solution that is optimal to achieve the goal and for their individual characteristics (e.g. height, skill level). The desired effects are reinforced and the learner is able to adjust their movements accordingly to match the desired goal. In this way, various co-ordination solutions within a single class of movements (e.g. tennis backhand shot) are found in order to achieve the desired goal. In comparison, more traditional prescriptive methods of instruction require the learner to minimize variability within a class of movements. Although not empirically verified, there is suggestion that this experience of various motor solutions to achieve a desired target outcome is actually the more robust method of learning (Schöllhorn *et al.*, 2006). In research where one of us has examined how people acquire novel, two-handed co-ordinated movements, initial variability in the way the person approaches the learning situation was shown to be related to their ability to learn the task (Hodges & Franks, 2000).

Methods of training that emphasize ball flight and the target-goal, rather than the desired movement form, appear to be useful constraints to emphasize in order to bring about a desired movement form. If a novice performer displays an incorrect technique (e.g. standing foot is placed well behind the ball when kicking), then any instructional interventions to correct this should be expressed in an externally focused manner (e.g. wait until you're over the ball). It might be necessary to encourage beginners to try various functional movement solutions to achieve the desired action effect goal. We have found that some individuals appear to demonstrate quite persevering behaviours in the face of failure and in the absence of task-specific movement instructions (Hodges *et al.*, 2000). External task goal constraints and actions-effects related information (such as desired ball flight) might not be sufficient to encourage a change in behaviour, without additional prompting or encouragement. Instructions and informational manipulations should be designed to take into account the individual's experience with the skill. A decision might be made to first provide a combination of movement-related, internal instruction with external action-effects related information to encourage change and an optimal control focus. Case Study (p. 208) illustrates the practical implications of action-effects research.

Action-percepts

If a novice soccer player practices the skill of kicking by constantly focusing on the action-effect of ball trajectory, then when he/she comes to play the game itself,

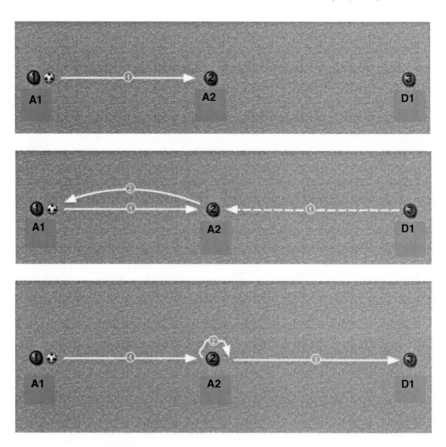

Figure 17.3 Soccer drill that retains the information-movement couplings inherent in playing a soccer game. Attacker 1 (A1) and Attacker 2 (A2) must combine to get the ball past Defender 1 (D1) to an end line. To start, (a) A1 passes to A2, (b) D1 can either run toward A2 or (c) D1 can stay still. D1 is free to decide on either option but cannot touch the ball or opponent, or move in front of A2. A2 must select and execute an appropriate motor skill based on D1's position and anticipating that D1 will tackle. The practice repeats from D1 (who now becomes A1).

he/she will continue to focus on the ball and will be less likely or unable to gather perceptual information related to the position and movements of teammates and opponents (a strategy that is most effective in soccer). Therefore, novice soccer players need to practice under conditions that retain the information-movement couplings that are normally present in the game (i.e. teammates, opposition, space, ball), but the task may need to be simplified (e.g. small-sided games, adapted drills, see Davids *et al.*, 2008). The links between perceptual and motor skills appear to be set in the early stages of development, so it would seem important that novices are exposed to activities that maintain these information-movement couplings. Movement co-ordination will still occur through anticipation of effects, but these effects will be based on and linked to inherent perceptual information within the performance environment (i.e. a combination of action-effects and action-percepts).

These implications also extend to net and field sports, as well as other invasion sports. For example, in tennis, a player must select and execute each shot based on the position, strengths, and tactics of their opponent (and themselves), as well as the position and movements of the ball. Similarly, in cricket, a batter must select and execute shots within their repertoire based on the bowler's delivery of the ball and the positioning of their opponents in the field. Therefore, in both these cases there is a need for performers to practice under conditions that retain those information-movement couplings that are normally present in the game, although the task needs to be simplified for learners. The Case Study: Practising ball control (p. 208) illustrates these ideas (see also Figure 17.3).

In summary, researchers have shown that both external action-effects and external-percepts are important for the planning, initiation and execution of motor skills in actual dynamic sports play, as well as for the learning of skill in these sports. Coaches and practitioners should ensure that practice retains the information-movement couplings inherent in the game and that instruction is directed where possible to external, skill and game-related information.

These case studies illustrate the practical implications of action-effects research and can be interpreted in relation to Figure 17.3.

Case Study: Practising kicking skills

A novice child or adult is practising kicking skills, and is having difficulty lifting the ball in the air. One simple constraints-based method of instruction would be to change the attentional focus of the child so that he/she now focuses on the desired ball flight rather than the desired movement form. This is best encouraged through a demonstration (and emphasis) on the characteristics of the desired ball flight. Ideally, augmented feedback should be provided about the ball (e.g. video feedback, coach feedback emphasizing components of the ball flight). Other methods could be used which encourage the visualization of the desired ball trajectory (e.g. lift the ball, rather than lift your foot). Alternatively, another simple constraint-based method would be to place a height barrier (or a person) directly in front of the kicker, so that they are required to adjust their movement form to clear the barrier. We have heard anecdotal evidence that this technique is used to encourage players attempting to chip a ball onto the green in golf, as well as past opposing players in soccer.

Case Study: Practising ball control

A soccer player is slow making decisions about what to do with the ball after its reception. This person shows little anticipatory search of the environment before and during ball reception. In this case it is necessary for the player to practise ball control skills in conditions where the information-movement couplings inherent in soccer are retained. One example of a method designed to improve visual search is shown in Figure 17.3. In this soccer drill, Attacker 1 (A1) and Attacker 2 (A2) must combine to get the ball past Defender 1 (D1) to an end line. To start, Attacker 1 must pass to Attacker 2 and as this happens the defender can either run toward the second attacker or stay still (see Figure 17.3). The defender is free to decide on either option but cannot touch the ball or opponent, or move in front of Attacker 2. Attacker 2 must select and execute an appropriate motor skill based on the defender's position and anticipating that this person will tackle. To complete this task, Attacker 2 must look over his/her shoulder at the defender as the ball travels from Attacker 1. This means that Attacker 2 is performing a visual monitoring task, in order to make a decision as to what motor skill to perform, based on whether the defender runs towards him/her (see Figure 17.3), Attacker 2 passes back) or stays still (see Figure 17.3), Attacker 2 turns and dribbles. In this practice, Attacker 2 is using his/her perceptual skills as they would in a match, by gathering information on the movements of other players and selecting appropriate motor skills based on this information. The practice repeats with a rotation of player positions (i.e. the defender now becomes Attacker 1, etc.). This practice can be progressed into a 2 vs 1 directional game. To simplify this game for lesser-skilled players in order to focus on the main goal of improving the linkage between actions and action-percepts, various task constraints can be manipulated. The size of the playing area could be increased, or tackling could be banned, so that players have a little more time to make decisions, but they still face the same perceptual constraints.

References

Beilock, S. L., Carr, T. H., MacMahon, C. & Starkes, J. L. (2002). When Paying Attention becomes Counterproductive: Impact of Divided Versus Skill-focused Attention on Novice and Experienced Performance of Sensorimotor Skills. *Journal of Experimental Psychology: Applied*, 8, 6–16.

Castaneda, B., & Gray, R. (2007). Effects of Focus of Attention on Baseball Batting Performance in Players of Differing Skill Levels. *Journal of Sport & Exercise Psychology*, 29, 60–77.

Davids, K., Button, C. & Bennett, S. J. (2008). *Dynamics of Skill Acquisition: A Constraints-led Approach*. Champaign, Illinois: Human Kinetics.

Drost, U. C., Rieger, M., Brass, M., Gunter, T. C. & Prinz, W. (2005). Action-effect Coupling in Pianists. *Psychological Research*, 69, 233–241.

Ford, P., Hodges, N. J. & Williams, A. M. (2005). On-line Attentional-focus Manipulations in a Soccer-dribbling Task: Implications for the Proceduralization of Motor Skills. *Journal of Motor Behavior*, 37, 386–394.

Ford, P., Hodges, N. J. & Williams, A. M. (2007). Examining Action-effects in the Execution of a Skilled Soccer Kick through Erroneous Feedback. *Journal of Motor Behavior*, 39, 481–490.

Ford, P., Hodges, N. J., Huys, R. & Williams, A. M. (2006). The Role of External Action-effects in the Execution of a Soccer Kick: A Comparison Across Skill Level. *Motor Control*, 10, 386–404.

Ford, P., Hodges, N. J., Huys, R. & Williams, A. M. (2009). Evidence for End-point Trajectory Planning during a Kicking Action. *Motor Control*, 13, 1–24.

Hodges, N. J. & Franks, I. M. (2000). Attention-focusing Instructions and Co-ordination Bias: Implications for Learning a Novel Bimanual Task. *Human Movement Science*, 19, 843–867.

Hodges, N. J., Hayes, S. J., Eaves, D., Horn, R. & Williams, A. M. (2006). End-point Trajectory Matching as a Method for Teaching Kicking Skills. *International Journal of Sport Psychology*, 37, 230–247.

Hodges, N. J., Huys, R. & Starkes, J. L. (2007). A Methodological Review and Evaluation of Research of Expert Performance in Sport. In G. Tenenbaum & R. Eklund (eds), *Handbook of Sport Psychology*, 3rd edn. New York: Wiley, pp. 161–183.

Hodges, N. J., Oakey, M., Mussell, L. & Franks, I. M. (2000). The Role of Visual Information Pertaining to Ball Flight when Learning and Performing a Golf Chip. *Journal of Sport & Exercise Psychology*, 22, S52.

Hommel, B. (2004). Event Files: Feature Binding in and across Perception and Action. *Trends in Cognitive Sciences*, 8, 494–500.

James, W. (1981). *The Principles of Psychology, Volume 2*. Cambridge, MA: Harvard University Press.

Koch, I., Keller, P. & Prinz, W. (2004). The Ideomotor Approach to Action Control: Implications for Skilled Performance. *International Journal of Sport & Exercise Psychology*, 2, 362–372.

Kunde, W. (2001). Response-effect Compatibility in Manual Choice Reaction Tasks. *Journal of Experimental Psychology: Human Perception and Performance*, 27, 387–394.

Kunde, W., Hoffman, J. & Zellmann, P. (2002). The Impact of Anticipated Action Effects on Action Planning. *Acta Psychologica*, 109, 137–155.

Kunde, W., Koch, I. & Hoffmann, J. (2004). Anticipated Action Effects Affect the Selection, Initiation and Execution of Actions. *The Quarterly Journal of Experimental Psychology. Section A: Human Experimental Psychology*, 57A, 87–106.

McNevin, N. H., Shea, C. H. & Wulf, G. (2003). Increasing the Distance of an External Focus of Attention Enhances Learning. *Psychological Research*, 67 (1), 22–29.

Prinz, W. (1997). Perception and Action Planning. *European Journal of Cognitive Psychology*, 9, 129–154.

Schöllhorn, W. I., Beckmann, H., Michelbrink, M., Sechelmann, M., Trockel, M. & Davids, K. (2006). Does Noise Provide a Basis for Unification of Motor Learning Theories? *International Journal of Sport Psychology*, 37, 186–206.

Smith, M. D. & Chamberlin, C. J. (1992). Effect of Adding Cognitively Demanding Tasks on Soccer Skill Performance. *Perceptual and Motor Skills*, 75, 955–961.

Williams, A. M., Davids, K. & Williams, J. G. (1999). *Visual Perception and Action in Sport.* London: E. & F. N. Spon.

Wulf, G. (2007). *Attention and Motor Skill Learning.* Champaign, Illinois: Human Kinetics.

Wulf, G. & Su, J. (2007). An External Focus of Attention Enhances Golf Shot Accuracy in Beginners and Experts. *Research Quarterly for Exercise and Sport*, 78, 384–389.

Wulf, G. & Prinz, W. (2001). Directing Attention to Movement Effects Enhances Learning: A Review. *Psychonomic Bulletin & Review*, 8, 648–660.

18 A constraints-based training intervention in boxing

Robert Hristovski

Introduction

Boxing is a non-co-operative skill contest between two people in which the global goal is either to win more points by applying successful punches to an opponent's head or body, or alternatively to win the match with a knockout. According to expert literature in boxing (see Kajchevski *et al.*, 2003), one of the most important abilities of skilled boxers with tactical significance, is the ability to apply diverse punches with relatively high frequency at close and medium distances from an opponent on the basis of perceived distance and the guard of the opponent. Diversity of punches constrains the opponent to depend on probabilistic perceptual judgments for decision-making rather than accurate knowledge of an opponent's actions. Additionally, the opponent would have to maintain a very high level of alertness and attention in order to evade or block an attack, which is why experienced boxers with well-developed punching diversity usually capture the attention of an opponent with a deceptive movement before starting a series of punches within close range. Alternatively, punching diversity is used when the opponent has already lost his/her alertness as a result of being close to a knockdown state or as a consequence of exhaustion.

When combined with high frequency diversity, more often than not, at least one punch of the combination will succeed in hitting one of the opponent's target zones. Punching frequency depends on the category of boxers and is usually higher in lighter categories (Kajcevski *et al.*, 2003). It is important to note that high-frequency diversity of punches, especially those with higher impact energy demands, needs a developed whole leg-trunk-arm kinetic chain (i.e. synergy) switching ability with highly developed control of inertial forces to prevent loss of balance. High-frequency switching ability between e.g. contralateral or ipsilateral hooks and uppercuts is a different quality to the high-frequency punching of mirror symmetry punches (e.g. left-right jab or left-right hook), which are evolutionary stabilized patterns. Therefore, systematic and long term practice is needed to establish and maintain perception-action couplings of this type. Perceptions and actions are dynamically coupled in the online regulation of co-ordinated movements and are instrumental in ensuring stable adaptive action patterns with respect to the situation demands, of utmost importance in contests like boxing.

Constraints-based research on boxing diversity and punching frequency

In accordance with the constraints-based framework on motor learning and performance (Davids, Chapter 1; Davids et al., 2008; Araújo et al., 2004; Newell, 1986) research in boxing has been conducted with the aim of capturing some of the key constraints that mold the punching activity of boxers with respect to targets (see Hristovski et al., 2006a; Hristovski et al., 2006b; Araújo et al., 2006). It has been shown that one of the key "control" parameters, (i.e. constraints) in attacking and defending behaviour in boxing is not physical distance but scaled distance to a target. Scaled distance is the ratio of the physical distance and the arm length of the attacker, to a target/opponent. Hence, it has been concluded that boxers use an intrinsic, body scaled metric of distance, rather than an objective physical distance in punching a target. Moreover, it has been shown that what boxers perceive for guiding their behaviour are the affordances (i.e. perceived opportunities for specific punching actions). Punching actions have been defined as angles (directions) of impact of an attacker's fist with the target and were considered as "order" parameters (see Newell & Ranganathan, Chapter 2), (i.e.

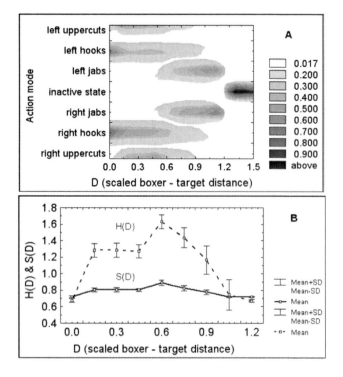

Figure 18.1 A. Abrupt and continuous changes of the probabilities of punching actions. B. The unpredictability (H) and diversity (S) of actions change as a function of the scaled boxer-target distance (D). It is maximized around D = 0.6.

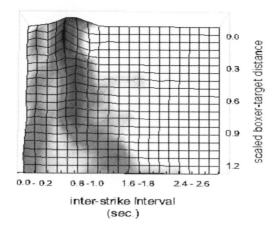

Figure 18.2 Probabilities of the inter-strike time intervals (inverse punching frequencies) as a function of the scaled boxer-target distance. Darker areas correspond to high-probability levels and lighter areas to low-probability levels of between-punch time intervals (inverse punching frequencies).

variables that contain the collective information of the organization of the upper limbs of the attacker with respect to a target). In other words, the direction of fist-target impact is most probably a variable that organizes the trajectory formation of different punches. In Figure 18.1A one can see that punching actions emerge and vanish for certain values of the scaled distance to the target.

In subsequent studies (Chow *et al.*, 2009; Hristovski *et al.*, 2009) it has been shown that besides the direction (i.e. angle) of the fist-target impact, the frequency and the relative phase of punching activity also play a role as order parameters that inform the low dimensional temporal dynamics of boxing actions. Moreover, the frequency of attacking actions can play a role as a control parameter in the defensive actions of an opponent (Hristovski *et al.*, 2009).

From Figure 18.2 one can see that for all scaled boxer-target distance values there are two probability ridges of punching frequencies (darker shadowed regions) divided by a low-probability valley (lightly shadowed regions). At scaled distances larger than 1.35 m the inter-strike time interval becomes infinite, since after a punch body balance is typically lost. At slightly lower scaled boxer-target distances above 0.9 m, that is, distances significantly larger than one extended arm length, the low-probability (lightly shadowed) punching frequency valley is wider due to the large amplitude of oscillation of the body toward and from the target. So the boxers either threw single or coupled anti-phase left-right or right-left jab/straight punches or then leaned backwards until the next forward oscillation, which takes some stochastically distributed period of time. The single-punch time intervals (i.e. those without a stable phase relationship between them) are concentrated on the right probability ridge, that is the one with higher inter-strike intervals, or lower punching frequencies. The high-frequency coupled left-right or right-left punches are concentrated in the left probability ridge, and those punches fluctuated around the stable anti-phase mode. The narrowing of the low-punching frequency valley is a function of the scaled boxer-target distance, since closer to the heavy bag, the forward and backward oscillations of the body became smaller and eventually ceased to exist at scaled distances smaller than 0.9 m–0.8 m. The low-probability (lightly shadowed) valley for lower-scaled boxer-target distance values than 0.8 m is a result of the intrinsic dynamics tendencies (Kelso, 1995) of the boxers, which needs further investigation.

Another important characteristic of both high- and low-punching average frequencies is that they became almost constant for smaller-scaled distance values (lower than 0.8 m). Hence, by combining the characteristics of diversity of punches (see Figure 18.1A) and the frequency characteristics of punches (Figure 18.2) one can see that at D = 0.6 m, high-frequency punching diversity is maximized.

Several more specific observations were made:

1   Perceived efficiences (i.e. perceptual judgments of good impact with the target) of specific punches depended on the scaled distance from the target and strongly constrained the probabilities of occurrence of the actions, enhancing the probabilities of the associated punches and reducing the probabilities of concurrent punches. For example, high-perceived efficiency of jabs enhanced the occurrence of jabs and suppressed the occurrence probabilities of hooks and uppercuts and vice versa.

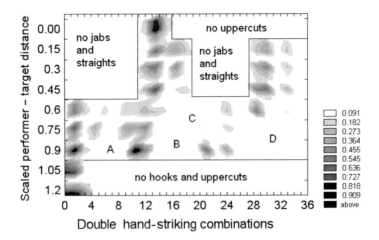

Figure 18.3 Intrinsic punching combination tendencies of T.K. dependent on the scaled distance from the heavy bag. Regions inside bordered areas signify absence of particular punches. Regions A, B, C and D outside these areas signify that single punches of certain types are present but that combinations are missing. Dark grey areas are more probable and light grey areas signify less probable combinations.

2   The coupling of punches was highly sensitive to scaled distance, so, often a minute change in the scaled distance brought about a substantial change of inter-punch couplings.

3   The scaled distance D = 0.6 m afforded maximum diversity H (i.e. inter-mode variability or unpredictability) of punching activity. Around this distance the boxers have least constrained opportunities for combining various punches.

4   The scaled distance D = 0.6 m afforded maximum efficiency ratio E of punching activity, which increased if the sum of the perceived efficiencies increased and the sum of the perceived efficiency differences decreased (see Hristovski et al., 2006a for a detailed explanation of this measure). Around this distance the efficiencies of all types of punches exhibited the closest values, meaning that their differences were minimal.

5   There were pronounced asymmetries between the left and right uppercut punches, i.e. their onset occurred at different scaled distances from the target, which was less frequently observed in jabs (straights) and hooks.

This data witnesses the strong perception-action coupling in boxing activity and the training of boxers should adhere to this fundamental characteristic. In other words, by changing the distance to the target in practice, what is learned is the coupling between the scaled distance – punching efficiency – punch type – punching frequency. By intentionally changing the distance to a target, boxers may ensure the efficiency (i.e. impact energy) of a specific type of punching and consequently change the probabilities and frequency of their occurrence. A partial multiplicative measure of boxing performance potential stems from these findings (see Simonton, 2003; Abbott, Button, Pepping & Collins, 2005).

$$P = H <\omega> E;$$

where H is the diversity of boxing punches, $<\omega>$ is the average frequency of punches, where double brackets $< >$ designate a statistical average and E is the efficiency ratio of punches that measures the closeness of the fist-target energy of impact[1] of different punches. It is a partial measure because overall boxing performance potential depends on more dimensions than these three alone.

Diversity, as measured by the entropy measure H would be maximal if a boxer uses with equal probability all of the available punches (see Hristovski, 2006a and Hristovski, 2006b for detailed calculation of this measure). For 6 different types of punches its maximal value is $H = \ln 6 = 1.792$ natural units, where $(\ln)$ is a natural logarithm. For example, if the boxer performs 60 punches in total and every type of six different types of punches (i.e. left-right jab (straight), left-right hook, left-right uppercut) has been used exactly 10 times, then the diversity is maximal. If any of the punches is statistically represented more than others, which is usually the case, the diversity is less than maximal. By definition, the punching frequency ω is larger when the time between the punches (i.e. the inter-strike time interval) is smaller. The smallest inter-punch intervals were observed when boxers performed in an anti-phase fashion (see Figure 18.2), when just after the punch with one fist, at the start of its withdrawal towards the body, the other arm was activated toward the target. These time periods are usually between 150 and 300 m.

Since punching frequency ω is an inverse of the time interval τ between punches, it is obvious that relation (1) can be written as: $P = H/<\tau>E$, where $< >$ designates a statistical average and $H/<\tau>$ represents the diversity production of the boxer per unit of time. In other words, the partial punching performance potential P depends on the punching diversity production and the efficiency ratio of the boxer. It is very important to realize that this measure depends on the scaled boxer-target distance D, which constrains its values and maximizes them around scaled distance D = 0.6 m (for details see Hristovski *et al.*, 2006a and Hristovski *et al.*, 2006b).

The efficiency ratio E is maximal if all punches have the same impact energy with the target. The performance potential P is never maximal, although it is better if it has higher values. Some successful boxers usually maximize one or two of these components and base their strategy on them, which means that they might still improve by paying attention to the other components of the punching activity. Hence, to maximize the partial punching performance potential P, one may need to increase the values of the 3 variables on the right hand side of relation.

Case Study: Boxing: constraints-based practice of a boxer novice or how J. R. and T. K. were learning together

Identify the problem

Lack of experience.

Setting

Practise in an amateur boxing club.

Primary constraints

The task set was practising single and combinatory punches.

Identifying the intrinsic coordinative tendencies of single punches in a novice T. K.

T. K. was a newcomer to the boxing club in which J. R. was a personal trainer. In an initial conversation, J. R. established that T. K. was interested in boxing and had watched a lot of matches, but had no personal experience. Aged 11, he wanted to learn some boxing techniques and to join the amateur club to develop his skills. He had been motivated to learn boxing after one of his city mates had won first prize in an international competition. J. R. decided that he needed to learn the basics first, for example, elementary punches, footwork and the stance.

In order to establish T. K.'s co-ordination when punching, J. R. decided to physically demonstrate the moves, rather than verbally explaining them. J. R. asked T. K. to hit his open palm with his fists, at first lightly and then more forcefully. J. R. held his palm at different angles in relation to T. K.'s visual line. By changing the orientation of his palm, J. R. succeeded in constraining T. K.'s action system to form, as yet unskilfully, patterns that generally looked like jabs, hooks and uppercuts. The configuration of the perceptual information coming from J. R.'s palm position managed to regulate T. K.'s punches in general action patterns. J. R. then demonstrated the best position to hold the fist in relation to the forearm that prevents injuries. T. K. quickly got the point. "When will be the first session?" asked T. K. "Well, we've already started mate" answered J. R.

Constraints-based intervention on elementary punches

Main goal of the practice   Acquisition of basic attacking co-ordination patterns (punches) with a target satisfying the need for accuracy and high energy of impact, i.e. punching efficiency constraints. Three different sessions were designed for T. K.

Session 1: Equipment used   Heavy bag, double-end bag, hand pads and body opponent.
In the next few sessions J. R. organized the following "target practice" for T. K. First, the heavy bag and double-ended bag were used with larger-area target markers, inviting punches such as jabs (straights), hooks and uppercuts. The instructional constraint was to land punches on the marked areas of the heavy bag and subsequently withdraw the fists to a guard position. The attention-focusing instruction was for T. K. to explore and find by himself the best distance at which he could perform all the punches with optimal energy of impact. These instructions constrained T. K. to co-ordinate his upper limbs with differing degrees of freedom, allowing him to hit the targeted areas effectively. This helped him to explore the power of his punches at differing distances, so that he could find the best distance at which to execute all punches. Since the heavy bag did not possess surfaces that would afford efficient uppercut punches, J. R. posed it at a height that would allow T. K. to hit the underside of the bag too.

Session 2: Equipment used   Heavy bag.
Next, there were several bouts of continuous fast throwing of single punches whilst changing the distance from the heavy bag and basic footwork.
J. R. knew that quick punches contribute to the energy of the impact. Since impact energy is nothing more than kinetic energy that depends on the mass and the velocity squared of the fist, by increasing the fist velocity a greater impact is achieved. So J. R. encouraged T. K. to throw punches as quickly as possible.

Session 3: Equipment used   Double end bag.
Then J. R. set up a session consisting of several bouts of power punches, such as the hook, straight (i.e. cross) and uppercut. This enabled T. K. to explore the differing distances that would enable the greatest impact.
J. R. paid specific attention to the leg-trunk-arm chaining and the transfer of

weight from the rear to the front leg as he tried to satisfy the punch-power task constraint. He quickly noticed that T. K. had problems with that specific co-ordination pattern, as most beginners do. Instead of verbally explaining to T. K. the details of the leg-trunk-arm co-ordination, angles and so on, he asked T. K. to try to push *as quickly and as forcefully as possible* with his left or right fists the heavy bag that he (J. R.) was holding firmly. "Try to push me quickly together with the bag," he said. T. K. positioned himself a bit to the side of the vertical axis of the heavy bag and did what J. R. asked him to do. The closed kinetic chain of T. K.'s body with the fixed heavy bag did the job. As T. K. pressed quickly and forcefully with his right fist on the heavy bag his right rear leg and the trunk self-assembled into quick rotation counter clockwise. T. K. tried that several times for different "simulated" punches, pressing on left or right, forward, or bottom-up and saw that it worked. Afterwards he moved to the double-ended bag again to finish the bout. Although not perfectly co-ordinated, he performed much better than he had a few minutes before. Instead of basing the instructional constraint on verbal information, J. R.'s method was to use an external focus of attention to develop a metaphor for power punching. The "pushing metaphor" worked for T. K. J. R. liked to use metaphors and analogies and said, "Try to be a whirlpool on top of which are your arms".

Afterwards, T. K. was introduced quickly to the hand pad and body oppo-nent work. However, J. R. was particularly interested in the intrinsic punching combinatorial tendencies of T. K. Learning about the learner was the best way to teach him.

Identifying the intrinsic coordinative combination tendencies of T. K.

J. R. noticed that T. K. was using some punching combinations more often than others. It was much harder, however, to diagnose more precisely which punching combinations T. K. was using rarely or not using at all and why. Being aware that punching diversity with high frequency is of crucial tactical importance in fights at close distance and clench positions, he decided to study T. K.'s intrinsic punching combination tendencies. To achieve this, he decided to film his punching activity at a fixed heavy-bag from different distances. It was a cumbersome procedure, but he enjoyed it. He instructed T. K. to perform a series of 60 power punches at several distances from the heavy-bag separated by 10 cm each time, using the light diagonal (i.e. close to parallel) stance of the feet. Although the parallel or light diagonal stance is not the most common boxing stance, he instructed T. K. to use it because it does not introduce asymmetry of punches in advance. By using this instructional constraint he released the strong constraint of the diagonal stance since he was seeking to provide an equal opportunity for left-arm and right-arm punches to be used, before drawing conclusions about the intrinsic coordinative tendencies of T. K.

T. K.'s intrinsic combination tendencies at different scaled distances from the heavy-bag showed the existence, on the one hand, of strongly coupled punches, and on the other hand, rarely emerging or missing combinations. Hence, J. R.'s goal was to decouple some of the combinations and to form stronger couplings among the others, so that T. K.'s diversity of punching could be enhanced.

Primary constraints of T. K.

Personal   Lack of diversity of punching.

Task   Action selection diversity satisfying frequency, accuracy and energy of impact requirements.

Main goal of the practice   To maintain important perception-action couplings while increasing the decision-making abilities and diversity of punches.

Equipment used   Body opponent (mannequin), hand pads.

In contrast to many boxing trainers J. R. used to play with the body mannequin by moving the torso irregularly in different directions using its elastic characteristics. Irregular variation of the torso-head of the body opponent spontaneously generated irregular variability of T. K.'s movements through the strong perception-action couplings. The variability of each class of punches, i.e. straights, hooks or uppercuts, was evident from the aborted movements up to fully developed punches. "Keep the best distance from which you can use all of your arsenal," said J. R. "Keep the focus on its head and punch any part you can." T. K. was constrained to move forward and backward and to use a large variety of punches. What the predictable heavy bag did not succeed in achieving, the irregularly moving mannequin did. Many of the punching combinations that were not present before emerged as a consequence of the manipulation of the distance and strikeable surfaces on the mannequin.

Next, J. R. moved on to hand pads work. In order to give T. K.'s punches an increased force, he was holding the hands close to his own body and was pressing them toward coming punches. Moving around and changing the elevation and direction of the palms constrained T. K. to assemble his punches in different combinations. Over the next month and half J. R. slowly increased the frequency of combining different directions of his palms and T. K. became increasingly successful at the task. Sometimes J. R. was substituting hand pad work with situational sparring with some of T. K.'s more advanced club-mates. For T. K., specific high frequency combinations were encouraged by *very short time exposure* to a sparring partner's undefended body surfaces. "Try to hit him more than twice on any undefended surface ... of course above the belt," grinned J. R.

After a month and a half or so of these exercises, T. K. was prepared to perform his first all-out sparring session.

Note

1 For a given kinetic energy of the fist and a static target the impact is maximal if it is applied under 90 degrees with respect to the impact surface.

References

Abbott, A. J., Button, C., Pepping, G. J. & Collins, D. (2005). Unnatural Selection: Talent Identification and Development in Sport. *Nonlinear Dynamics, Psychology and Life Sciences*, 9(1), 61–88.

Araújo, D., Davids, K. & Bennett, S. (2004). Emergence of Sport Skills under Constraints. In A. M. Williams & N. J. Hodges (eds), *Skill Acquisition in Sport: Research, Theory and Practice*, London: Routledge, pp. 409–433.

Araújo, D., Davids, K. & Hristovski, R. (2006). The Ecological Dynamics of Decision making in Sport. *Psychology of Sport and Exercise*, 7(6), 653–676.

Chow, J. Y., Davids, K., Button, C., Rein, R., Hristovski, R. & Koh, M. (2009). Dynamics of Multi-articular Co-ordination in Neurobiological Systems. *Nonlinear Dynamics, Psychology & Life Sciences*, 13(1), 27–56.

Davids, K., Button, C. & Bennett, S. J. (2008). *Dynamics of Skill Acquisition: A Constraints-led Approach*. Champaign, Illinois: Human Kinetics.

Davids, K. (2010). The Constraints-based Approach to Motor Learning: Implications for a Non-linear Pedagogy in Sport and Physical Education. In K. Davids and I. Renshaw (eds), *A Constraints-led Approach to Motor Learning: Designing Effective Practice*. London: Routledge.

Hristovski, R., Davids, K., Araújo, D. & Button, C. (2006a). How Boxers Decide to Punch a Target: Emergent Behaviour in Non-linear Dynamic Movement Systems. *Journal of Sports Science and Medicine*, CSSI, 60–73.

Hristovski, R., Davids, K. & Araújo, D. (2006b). Affordance – Controlled Bifurcations of Action Patterns in Martial Arts. *Nonlinear Dynamics, Psychology, and Life Sciences*, 10(4), 409–444.

Hristovski, R., Davids, K. & Araújo, D. (2009). Information for Regulating Action in Sport: Metastability and Emergence of Tactical Solutions under Ecological Constraints. In Araújo, D., Ripoll, H. & Raab, M. (eds), *Perspectives on Cognition and Action in Sport*, New York: Nova Science Publishers, pp. 43–57.

Kajchevski, A. Nastevski, V. & Kostovski, Z. (2003). *Boxing*. Skopje: St. Cyril and Methodius University Press (In Macedonian).

Kelso, J. A. S. (1995). *Dynamic Patterns: The Self-organisation of Brain and Behaviour*. Cambridge, MA: MIT Press.

Newell, K. M. (1986). Constraints on the Development of Co-ordination. In M. G. Wade & H. T. A. Whiting (eds), *Motor Skill Acquisition in Children: Aspects of Co-ordination and Control*, Amsterdam: Martinies NIJHOS, pp. 341–360.

Newell, K. M. & Ranganathan, R. (2010). Instructions as Constraints in Motor Skill Acquisition. In K. Davids and I. Renshaw (eds), *A Constraints-led Approach to Motor Learning: Designing Effective Practice*. London: Routledge.

Simonton, D. K. (1999). Talent and Its Development: An Emergenic and Epigenetic Model. *Psychological Review*, 106, 435–457.

19 Researching co-ordination skill

Dana Maslovat, Nicola J. Hodges,
Romeo Chua and Ian M. Franks

Co-ordination skills

In our daily lives, we often perform movements that require complex co-ordination of our limbs, such as tying our shoes, washing dishes, or walking down a crowded street. Similarly, effective sport performance is often characterized by the production of very specific co-ordination patterns. The purpose of this chapter is to provide a brief overview of research pertaining to the learning of new co-ordination patterns and skills. The majority of the research we will summarize involves laboratory-based tasks in which the required co-ordination pattern can be controlled and measured; however we believe the results of these studies can be applied to many sport scenarios where individuals are required to learn or modify a co-ordination pattern. It is our hope that this chapter will aid in the understanding of the production of new co-ordination patterns as well as provide valuable practical information to accelerate the learning process.

The first part of this chapter will focus on what we will refer to as "intrinsic" constraints. This will include a discussion of factors thought to affect natural co-ordination patterns (those that can be performed without practice), how new patterns are learned, as well as individual differences in the skill acquisition process. The second part of this chapter will focus on what we will refer to as "extrinsic constraints". This will include a discussion of various practice conditions that have a relatively permanent effect on performance of co-ordination skills, such as instructions, demonstrations, feedback, as well as practice amount and quality. In view of the expertise of the authors, the majority of the chapter will focus on these extrinsic constraints.

Intrinsic constraints

One consistent finding in the examination of co-ordination between limbs is that although hypothetically the number of possible movements is limitless, only a few are usually selected and can be performed without practice (for a review see Kelso, 1981, 1984, 1995). These "natural" patterns include in-phase movements (i.e. 0°

relative phase) and anti-phase movements (i.e. 180° relative phase), which can either be defined egocentrically or allocentrically (Swinnen, 2002). Egocentric definitions involve symmetry of muscle contraction (i.e. in phase is considered synchronous contraction of homologous muscles, whilst anti-phase is considered alternating contraction of homologous muscles), while allocentric definitions involve symmetry of direction in extrinsic space (i.e. in phase is considered movement in the same direction, whilst anti-phase is considered movement in opposite directions). In-phase co-ordination has been shown to be more stable than anti-phase, as evidenced by a spontaneous transition from anti-phase to in-phase with increasing movement speed. The stability of these intrinsic patterns has been attributed to different loci, including neuromuscular-skeletal constraints (Carson, 1996; Carson *et al.*, 2000), neural cross-talk (Cattaert, *et al.*, 1999), and perceptual constraints such as visual or proprioceptive feedback (Mechsner *et al.*, 2001; Mechsner & Knoblich, 2004).

Although there appear to be only a very few intrinsic patterns (e.g. in-phase and anti-phase), new co-ordination patterns can be learned given sufficient practice and appropriate feedback (see Fontaine *et al.*, 1997; Schoner *et al.*, 1992). The acquisition of a new co-ordination pattern may cause a relatively persistent (Zanone & Kelso, 1992) or temporary (Fontaine *et al.*, 1997; Lee *et al.*, 1995) destabilization of more natural, intrinsic movement patterns. As participants learn, there are changes in performance of existing movement patterns or previously learned movements showing that learning is a general phenomenon affecting more than just the stability of the practiced movement (see Maslovat *et al.*, 2005; Swinnen *et al.*, 1997).

The research involving intrinsic patterns highlights important applications to practitioners trying to teach someone a new co-ordination pattern. First, it is important to note that certain co-ordinated movements will be easier to perform than others, due to the various constraints of the limbs, perceptual sensitivities, and task-related factors. In addition, there is a strong "attraction" to patterns that we can already perform and during skill acquisition the learner may revert to these patterns (or habits) until such time as the new movement pattern is "stable". Second, and perhaps less intuitive, is that the learning of a new pattern can disrupt a movement that the learner already has in their repertoire. Learning is not simply the addition of a new pattern to those already acquired but rather involves a reorganization of the entire pattern inventory a learner possesses at any given time (for a more detailed review see Newell *et al.*, 2008; Zanone & Kelso, 1994). Thus, to determine how a learner will acquire a new skill it is necessary to know what skills he or she can already perform. These considerations highlight the importance of an individualistic approach to skill assessment and evaluation. As skill acquisition is dependent on the current state of the learner, it is also necessary to consider individual differences in the way individuals allocate attention to various components of the task (Temprado *et al.*, 2002), their level of anxiety (Court *et al.*, 2005), and handedness (Amazeen *et al.*, 2005). These factors all have been shown to affect the rate of learning of new co-ordination movements.

Extrinsic constraints

Practitioners have the most control over constraints that occur within the practice environment. Practice organization and the interaction of the instructor with the learner have a large impact on the rate of acquisition of a newly learned co-ordinated movement. We will separate this section into three sub-areas: organization of practice (including amount of practice and skill presentation schedule); skill presentation methods (including instructions and demonstrations); and augmented feedback (including attentional cues and feedback modalities). Once we have summarized the pertinent research in each area we will explain how these findings can be practically applied to the learning environment to optimize learning.

Practice organization

One of the critical factors in skill acquisition is the amount of time spent practicing. All other factors being equal, more practice will lead to better skill performance. However, along with the *quantity* of practice engaged by the learner the *quality* (i.e. context) of practice can also have a large effect on learning. For example, if a number of skills are to be learned, the order in which the skills are presented to the learner has been shown to affect retention and transfer performance. Learning is enhanced if the learner is required to perform the skills in a random order rather than a blocked order, where a skill is repeated over and over before moving on to the next skill. Overcoming the unpredictability of a random skill presentation causes the learner to be more engaged in the learning process. This results in better long term learning effects, although often at the expense of short term gains. This effect is known as *contextual interference* and has been shown to occur for a wide variety of tasks (see Brady, 1998; Magill & Hall, 1990 for reviews), including the learning of novel co-ordination movements (Maslovat *et al.*, 2004; Tsutsui *et al.*, 1998).

To examine the effects of amount of practice and practice schedule on learning, we recently (Maslovat *et al.*, 2004) examined if a random or blocked presentation schedule of two tasks had a greater effect on learning compared to practicing a single task for twice as many trials. We found that the contextual interference provided by practicing two tasks in a random order produced the same learning benefits as practicing a single task for double the practice time. This result suggests that rather than increasing practice time on a specific task, equal benefit can be derived from the introduction of a second, related task randomly interspersed (with a secondary benefit of getting practice trials on another task). It also suggests that while amount of practice is important for learning, changing the context of practice can have a similar effect such that less practice is needed to achieve a similar level of skill efficiency.

Skill presentation

In addition to practice organization, the way a skill is presented to the learner can impact the learning process. The goal of skill presentation is to transfer information from the instructor to the learner and this can be achieved in a number of ways, such as verbal instructions or physical demonstrations. While both these methods of skill presentation are thought to assist learning for many types of tasks, they appear to be less effective for co-ordination tasks. In a series of studies examining the learning of a continuous bimanual task, demonstrations and instructions had little effect on acquisition of the overall movement pattern, and at times both instructions and demonstrations actually hindered the acquisition process (see Hodges & Franks, 2002, 2004, for reviews). The authors concluded that it was more effective to withhold prescriptive "how to" information and provide a more abstract reference template with task-relevant feedback. When the learner is not experienced enough to verbalize or understand the movement pattern, the information provided by the coach/instructor can be difficult to use and might result in an undesirable movement or strategy despite instructions to the contrary. For example, one consequence of prescriptive "how to" information early in learning is a lack of variability in initial movement attempts. This can have the adverse effect of hindering the participant from breaking away from more novice, or intrinsic movement patterns.

There have also been researchers who have shown benefits from providing demonstrations for the learning of novel co-ordination tasks. The effectiveness of prescriptive information appears to depend upon the complexity of the task (in terms of its physical constraints and amount of movement options), the richness of feedback available about movement correctness, in addition to the type of comparisons made. For example, Magill and Schoenfelder-Zohdi (1996) found that a visual demonstration was more effective than verbal instructions for the acquisition of a rhythmic gymnastics' skill. Similarly, Hayes et al. (2008) showed benefits of combining instructions with demonstrations for learning three-ball cascade juggling. This may be because when the task or skill is relatively restricted (e.g. the movement can take place only in one plane), then instructions are less likely to be needed to act as an additional constraint, and in fact may negatively impact on performance and learning. However, if the number of possible task solutions is many and the skill to be acquired is highly unconstrained, then more instruction will be necessary in the absence of additional physical constraints or prescriptive feedback (see Fowler & Turvey, 1978).

There have also been manipulations to the amount of practice accompanying visual demonstrations, in order to look at the effectiveness of demonstrations as a teaching aid in the absence of any physical practice, so termed observational practice (Vogt & Tomascheke, 2007). Using a unimanual co-ordination task in which participants had to co-ordinate movements of the wrist and elbow joint, Buchanan et al. (2008) showed that observational practice benefited later performance of a novel co-ordination skill. In contrast to the research detailed above, Buchanan et al. (2008) had participants watch a model that was gradually improving at the task (i.e. a learning model). Thus the authors could not determine if the positive effects of observation were attributed to the task (within limb co-ordination) or the model type. We have recently collected data to differentiate between these explanations. No beneficial effects were observed from merely watching a learning model practice a novel two-handed co-ordination movement, suggesting that movement complexity (i.e. single or dual limb co-ordination) is a significant factor in determining the effectiveness of instructions and demonstrations (Maslovat *et al.*, 2008).

Collectively, the results of these studies lead to the suggestion that practitioners should carefully consider the method of skill presentation. Early in the learning process the learner may not be able to visualize or verbalize the movement pattern and thus may not benefit from complex instructions or complicated demonstrations. A combination of methods may also prove beneficial as different details are provided by different presentations. Furthermore, it is important that the learner understand the goals of the movement and information is presented clearly. It may also be useful to avoid the temptation of presenting too much information which may overwhelm the learner. However, if demonstrations are not deemed to be useful the practitioner needs another method to transfer information to the learner.

Feedback

Thus far we have shown that demonstrations and instructions can be overly constraining or not constraining enough, depending on the type of skill to be learned. For movements involving complex interactions between the limbs it may be necessary for the learner to get direct information about their movements as they perform the task, known as *concurrent feedback*. For example, in a series of experiments Wulf *et al.* (1998) showed that increased concurrent feedback improved learning to ride on a ski-simulator. For bimanual co-ordination tasks, an effective method of acquisition is to provide a graphical reference template of the action, which provides the learner with information about the relationship between the limbs. This is typically achieved by merging the movement of both limbs into a single feedback source, whereby movement of the right limb moves a cursor on the screen in the horizontal direction while movement of the left limb moves the cursor in the vertical direction (see Lee *et al.*, 1995). Thus the required co-ordination pattern can be represented as a shape on the screen referred to as a Lissajous Figure (see Figure 19.1). This method of feedback appears to help constrain the limbs in a relatively simple to understand manner. The learner now has a tangible goal to achieve; that is to produce the pattern/shape on the screen, rather than simply copying an abstract movement. Numerous researchers have shown positive effects of using such a reference template when compared to demonstrations and other types of feedback sources (see Maslovat *et al.*, 2009; for a review).

Although providing a reference template and augmented feedback can accelerate the skill acquisition process practitioners must be careful with the amount of feedback they provide, especially in the later stages of learning. There is a substantial body of research that has shown that performers can become dependent on

Counter-clockwise – right-hand leading

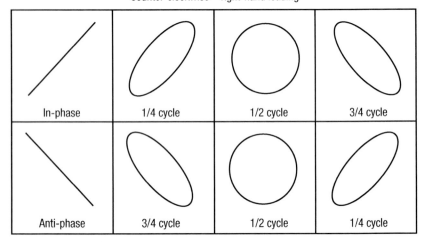

Clockwise – left-hand leading

Figure 19.1 A visual display of reference templates for various relative phase co-ordination patterns, with corresponding direction and criteria shown.

information available during practice, resulting in a decrease in performance when the feedback is removed. This theory is known as the *guidance hypothesis*, and has been shown for a variety of tasks (see Wulf & Shea, 2004 for a review). We have recently examined the guidance hypothesis in the acquisition of a new bimanual movement (Maslovat *et al.*, 2009). Results from this study indicated that participants that had high amounts of concurrent feedback during training (continuous group) were unable to adapt and perform the learned pattern when feedback was changed or removed relative to a group that received less feedback (discrete group) (Figure 19.2). Thus although feedback about the movement pattern can provide valuable information early in the skill acquisition process, this feedback should be gradually withdrawn to avoid over-dependence by the learner.

Another type of feedback that has been examined is the use of an auditory template to provide the learner with information as to *when* the limbs should be in a particular location. This is typically achieved by requiring the learner to synchronize a particular point in the movement pattern to a metronome pulse, which provides "anchors" for the movement and thus increases movement consistency. Although originally considered for juggling performance (Beek, 1989), anchoring to a metronome has been more recently investigated to determine if it can speed the acquisition process of a new bimanual movement. Positive effects of an auditory template have been shown for the re-learning of walking in patients who have experienced a stroke, Parkinson's Disease and traumatic brain injury (see Maslovat *et al.*, 2009 for a review). Initial acquisition of a novel dance sequence has also been shown to be accelerated through the use of an auditory model (Wuyts & Buekers, 1995). However, we (Maslovat *et al.*, 2006, Maslovat *et al.*, 2009) have

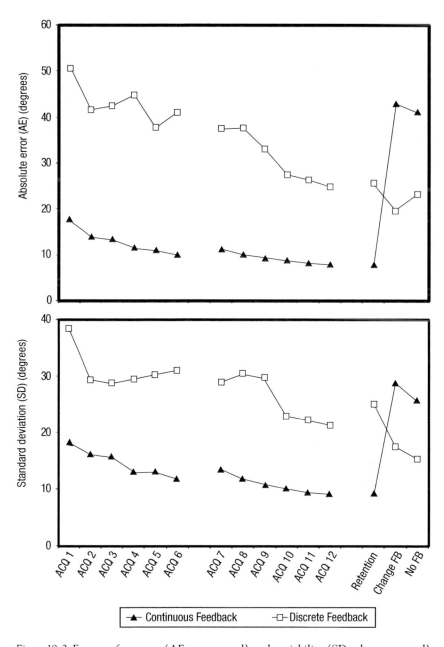

Figure 19.2 Error performance (AE – top panel) and variability (SD – bottom panel) during 12 acquisition blocks (ACQ), retention, and transfer to a change and removal of feedback (FB). Note the large change in performance by the continuous feedback group during transfer. Adapted from Maslovat *et al.* (2009).

tried to extend these findings to a novel co-ordination pattern and have failed to find positive learning effects. Using a 90 degree pattern (halfway between in-phase and anti-phase), we required participants to synchronize one, two or four reversal points of the limbs to a metronome. As stated, pattern stability and rate of acquisition were not positively affected as a result of the anchoring method. While we attributed the lack of assistance of the metronome to the specific timing requirements of the to-be-learned task, more research is needed to determine the characteristics of a movement pattern that allow an auditory template to provide learning benefits.

Summary

The purpose of this chapter was to provide an overview of the research examining the acquisition of new co-ordination movements, with a focus on extrinsic task constraints that promote learning. The performance and learning of these movements results from a complex interaction of constraints imposed by intrinsic and extrinsic factors pertaining to both the individual and the practice environment. While the intrinsic constraints are largely out of the practitioner's control, it is important that he or she be aware of them as this will enable them to understand why a particular learner may have difficulty with a specific skill or situation. In the consideration of extrinsic constraints, we summarized research findings pertaining to practice organization, skill presentation, and feedback. All of these factors are directly in control of the practitioner (and performer) and have a major impact on the performance and skill retention capabilities of the learner. Even though amount of practice is an important determinant of learning, we argue that effective practice organization can overcome some of the time limitations faced by the learner. In addition, how the skill is presented and how feedback is given to the learner are critical components within the practice environment that must be carefully planned and considered depending on the type of task being presented and the skill level of the learner. Early in practice, demonstrations and instructions may be less critical than effective feedback presented in a way that helps the learner understand the goals of the movement. However, as learning progresses it is necessary to gradually remove the feedback to ensure a lack of dependence on the feedback source. This ensures the learner can reproduce the acquired movement in a variety of environmental conditions, typically the ultimate goal of practice.

References

Amazeen, E. L., Ringenbach, S. D. & Amazeen, P. G. (2005). The Effects of Attention and Handedness on Co-ordination Dynamics in a Bimanual Fitts' Law Task. *Experimental Brain Research*, 164, 484–499.

Beek, P. J. (1989). *Juggling Dynamics*. Ph.D. Thesis. Amsterdam: Free University Press.

Brady, F. (1998). A Theoretical and Empirical Review of the Contextual Interference Effect and the Learning of Motor Skills. *Quest*, 50, 266–293.

Buchanan, J., Ryu, Y., Zihlman, K. & Wright D. (2008). Observational Practice of Relative but not Absolute Motion Features in a Single-limb Multi-joint Co-ordination Task. *Experimental Brain Research*, 191, 157–169.

Carson, R. G. (1996). Neuromuscular-skeletal Constraints upon the Dynamics of Perception-action Coupling. *Experimental Brain Research*, 110, 99–110.

Carson, R. G., Riek, S., Smethurst, C. J., Parraga, J. F. L. & Byblow, W. D. (2000). Neuromuscular-skeletal Constraints upon the Dynamics of Unimanual and Bimanual Co-ordination. *Experimental Brain Research*, 131, 196–214.

Cattaert, D., Semjen, A. & Summers, J. J. (1999). Simulating a Neural Cross-talk Model for Between-hand Interference during Bimanual Circle Drawing. *Biological Cybernetics*, 81, 343–358.

Court, M. L. J., Bennett, S. J., Williams, A. M. & Davids, K. (2005). Effects of Attentional Strategies and Anxiety Constraints on Perceptual-motor Organization of Rhythmical Arm Movements. *Neuroscience Letters*, 384, 17–22.

Fontaine, R. J., Lee, T. D. & Swinnen, S. P. (1997). Learning a New Bimanual Co-ordination Pattern: Reciprocal Influences of Intrinsic and To-be-learned Patterns. *Canadian Journal of Experimental Psychology*, 51(1), 1–9.

Fowler, C. A. & Turvey, M. T. (1978). Skill Acquisition: An Event Approach with Special Reference to Searching for the Optimum of a Function of Several Variables. In G. Stelmach (ed.), *Information Processing in Motor Control and Learning*. New York: Academic Press, pp. 1–40.

Hayes, S. J., Ashford D. & Bennett, S. J. (2008). Goal-directed Imitation: The Means to an End. *Acta Psychologica*, 127, 407–415.

Hodges N. J. & Franks, I. M. (2002). Modelling Coaching Practice: The Role of Instructions and Demonstrations. *Journal of Sports Sciences*, 20, 1–19.

Hodges, N. J. & Franks, I. M. (2004). Instructions, Demonstrations and the Learning Process: Creating and Constraining Movement Options. In A. M. Williams & N. J. Hodges (eds), *Skill Acquisition in Sport: Research, Theory and Practice*. London, UK: Routledge, pp. 145–174.

Kelso, J. A. S. (1981). On the Oscillatory Basis of Movement. *Bulletin of the Psychonomic Society*, 18, 63.

Kelso, J. A. S. (1984). Phase Transitions and Critical Behavior in Human Bimanual Co-ordination. *American Journal of Physiology: Regulatory, Integrative and Comparative*, 15, R1000–R1004.

Kelso, J. A. S. (1995). *Dynamic Patterns: The Self-organization of Brain and Behavior*. Cambridge, MA: MIT Press.

Lee, T. D., Swinnen, S. P. & Verschueren, S. (1995). Relative Phase Alterations during Bimanual Skill Acquisition. *Journal of Motor Behavior*, 27, 263–274.

Magill, R. A. & Schoenfelder-Zohdi, B. (1996). A Visual Model and Knowledge of Performance as Sources of Information for Learning a Rhythmic Gymnastic Skill. *International Journal of Sport Psychology*, 27, 7–22.

Magill, R. A., & Hall, K. G. (1990). A Review of the Contextual Interference Effect in Motor Skill Acquisition. *Human Movement Science*, 9, 241–289.

Maslovat, D., Bredin, S. S. D., Chua, R. & Franks, I. M. (2005). Evaluation of Scanning Methodology in Bimanual Coordination. *Motor Control*, 9, 310–329.

Maslovat, D., Brunke, K. M., Chua, R. & Franks, I. M. (2009). Feedback Effects on Learning a Novel Bimanual Coordination Pattern: Support for the Guidance Hypothesis. *Journal of Motor Behavior*, 41, 45–54.

Maslovat, D., Lam, M. Y., Brunke, K. M., Chua, R. & Franks, I. M. (2009). Anchoring in a Novel Bimanual Co-ordination Pattern. *Human Movement Science*, 28, 28–47.

Maslovat, D., Chua, R., Lee, T. D. & Franks, I. M. (2004). Contextual Interference: Single Task Versus Multi-task Learning. *Motor Control*, 8, 213–233.

Maslovat, D., Chua, R., Lee, T. D. & Franks, I. M. (2006). Anchoring Strategies for Learning a Bimanual Co-ordination Pattern. *Journal of Motor Behavior*, 38(2), 101–117.

Maslovat, D., Hodges, N. J., Chua, R. & Franks, I. M. (2008). *Observational Practice of a Learning Model During the Acquisition of a Novel Coordination Skill*. Paper presented at the Canadian Society for Psychomotor Learning and Sport Psychology Conference, Canmore, Canada.

Mechsner, F., Kerzel, D., Knoblich, G. & Prinz, W. (2001). Perceptual Basis of Bimanual Co-ordination. *Nature, 414*, 69–73.

Mechsner, F. & Knoblich, G. (2004). Do Muscles Matter for Co-ordinated Action? *Journal of Experimental Psychology: Human Perception and Performance*, 30, 490–503.

Newell, K. M., Liu, Y.-T. & Mayer-Kress, G. (2008). Landscapes Beyond the HKB Model. In A. Fuchs & V. K. Jirsa (eds), *Coordination: Neural, Behavioral and Social Dynamics*. Berlin: Springer Verlag, pp. 27–44.

Schoner, G., Zanone, P. G. & Kelso, J. A. S. (1992). Learning as Change of Co-ordination Dynamics: Theory and Experiment. *Journal of Motor Behavior*, 24, 29–48.

Swinnen, S. P. (2002). Intermanual Co-ordination: From Behavioural Principles to Neural-network Interactions. *Nature Reviews Neuroscience*, 3, 350–361.

Swinnen, S. P., Lee, T. D., Verschueren, S., Serrien, J. & Bogaerds, H. (1997). Interlimb Co-ordination: Learning and Transfer under Different Feedback Conditions. *Human Movement Science*, 16, 749–785.

Temprado, J. J., Monno, A., Zanone, P. G. & Kelso, J. A. S. (2002). Attentional Demands Reflect Learning-induced Alterations of Bimanual Co-ordination Dynamics. *European Journal of Neuroscience*, 16, 1390–1394.

Tsutsui, S., Lee, T. D. & Hodges, N. J. (1998). Contextual Interference in Learning New Patterns of Bimanual Co-ordination. *Journal of Motor Behavior*, 30, 151–157.

Vogt, S. & Thomaschke, R. (2007). From Visuo-motor Interactions to Imitation Learning: Behavioural and Brain Imaging Studies. *Journal of Sports Sciences*, 25(5), 3–23.

Wulf, G, Shea, C. H. & Matschiner, S. (1998). Frequent Feedback Enhances Complex Motor Skill Learning. *Journal of Motor Behavior*, 30, 180–192.

Wulf, G. & Shea, C. H. (2004). Understanding the Role of Augmented Feedback: The Good, the Bad and the Ugly. In A. M. Williams & N. J. Hodges (eds), *Skill Acquisition in Sport: Research, Theory and Practice*. New York: Routledge, pp. 121–144.

Wuyts, I. J. & Buekers, M. J. (1995). The Effects of Visual and Auditory Models on the Learning of a Rhythmical Synchronization Dance Skill. *Research Quarterly for Exercise and Sport*, 66(2), 105–115.

Zanone, P. G. & Kelso, J. A. S. (1992). Evolution of Behavioural Attractors with Learning: Nonequilibrium Phase Transitions. *Journal of Experimental Psychology*, 18, 403–421.

Zanone, P. G. & Kelso, J. A. S. (1994). The Co-ordination Dynamics of Learning: Theoretical Structure and Experimental Agenda. In S. P. Swinnen, H. Heuer, J. Massion & P. Casaer (eds), *Interlimb Coordination: Neural, Dynamical, and Cognitive Constraints*. New York: Academic Press, pp. 461–490.

20 Skill acquisition in tennis

Equipping learners for success

Damian Farrow and Machar Reid

Introduction

Tennis is a dynamic interceptive-skill sport that requires players to respond under restrictive time demands. These qualities make tennis a relatively difficult sport to learn for those in the co-ordination stage of learning (Newell, 1985). These constraints are magnified for children tackling the game for the first time. Often children are first introduced to the sport by their parents and as a result borrow their mum or dad's racquet and step out on a full-sized court for their first experience. The child is then required to wield an overly long racquet and make contact with a ball that can easily bounce over their head, meanwhile the net seems as high as they are tall, the opposing court is full of confusing line markings, and not only do they have to contact the ball, but are required to cover the large amounts of distance of a full-size court to do it.

Such a scenario has long established the need for tennis to be scaled to meet the needs of children from an enjoyment and participation perspective. Equally, scaled equipment can be used to constrain a learner's movement pattern to promote skill acquisition (Davids *et al.*, 2008, see also Renshaw Chapter 3). The constraints framework (Davids *et al.*, 2008) is a useful paradigm for examining the issue of task and/or equipment scaling (Davids *et al.*, 2008). Specific task constraints can be used to enable learners to cope with restrictive time demands and to allow them to focus on the emergence of specific information-movement couplings.

Empirical attention has been paid to task constraints such as tennis racquets (Beak *et al.*, 2002; Pellet & Lox, 1997; Gruetter & Davis, 1985; Blanksby *et al.*, 1979); court size (Coldwells & Hare, 1985; Lee *et al.*, 1984) and the influence of ball compression on skill development (Hammond & Smith, 2006). Tennis also recently introduced three ball types for use in tournament play. In addition to a regulation or medium-paced ball (Type 2), faster (Type 1) and slower (Type 3) balls have been recommended for different conditions. The Type 3 ball is 6% bigger than the Type 1 and 2 balls, increasing its drag and subsequent flight time, slowing the game of tennis accordingly (Metha & Pallis, 2001). From a skill learning perspective research has demonstrated, and subsequently recommended, that the Type 3 ball may be beneficial for beginner level players (Cooke & Davey, 2005). Unfortunately, this body of extant research is limited and its findings inconclusive;

largely constrained by research designs that failed to match the control and experimental groups for age and skill, and lacked sufficient control over the influence of the coaching process (Coldwells & Hare, 1994; Hammond & Smith, 2006). As a result there is a lack of empirical evidence to guide the degree of initial scaling and/or progression required as skill develops.

This lack of firm evidence to guide the use and interaction of scaled racquet sizes and court dimensions/fixtures (i.e. net height) in tennis is topical. The sport's governing body, the International Tennis Federation (ITF), has recently and successfully launched a worldwide coaching/participation initiative – the "Play and Stay" program – based on task and equipment scaling. The broad aim of the program is to encourage coaches to get players to "play" the game rather than to simply teach technique. This emphasis is consistent with recent critiques of sport pedagogy that have underlined the benefits of less prescriptive coaching approaches (Davids et al., 2008). The program recommends the use of scaled racquets and balls on three different-sized courts within a variety of competition formats. Yet the guidelines as to the most appropriate ball type and court size for players of different ages and/or skill levels appear arbitrary; their interpretation internationally more arbitrary still. By way of example, in embracing the initiative, the United States Tennis Association (USTA) separates children into two age categories, under 8 and under 10 years old. Under 8 incorporates smaller racquets, very low compression balls, a lower than normal net, and a court close to half that of normal size. As the kids increase in age all of these features increase to full size. The Lawn Tennis Association (LTA) in the UK is more descriptive with their underage constraints, with various low compression balls colour-coded for children aged under 8 (red), under 9 (orange), and under 10 (green). Again net heights, court size, and racquet sizes increase with age with full-court dimensions suggested for children 10 years and above. While in Belgium, the Flemish Tennis Association advocate the use of four different-sized courts and four different balls across four different ages (<7 years, 8 years, 9 years and 10 years) and three different skill levels (beginner, experienced or talented).

In spite of this approach to ball, court, and racquet selection, the initiative has been enthusiastically welcomed and promoted by the global tennis fraternity. Its support is most tangible in England, where the LTA have developed a national competition structure consistent with its recommended age-based constraints. While the introductory vignette described a sport handcuffed by constraints in the form of rules and tradition, those constraints are now being redefined. The challenge now lies in establishing some practical scaling recommendations that help to foster a love for the game and expedite skill acquisition.

Court and ball constraints

Farrow and Reid (in press) examined the effect of a decompressed tennis ball and a reduced court size on the skill acquisition and associated psychological responses of young children in a structured tennis coaching program. The experimental design consisted of a rally performance pre-test used to record the number of balls the participants could hit back to a coach and to also allow a qualitative assessment of stroke production. This was followed by a five-week training period, where participants were assigned to one of four practice conditions that involved the manipulation of ball compression and court size. One week after the final practice session a post-test identical to the pre-test was completed. In addition to the pre-testing and post-testing, within practice session data such as the volume of strokes hit by each participant were recorded. Furthermore, at the completion of each practice session, participants rated their level of engagement during the practice session based on the findings of Seligman *et al.* (2005), who demonstrated that engaging activities facilitated happiness and promoted adherence to the activity.

All testing sessions were conducted on a regulation outdoor (synthetic grass) tennis court. The two balls used for the rally assessment, and throughout the research design, were a standard Slazenger tennis ball (standard ball) and a Wilson "red" decompressed (scaled) ball (<50% of standard ball compression, or, 56% lighter, 10% bigger and 37% less bouncy than standard balls, ITF, 2008). The courts selected for the assessment, and throughout the study, were a full-sized court (23.77 m × 10.97 m) and a scaled court (11 m × 5.5 m). Consistent with the reduction in width and length, net height was decreased to 0.8 m in the scaled-court condition. All players used 53 cm aluminium Wilson tennis racquets. The modifications utilized were in accordance with the ITF's recommendations for the age and skill level of the participants (http://www.tennisplayandstay. com/#Progression).

All groups completed one 30-minute practice session per week for five weeks within one of four practice conditions: a standard ball-scaled court, scaled ball-scaled court, standard ball-standard court or scaled ball-standard court. Each practice group used the same tennis racquet and completed identical activities within each practice session. The activities formed part of Tennis Australia's (TA) "Hot Shots" training program. The "Hot Shots" program is based on the principles of the ITF's "Play and Stay" initiative, and its activities largely comprise of game play, where players are presented with a combination of co-operative rally situations and competitive playing opportunities with a partner. The same TA qualified coach administered all practice sessions, hence the only difference between each practice group was the combination of ball type and court utilized.

The primary conclusion drawn from the results was that the standard ball/ standard court practice condition (or the group that practiced under adult game constraints) affected a negative learning experience for the participants relative to the other ball-court scaling combinations. In particular, the standard/standard intervention group recorded significantly less hitting opportunities on the fore-hand side than both the scaled-court conditions (Figure 20.1) with a similar story evident on the backhand side. The decreased hitting opportunities experienced within the standardized adult conditions then flowed into the hitting success measures, where fewer forehands were successfully hit into court relative to some of the scaled practice conditions (Figure 20.1). A final piece of corroborating evidence that the adult standardized practice conditions were inappropriate for the children's skill acquisition was that the children rated the scaled ball/scaled-court

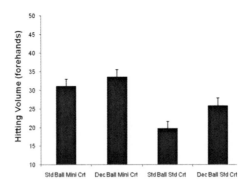

Figure 20.1 The mean number of forehand opportunities (left panel) and forehands hit successfully (right panel) for each practice group. Errors bars represent standard error.

intervention a significantly more engaging experience than the standard ball/ standard court condition. Cumulatively these results suggest a cyclical pattern of behaviour where restricted opportunity, and in turn success, leads to poorer engagement in the learning process.

Such findings are probably not that surprising to many tennis coaches. However, the traditional solution has been for coaches to attempt to control the practice environment through task decomposition rather than simplification. In other words, a coach may elect to carefully feed balls into the learner's hitting zone so that they gain a degree of success. A period of skill stability is soon reached by the learner (and coach!) where the learner settles on a stroke pattern that provides them success in the relatively benign practice conditions. Forays into more open game-based conditions typically result in one-stroke rallies where the coach often concludes the player's technique is simply not ready to withstand competitive play. An alternate and more theoretically sound approach, now being advocated by many national tennis bodies, is one of task simplification. Instead of decoupling the task of stroke production from gameplay, the two are allowed to freely interact through the implementation of scaled equipment that leads to representative practice conditions. Importantly, co-operative and competitive play against a peer is favoured over coach-fed hitting practice and as a result players have a much greater opportunity to educate their attention through attunement to key affordances for action. New solutions are actively sought rather than reliance on ultimately non-specifying information.

Farrow and Reid (in press) also highlighted that the scaling of court size exerted a more significant influence on skill development relative to that of the ball. Resultant analyses that considered the specific influence of the court scaling (irrespective of ball type) demonstrated an obvious advantage for the participants practising on a scaled-court relative to the standard court. To the tennis coach, the notion of scaling court and ball size, more so than racquet size, has had lasting appeal. Anecdotes of coaches using the service boxes as surrogate playing areas are as time-honoured as they are unstructured. The same can be said of the puncturing of tennis balls to lower their bounce or the enclosing of balls in plastic bags to slow their travel (by heightening their drag coefficient). Nonetheless, in practice, it is the scaling of the court that has traditionally proven most intuitive. In these instances, players often modify swing shapes and speeds to combat a scaled, smaller court but coupled with a non-scaled, standard ball. Therein lies the theoretical rationale for advocating the use of a lower-compression ball to create representative practice conditions, where players can develop more complete technical and tactical repertoires uninhibited by courts that are too large, racquets that are too big and heavy, and balls that are too bouncy. It is important to note that while the scaling of ball compression was not as influential as court scaling, the influence of the ball should not be discounted. In particular the size of the ball coupled with its relative decompression requires further systematic examination (Farrow & Reid, in press).

From the data presented it is clear that scaling is a useful vehicle for simplifying the task for the learner while allowing the key information sources within the practice enviornnment to be presented in a perception-action coupled manner. In a sport such as tennis, where perceptual, decision-making and technical skills are inextricably linked, such a practice approach provides a coach with the greatest opportunity to simultaneously develop these key skills. In the following section we will draw attention to other ways in which scaling can, and is, being utilized. Furthermore, we present a number of constraints-based strategies for the development of the core tennis skills of the serve and baseline play.

A constraints-based approach to tennis skill acquisition

In tennis, the scaling of equipment is not confined to young beginners and the acceleration of their skill acquisition. Among the professional playing population, players' rackets are "scaled" to accommodate their personal preferences (haptic information), anthropometry, and swing mechanics, as well as the manufacturing idiosyncracies of different racket brands. Inexperienced or young players have been shown to be less attuned to variation in the haptic information (inertial qualities) that characterizes different racket specifications (Beak, *et al.*, 2002; Brody, 2000). These findings are consistent with the proposed positive relationship between increased task-specific expertise and the ability of individuals to exploit richer information sources in the environment (e.g. information available from haptic and visual sources) (Gibson, 1979). It follows that many professionals choose to invest vast sums of money into their attunement to haptic information, or in more practical terms, the customizing of racquet design. To this end, players are chiefly concerned with, and sensitive to, changes to the racquet's swing weight (or swing moment of inertia) as it accounts for much of how the swung racquet feels and also the speed with which an individual player can expect to hit the ball (Brody *et al.*, 2002).

Table 20.1 Examples of specific constraints/interventions to elicit technical improvements in the tennis serve.

Behavioural constraints	Source	Practical intervention	Desired technical change
Task	Conditions or rules	Serve to backhand only	Limit excess axial trunk rotation when serving
		Serve from service line	Increase wrist flexion or 'snap'
		Play points with kick serves only	Better engage trunk rotation in the sagittal plane
	Court dimensions	Play half court tennis (down-the-line)	Vary swing trajectories but with consistent ball toss
		Serve from 2 m behind the service line	Reduce distance of ball toss in to the court
	Equipment	Use heavier racquets	Enhance velocity of segment rotation
		Increase diameter of the ball	Improve control of toss (minimize superfluous wrist flexion)
Environment	Surface	Sand serving	Improve lower limb drive
	Access to sensory information	Occlusion of ball flight (serve with eyes closed)	Heighten awareness of body position and rhythm
Player	Segment co-ordination	Serve off front leg	Improve balance/ involvement of rear leg
		Start abbreviated: in the 'trophy' position	Minimize extraneous racket movement in the backswing
		Stagger tossing (down) and hitting (up) arms in the ready position	Create shoulder tilt

The search for the perfect racquet (and swingweight) among professional players is generally ongoing and, more often than not, occurs devoid of explicit instruction from the coach. This fits nicely with the ecological theories underpinning contemporary coaching, which encourage players to explore solutions to different movement problems and to learn more implicitly. That is, coaches who understand that players adjust their on-court movements, and more globally their performance, according to the imposed behavioural constraints, are challenged to assist a player develop through more than just the time-honoured verbal or visual feedback. Examples of how this type of constraint manipulation can be used to

Table 20.2 Examples of specific constraints/interventions to elicit tactical improvements in the use of a player's groundstrokes.

Behavioural constraints	Source	Practical intervention	Desired tactical change
Task	Conditions or rules	Cannot play consecutive shots in the same way	Ability to change rally tempo (spin and speed) and direction
		Play points; points can only be won by a forehand that bounces in the service box	Learn to use the drop shot
		Play points; the winner of the point is the player who has covered the least amount of court (as determined by number of steps)	Create space on the opponent's court
	Court dimensions	Play in doubles alleys	Flatten shot trajectory
		Increase net height (rope over net)	Improve use of the court length
	Equipment	Use shorter racquets	Learn to finish points more quickly
		Use a modified (bigger/ slower) ball	Improve ability to construct points in different ways; develop court craft
Environment	Surface	Play on 'boards'	Learn to play up the court, taking time and space away from the opponent
		4 × 15 minutes clay + 15 minutes hard	Reinforce 'invariant' tactical patterns
	Access to sensory information	Partial occlusion of ball flight	Refine ability to perceive cues
Player	Segment co-ordination	Elicit player fatigue	Challenge decision-making (tactical use of groundstrokes) under duress
		Rubber band between legs	Encourage player to dictate point from the outset

facilitate the learning of key technical characteristics in the tennis serve as well as tactics important to succesful baseline play are offered through Tables 20.1 and 20.2 respectively.

Beyond the regulations that govern scoring and court dimensions, the sport's rule book offers another very significant constraint that implicitly shapes player performance, the court surface. The ITF have upward of six approved court surfaces. Few if any other sports are presented with such a diversity in playing surfaces. The variation in playing characteristics of different court surfaces are so great that they are considered to underpin the development of all facets of the game, including tactics, technique, physical build, psychology, and technical skill. Further, the traditional categorization and characteristics associated with particular game styles, including "counter-punchers" and "serve and volleyers", remain virtually synonymous with the development of players on specific court surfaces (clay and grass in the above examples). With changes to the distribution of tournaments played per court surface in the modern professional game, anecdotal and empirical reports even point to the role of the predominant court surface upon which players develop their games as a factor contributing to their chances of future professional success (Reid *et al.*, 2007).

Figure 20.2 Environmental constraint manipulation. The half-clay, half-grass court used in Mallorca in an exhibition match between Roger Federer and Rafel Nadal.

Interestingly, it is rare to hear of coaches actively utilizing the court surface as a practice constraint. While somewhat understandable in that the playing charac-teristics of the different court surfaces can promote disparate strategy and therefore technical/movement skills, transferability of these skills is important. A prime example of the length to which some top professional players will go to maximize their chances of experiencing success across court surfaces is that of a former world number 1 who laid all four Grand Slam surfaces at a private academy in his home town. This afforded him the opportunity to practice on the surface specific to the most important tournaments of the year. A notion – different in intent – to that of using those surfaces as a form of "within practice session" constraint. Indeed, perhaps the most graphic example of the implicit use of court surface in this way was on display during a 2007 exhibition match between Roger Federer and Rafael Nadal. The match, played on a purpose-built court in Mallorca, was grass at one end and clay at the other (Figure 20. 2). From the need to adapt the way in which a heavily spun ball was hit or met, to decisions like when to approach the net, this court design presented a complex tactical and technical challenge. In application, infrastructure that provides easy access to more than one court surface affords coaches the opportunity to destabilize player learning, simply through a change in surface. Again, although it may not replicate the constraints presented on that court in Mallorca, the capacity to regularly change court surface, both within a session and/or within a training block, could be expected to expedite the acquis-tion of specific tennis skills.

It is common to see dispute between the controlled (perhaps overly) scientific evidence on a particular topic and coaching folklore. However, the vital role that task and equipment scaling can play in the tennis skill acquisition process is not such a topic. Coaches are encouraged to more actively consider how they can create representative practice conditions for their learners through the strategic manipulation of constraints such as ball compression and size, court dimensions, and racquet length. Appropriate progression through these task simplification approaches has been demonstrated to lead to increased learner practice opportu-nity, engagement and ultimately skill learning.

References

Beak, S., Davids, K. & Bennett, S. J. (2002). Child's Play: Children's Sensitivity to Haptic Information in Perceiving Affordances of Rackets for Striking a Ball. In J. Clark & J. Humphrey (eds), *Motor Development: Research and Reviews*. Minnesota: NASPE, pp. 120–141.

Blanksby, B., Elliott, B. & Ellis, R. (1979). Selecting the Right Racquet. *Australian Journal of Health Physical Education and Recreation*, 86, 21–25.

Brody, H. (2000). Player Sensitivity to the Moments of Inertia of a Tennis Racquet. *Sports Engineering*, 3, 145–148.

Brody, H. Cross, R. & Lindsey, C. (2002).*The Physics and Technology of Tennis*, Racquet Tech Pub., Solana Beach, USA.

Coldwells, A. & Hare, M. E. (1985). The Transfer of Skill from Short Tennis to Lawn Tennis. *Ergonomics*, 37(1), 17–21.

Cooke, K. & Davey, P. (2005). Tennis Ball Diameter: The Effect on Performance and the Concurrent Physiological Responses. *Journal of Sports Sciences*, 23, 31–39.

Davids, K., Button, C. & Bennett, S. (2008). *Dynamics of Skill Acquisition*. Human Kinetics.

Farrow, D. & Reid, M. (in press). The Effect of Equipment Scaling on the Skill Acquisition of Beginning Tennis Players. *Journal of Sports Sciences*, forthcoming.

Gibson, J. J. (1979). *The Ecological Approach to Visual Perception*. Boston, MA: Houghton-Mifflin.

Gruetter, D. & Davis, T. (1985) Oversized vs. Standard Racquets: Does it Really Make a Difference? *Research Quarterly For Exercise and Sport*, 56, 31–36.

Hammond, J. & Smith, C. (2006). Low Compression Tennis Balls and Skill Development. *Journal of Sports Science and Medicine*, 5, 575–581.

ITF. (2008). *ITF Approved Tennis Balls and Classified Court Surfaces – A Guide to Products and Test Surfaces*. London: ITF Ltd.

Lee, A., Edwards, P. & Smith, J. (1984). The Transition from Short Tennis to Lawn Tennis. *Journal of Sports Sciences*, 2, 163–164.

Metha, R., & Pallis, J. (2001). The Aerodynamics of a Tennis Ball. *Sports Engineering*, 4, 177–189.

Newell, K. M. (1985). Coordination, Control and Skill. In D. Goodman, R. B. Wilberg, & I. M. Franks (eds), *Differing Perspectives in Motor Learning, Memory and Control*. Amsterdam: Elsevier Science, pp. 295–317.

Pellet, T. K. & Lox, C. L. (1998) Tennis Racket Head Size Comparisons and their Effect on Beginning College Players' Achievement and Self-efficacy. *Journal of Teaching in Physical Education*, 17(4), 453–467.

Reid, M., Crespo, M., Santilli, L., Miley, D. & Dimmock, J. (2007). The Importance of the International Tennis Federation's Junior Boys' Circuit in the Development of Professional Tennis Players. *Journal of Sports Sciences*, 25, 667–672.

Schmidt, R. A. & Wrisberg, C. A. (2000). *Motor Learning and Performance*, 2nd edn. Champaign, IL: Human Kinetics.

Seligman, M. E. P., Steen, T. A., Park, N. & Peterson, C. (2005). Positive Psychology Progress: Empirical Validation of Interventions. *American Psychologist*, 60(5), 421.

Index

Note: page numbers in *italic* refer to figures and tables

action capabilities, changes across
    timescales 137
action-effects, practical implications
    207–8
adaptive behaviours, and movement
    disorders 174
adolescents, and growth spurts 35
affordances: definition of 110; body-
    scaled and action scaled 137; in boxing
    212; in canoeing 156; in children 34;
    recalibration 137
AFL *see* Australian Rules Football
    (AFL)
attention, and basketball shooting 47
attractor patterns, and learning 222
attunement 110: in rugby union 120; in
    sailing 137
Australian Rules Football (AFL) 144; case
    study 148

backyard games, advantages of 38
basketball: case study 53; shooting styles
    49–50
Bernstein 4, 24, 174; *see also* degrees of
    freedom
Bloom 37
body scaled metrics: and action
    capabilities 212; and skill acquisition in
    children 231
boxing 211: case study 216; constraints-
    based research in 212

calibration: and action capabilities 137
canoeing 152; discovery learning
    approach in 159; instructor-focused
    approaches 155; task simplification
    and decomposition in 156; traditional
    approaches 153–157

cerebral palsy (CP) 176
champions' model approach, limitations
    of 23
Chappell, Greg 38
children: hands-off approaches to
    coaching 38; non-linear pedagogy 33;
    skill acquisition 33; in tennis 231
coaching, individualizing 36
constraints: definition 174; attentional
    focus as 29; categories of 4–5; and
    children with movement difficulties
    173; degrees of freedom problem
    24; environmental 5, 37, 83–7;
    informational 6–7; manipulating *see*
    manipulating constraints; on movement
    in physical activity 18; organismic
    4, 88–92; role in the emergence of
    movement patterns 20; in swimming 83,
    87, 92; task 5, 87–8, 231
constraints-based research, in boxing 212
constraints-led approach: aim 3; to boxing
    216; in canoeing 153; for children
    with movement difficulties 180–4; and
    demonstrations 158; for developing
    decision-making in AFL 147; to
    football coaching 162–71; framework
    3; in swimming 83, 92; to tennis skill
    acquisition 235–9; theoretical basis of
    3–6
contextual interference 223
control parameters 26; in boxing 212; and
    mode parameters 26
co-ordination: as framework for creating
    changes 23; changes with practice 164;
    in football 164; in-phase and anti-phase
    222
co-ordination skills 221: and feedback 225;
    instructions and demonstrations 224

co-ordinative structures, implications for instructional strategies 24
Côté 37
creative play 39
cricket 109: case studies 105, 117; mental skills development 116–17; perceptual skills development 115–16; practice tasks 112–17; technical skills development 112

decision-making: in rugby union 120; in sailing 134–5; in team sports 144, 145
degeneracy: definition of 173; and functional variability in learning 173; and movement disorders 173
degrees of freedom: in cricket batting 114; freezing 135; in sailing 137
deliberate practice 37
demonstrations 23, 40, 155; role in the constraints-led approach 158
designing games for children 39–40
differential learning approach 70; stochastic perturbations 70; in track and field athletics 71–80
direct perception 174; *see also* Gibson
discovery learning approach, in canoeing 159

early play experiences, importance for expertise development 38
early specialization 37; and inherent risks 37 versus multi-dimensional approaches 37–9
education of attention: definition 136; attunement to affordances 110
emergent behaviours, children with movement difficulties 176–7
emergent functional adaptations 173
Ericsson 37
expertise, in sailing 134
Explanar® Golf Training System 187
exploration, manipulating degrees of freedom 135–6
external action: effects 199; percepts in football 204

Fajen 34
feedback: auditory 226; concurrent 225; and re-learning of walking 226
Flemish Tennis Association 232
focus of attention 200
football 161: case studies 169, 207, 208; chip pass 164, 202; perceptual

anticipation in 161; visual search strategies in 162–4, 204

Gibson 5–6, 29, 110, 133, 156, 164; perception-action cycle 6
goalkeeping 57: and the Müller-Lyer illusion 64; positioning for penalty kicks 64–6; visual search strategies in 163–4
golf 187–98; video feedback 187, 192
growth spurts 35–6, 35
guidance hypothesis 226

humans, as complex, neurobiological systems 3

individualizing the coaching *see* coaching, individualizing
information: and constraints on action *see* constraints, informational; coupling with movement 6–7; and instructions *see* instructions, information in; usefulness of 136
instructional control parameters, example 27
instructional strategies: definition 17; demonstrations 23; and intrinsic dynamics 21; use of metaphors or analogies 28
instructions: as a constraint 17–20; as control parameters 26; and creating phase transitions 27; focus of attention 28; information in 20–1, 48; and order parameters 24; presentation of 27–8; in swimming 130
International Society of Sport Psychologists: on childhood participation 38
intrinsic dynamics: definition 21; and affordances 34; and learning 34, 222

Jacobs and Michaels 6

kayaking 152
Kelso 25

Lawn Tennis Association (LTA) 232
learning design: for decision-making 12–14, 120; in canoeing 159; and informational constraints on action 7; and information-movement coupling 7–10; and task simplification 7
learning motor skills, description of 20

manipulating constraints: creating effective learning environments for

children 39; to develop tactical skills 125–7; to develop technical skills 127–9; to facilitate learning 42; for perceptual training 47; in rugby union 120; in swimming 92; to teach principles of play 124
medical model 183
Merloo South Junior AFL Club 148
Mosston & Ashworth 36
Müller-Lyer illusion 64
multi-dimensional approach to sporting development 38

Newell 25; *see also* constraints
non-linear pedagogy: and decision-making 121–2; developing technique 40; focus on the individual in 34, 36; key concepts 33; and movement disorders 173; principles xiv; and talent development 39
normative perspective, and idealized movement patterns of children 173

order parameters 24; relative phase of punching activity 213
outdoor education 152

penalty kicks 57; how to save or score 66–7; strategies for the kicker 61–64
perception-action coupling: in boxing 211; in team sports 145
perception-action skills: in cricket 100–5; video-based training of 101–5
perceptual attunement 136; *see also* education of attention
perceptual learning 29
perceptual skills: in cricket 100, 115; in football 164
perceptual training 47; in AFL 148–50; for basketball 51–54; in goalkeepers 60–61
perceptual-motor disorders173
phase transitions: characteristics of 27; and cricket batting 111
practice organization 223; benefits of open skills practice 145–7; implications of unopposed drills 147
punches, kinetic chain of 211

quiet eye (QE), and shooting at targets 50

rate limiters, in cricket batting 111–12
repetition without repetition: definition 74; in canoeing 159
representative practice tasks: and children 39; in cricket 110; specificity 164; in team sports144
representative task design 121
rugby union 159; learning design for decision-making in 12; manipulating task constraints in 120, principles of play in 121; sub-units 121
Ryan & Deci 36

sailing 131: case studies 140, 141; discovering solutions 137; expertise in 135; training the regatta start 138–9
self-organization of movements 41
skill acquisition: in children 62–77; in dynamic ball sports 199
spastic hemiparetic cerebral palsy (SHCP) 178
swimming: case studies 94; inter-limb co-ordination in 83–94
synergies *see* co-ordinative structures

talent identification, during growth spurts 36
task constraints *see* constraints, task
task de-composition 30: in canoeing 156; in cricket 110–11
task simplification 7; in canoeing 200
team sports, as complex dynamical systems 120
Tendulkar, Sachin 110
tennis 231, 286
transition information 27

United States Tennis Association (USTA) 232

variability, and exploration 190
video-based training, of perception-action skills 101–5
visual control: in basketball shooting 48–51
visual search strategies: in football 162, 204; of goalkeepers 162–4
video simulations 162

Woods, Tiger 37

LEARNING RESOURCES CENTRE